THE
REAL
WAR

THE REAL WAR

THE CLASSIC REPORTING
ON THE VIETNAM WAR
WITH A NEW ESSAY
BY JONATHAN SCHELL

PANTHEON BOOKS   NEW YORK 1987

LIBRARY OF CONGRESS CATALOGING IN PUBLICATION DATA

Schell, Jonathan, 1943–
    The real war.

    The village of Ben Suc originally published in 1967 by
Knopf; followed by The military half in 1968, also by the
same publisher.
    Contents: The real war—The village of Ben Suc—The
military half.
    1. Vietnamese Conflict. 1961–1975—Personal narratives,
American.   2. Vietnamese Conflict. 1961–1975—Destruction
and pillage.   3. Schell, Jonathan, 1943–   . I. Title.
DS559.5.S342   1988   959.704′3   87–43046
ISBN 0–394–75550–2 (pbk.)

Display typography by Quinn Hall

Manufactured in the United States of America

FIRST EDITION

CONTENTS

THE
REAL
WAR

More than a decade after its end, the Vietnam war refuses to lie quiet in its historical grave. Its whys and wherefores roil the scholarly community, its passions continue to spill out in books and plays and movies, its legacy vexes and divides our policymakers. Questions regarding the very nature of the war remain unresolved. Who, we are still wondering, was our enemy? Was it the National Liberation Front (N.L.F.)? Was it North Vietnam? Was it the Soviet Union? China? Both the Soviet Union and China? Or first one and then the other? Was it that still larger, if vaguer, entity "world communism"? Did we, in other words, face a local guerrilla force, or the conventional army of a small state, or a rival superpower, or a league of superpowers, or a coordinated global political movement? Or were we ourselves somehow the enemy? (President Nixon, for one, thought so. In his speech to the nation on November 3, 1969, in which he announced his secret "plan" for ending the war, he told the public, "North Vietnam cannot defeat or humiliate the United States. Only Americans can do that.") And what, correspondingly, was the character of the war? Was it a domestic revolution, a civil war, a war of aggression by a neighboring power, a war of subversion from without, or a strategic move by a global power bent on world domination? Or did we perhaps think it was one of these whereas in fact it was another? Why did we fight? Was it to defend the independence and freedom of a small country? Was it to defeat "wars of national liberation" in a "test case"? Was it to halt at the earliest possible moment a great power on the march, so as to prevent in our time a repetition of the mistake made by the democracies in 1939, in Munich, when they acquiesced in Hitler's invasion of Czechoslovakia? Or was it our goal not so much physically to stop an enemy as to preserve our reputation all around the world as a mighty nation ready and able to use its power to advance its interests and beliefs—to preserve what four presidents called the "credibility" of our power? Did our goal change during the war: did we perhaps enter the war for one reason but stay in it for another? How did we get into the war? Were we dragged reluctantly into an Asian "quagmire"? Or, on the contrary, did we carefully and calculatedly apply our power in accordance with theories of "limited war" that had been worked out well in advance by strategic analysts wrestling with the dilemmas of power in the nuclear age? And—perhaps the most baffling question of them all—why did we lose? How did it happen that the self-described mightiest power on earth could not prevail over forces mustered in tiny, poor, backward Vietnam? Was it because our military strategy was mistaken? Or was our military strategy correct, and did we in fact win with it, only to throw away the victory by prematurely withdrawing, under pressure from cowardly politicians, a duplicitous press, and a duped public? Did our political "establishment" suffer a "moral collapse," as Henry Kissinger has suggested, and is that why we lost? Or, on the contrary, did we leave, and lose, not because of any collapse but because we came to our senses and liquidated a hopeless and ruinous effort that we never should have launched? Finally, we ask ourselves, What does it all mean—what lessons, if any, should the United States draw from the experience? Is the lesson that there are certain limits on the usefulness of military force in imposing our will on other countries? Or is this lesson in fact a perilous "syndrome," a further symptom of the moral collapse that unnecessarily brought on the defeat; and is the proper lesson, therefore, that we should seek to revive our faltering will and assert ourselves militarily in the world? Because these questions concern the nature of the world we live in, and the nature of the United States' obligations in it, the debate is about more than the past; the present and the future are actively involved as well. In late 1966 and in 1967, I was in Vietnam as a reporter for *The New Yorker*; and from then until now I have found myself thinking and writing about the war in one way or another. In what follows, I will not try to address all the questions that have been raised by the war; instead, using the full benefit of hindsight, including material that has been made public in the years since the war's end, I will concentrate on the question why the United States lost in Vietnam. But I hope that in addressing this question I will be able to shed some light obliquely on the other questions as well.

THE VIETNAMESE THEMSELVES

"The Vietnamese themselves" was a phrase constantly on the lips of the Americans waging war in Vietnam when I arrived there in 1966. What the grammatically redundant "themselves" (characteristically spoken with extra emphasis) referred to indirectly was the Americans. The implicit meaning of the phrase was "not the Americans but the Vietnamese themselves." The Americans understood that there were certain things they could not do for their Vietnamese allies. The main one was to build a government that would command the allegiance of the Vietnamese people. The Americans could do many things in Vietnam, but not this; the Vietnamese *themselves* would have to do it.

In the summer of 1967, in the South Vietnamese province of Quang Ngai, I met an energetic, idealistic young American lieutenant-colonel who had responsibility for the Pacification Program in his area. He was profoundly discouraged with its progress so far. However, he had a program in mind that he believed might remedy the situation. The supporters of the N.L.F., he observed, were highly motivated, but the people who were "supposed to be on our side"—most of whom were refugees who had been driven into camps by American military operations in which their villages were destroyed—were "just blobs." The colonel didn't blame them. "Now they don't have any jobs, or houses, or anything that they can get excited about," he explained. To inspire their loyalty, a number of things would have to be done. First, security would have to be provided for the refugee camps. This could be accomplished by establishing a training program for local young men, who thereby would gain in self-confidence and competence. Then, the villages that had been destroyed in the American military operations would have to be rebuilt—"preferably by the villagers themselves." Next, democratic government would have to be set up in the villages. After that, the corruption that was rampant in provincial government would be eliminated. Finally, the military men now running the regime in Saigon would have to hand the government over to civilians, who would turn it into a full-fledged democracy. *Then* the discouraged people in the camps would have something to get excited about, and would go forth to defeat the N.L.F.

However, the colonel saw a serious obstacle to the fulfillment of his plan. "The Vietnamese have to do it themselves," he said, using the familiar formulation. "We can't try to do it for them." He went on: "I know what a tremendous temptation it is to give candy to kids. It makes you feel good inside. You're Number One . . . I have seen so many cases of Americans who want to play Santa Claus and feel warm all over, but this kind of thing is only corrupting, and it destroys the people's pride. If only we could learn."

The colonel's point was irrefutable. As he looked about him, not one of the steps in his hopeful plan had been accomplished. When I asked if I might spend the night in a secure village in the district, he said that I could not, for there was no such village. The temptation for the Americans to take things into their own hands was overwhelming. Yet if they did the South Vietnamese, shunted aside, would grow even weaker, for the more the Americans did things for the South Vietnamese the more dependent they became—a self-defeating result, since the point of the exercise was to strengthen them. Yet the plain fact was that if the Americans didn't do the things they wanted done, the things didn't happen. That was why the United States had felt it necessary to go into Vietnam in the first place. That was why there were almost half a million Americans in Vietnam when the idealistic colonel spoke to me. More than ninety per cent of the budget of the Saigon regime was being supplied by the United States; its armed forces were wholly supplied and trained by the United States; and every South Vietnamese official down to the level of district chief was provided with a full-time "adviser." In the words, in 1967, of General Creighton Abrams, who later became commander of the Military Assistance Command, Vietnam (the word "assistance" in the title expressed the wistful hope that "the Vietnamese themselves" would do most of the fighting),

"The in-depth U.S. advisory network became the 'glue' that held the situation together in many critical respects at the critical local level." Actually, the Americans were more than the glue; they were the structure as well. If the Americans didn't step in and hold the government together, it would collapse, but if they did step in, whatever independent strength it had was still further weakened and the regime's chances of ever standing on its own were further reduced. It's not an exaggeration to say that the whole American effort in Vietnam foundered on this contradiction.

VIETNAMIZING VIETNAM

President Nixon pursued a policy that he called Vietnamization. It was difficult to remember, sometimes, that the country to be Vietnamized was Vietnam. Did it require half a million Americans to turn Vietnam into itself? Wasn't Vietnam Vietnam already? In truth, it was not. It had, in a sense, been made a part of the United States—or, at any rate, the Saigon regime had, for it was wholly the creation and dependency of the Americans. It was all very well to say that "the Vietnamese themselves" should run their own country along the suggested lines; the trouble was that the ones saying this were Americans. Even the wish for Vietnam to be "independent" was an American one. Many paradoxical and comical scenes were enacted throughout the war in which Americans, maddened by their South Vietnamese allies' lack of initiative, ordered them, in effect, to be more independent. There was, however, a kind of Vietnamization that millions of Vietnamese, North and South, did passionately want, and that was the kind offered by the N.L.F. and the regime in the North. They wanted to expel all foreigners, including above all the Americans, and reunify their country. And this, as soon as the United States left, is what they did.

INTERVENING AND WITHDRAWING

The American government never quite made up its mind whether it was intervening in Vietnam or withdrawing. Usually, it was trying to do both at the same time. No sooner did it start to put troops in than it began to promise to get them out; no sooner did it start to take them out than it began to make dramatic and bloody "demonstrations" of its will to remain. During the long military buildup, officials constantly reported that the end was in sight. During the long withdrawal, President Nixon repeatedly reintervened, first by bombing and invading Cambodia, then by invading Laos, and then by blockading North Vietnam against Soviet and other shipping. It is a key fact about American policy in Vietnam that the withdrawal of American troops was built into it from the start. None of the presidents who waged war in Vietnam contemplated an open-ended campaign; all promised the public that American troops would be able to leave in the not-too-remote future. The promise of withdrawal precluded a policy of occupation of the traditional colonial sort, in which a great power simply imposes its will on a small one indefinitely—as, for example, the Soviet Union does in the countries of Eastern Europe—and it dictated the need, as a matter not so much of idealism as of basic strategy, to build a regime in South Vietnam that could survive the American departure. Had occupation been the policy, no independently strong regime would have been needed; a permanently dependent client state would have sufficed. American policy in Vietnam was called imperialistic. But it is a strange, crippled sort of imperialism that foresees departing its colonial possession even before it has seized it. At best, it is imperialism on the cheap, in which the colony is supposed, in a manner of speaking, to colonize itself.

WITHDRAWAL AND PUBLIC OPINION

The need to build withdrawal into American policy was dictated by domestic political considerations. The public, as the policy-makers well knew, had no appetite for an open-ended war, "limited" or otherwise. Fresh in everyone's mind was the memory of the Korean war, which, as it dragged on, quickly became unpopular with the public. It was after the Korean war that Secretary of State John Foster Dulles announced the policy of "massive retaliation," in which threats of nuclear retaliation would take over the task of responding to local aggression—a task that had been assigned to conventional forces in Korea. The new policy was designed to cost less—to give "more bang for the buck," in the phrase of the day—and to avoid arousing public opposition. Under President Kennedy and President Johnson, the government, nervous about a policy that courted the devastation of the world in every small crisis that might arise, swung away from this reliance on nuclear weapons and back to reliance on ground forces; but the limits on the public's patience with wars fought in faraway places for unclear goals had been demonstrated, and were remembered. Respect for—and fear of—public opinion was more than a limit placed on the government's freedom of action after the war was under way; it was built into the war policy from its inception. Standing always in the background of the decisions made by the American policy-makers in Vietnam was the basic fact that the United States was a democracy, in which the opinions of the public eventually had political weight and political consequences, including, notably, the policy-makers' possible expulsion from office.

PUBLIC OPINION IN ACTION

Two presidents—Johnson and Nixon—were driven from office because of the Vietnam war. As President Nixon's chief of staff H. R. Haldeman has rightly said, "Without the Vietnam war, there would have been no Watergate." But whereas Johnson, in the last analysis, respected the limits imposed on him by the democratic system and voluntarily left office, Nixon defied the limits and had to be forced out. Nixon, having promised in his election campaign of 1968 to end the war soon, instead protracted it for another five years. That effort was defeated not when South Vietnam fell to the Communists, in April of 1975, but eight months earlier, when Nixon resigned from office under pressure of impeachment proceedings, in which his conviction looked certain. His fall marked the irreversible collapse of any support in the United States for reintervention in Vietnam, as secretly promised by Nixon to President Nguyen Van Thieu. Once this was clear, the assault by North Vietnam, and its success, were assured.

TIME

> The war must be prolonged, and we must have time. Time is on our side—time will be our best strategist, if we are determined to pursue our resistance to the end.
> —TRUONG CHINH, Secretary General of the Communist Party of Vietnam, spring, 1947

We ran out of time. This is the tragedy of
Vietnam—we were fighting for time rather
than space. And time ran out.

> —NORMAN B. HANNAH, Foreign Service
> officer with experience in Vietnam,
> 1975

The puzzle of how the world's mightiest power was defeated by a tiny weak one begins to melt away once the
principle enunciated by Truong Chinh in 1947 and re-
affirmed, twenty-eight years and millions of lives later, by
Norman B. Hannah is entered into the equation. Successes
in the war for space—the capture of this or that Hamburger
Hill—meant nothing if, when it was all over and the Americans withdrew, the balance of Vietnamese forces was left
unchanged from what it had been when the United States
arrived. The same could be said of the military measuring
stick that the American command, vaguely aware that the
capture or defense of territory was not a meaningful measure, sought to employ in its stead: the body count. No
amount of success by either measure, short of a campaign
of genocide, which the United States was never willing to
undertake, could alter an elementary fact: that the Vietnamese lived in Vietnam whereas the Americans lived on
the other side of the globe. The American intervention
was expeditionary and therefore, almost in the nature of
things, bound one day to end. The geography that mattered
in the Vietnam war was not the position of the troops in
the field, it was the position of the countries on the earth.
Whatever the nature of things might be, however, the
United States had made known its intention to depart the
day it arrived, and the Vietnamese adversary had only to
wait. The Vietnamese were well-versed in the strategies of
time. The Americans, hardly able to see beyond the next

election, could at best look four or five or six years ahead. A decade was already off the political map. The Vietnamese were accustomed to thinking in decades, even in centuries. In March of 1946, Ho Chi Minh agreed to let the French put troops into Vietnam and keep them there for five years in exchange for the withdrawal of Nationalist Chinese troops, which had been stationed in the northern part of the country at the end of the Second World War. Some of Ho's colleagues took him sharply to task for having agreed to let the former colonial ruler back into the country. "You fools!" Ho answered. "Don't you realize what it means if the Chinese remain? Don't you remember your history? The last time the Chinese came, they stayed a thousand years. The French are foreigners. They are weak. Colonialism is dying. The white man is finished in Asia. But if the Chinese stay now, they will never go. As for me, I prefer to sniff French shit for five years than eat Chinese shit for the rest of my life."

WILL

If time was the unit of strategic gain that counted most in the Vietnam war, the force that counted most—the fire-power, so to speak, in this war for time—was political will. Will—the resolve and fortitude of a people—is always an important factor in war, but in the Vietnam war it was paramount. There were three peoples whose will mattered: the South Vietnamese, the North Vietnamese, and the Americans. Most important, for purposes of the American war effort, was the will of the South Vietnamese. If their will could not be shaped according to American wishes, then nothing the United States did, whether of a civilian or a military nature, could amount to anything. It was not enough, as the colonel in Quang Ngai realized, for the

Americans to impose their will on the South Vietnamese—
to bend their resisting will to American purposes; the
Americans needed to *awaken* the will of the South Vietnamese to actively want what the Americans wanted for
them. Only then would there be any chance that the regime
in the South could survive the intended American withdrawal. If it fell, all American hopes and accomplishments
would fall with it.

NATION-BUILDING

No project was more fundamental to American policy in
Vietnam than the effort, which came to be called "nation-
building," to create a strong government in the South, but
none was more unlikely of accomplishment. As the name
suggests, there was no nation in South Vietnam when the
United States began sending in its troops. One had to be
built. None ever was. In the end, "South Vietnam" did not
so much collapse as fail ever to be born. The government
could not be defended because it never existed. In politics,
as in nature, there are forces that clear the scene of organ-
isms whose strength has declined to a certain point. Again
and again, the Saigon regime declined to that point and
beyond. Again and again, it came to the end of its natural
life. Again and again, it collapsed. But again and again the
United States hoisted the cadaver to its feet and tried to
breathe artificial life into it. Like a ghost that is denied a
grave to rest in, this regime stalked the earth posthumously.
Normally, there are certain limits on the ills that afflict
governments, placed there by the governments' demise. But
in the artificially propped-up Saigon regime these ills—
corruption, intrigue, internal warfare—were, like the government itself, given an unnatural lease on life, and at-
tained fantastic, unreal proportions. The chief activity of

its top personages was not to govern but to plot against one another. Between November of 1963, when President Ngo Dinh Diem was overthrown in an American-backed coup and murdered, and February of 1965, five governments succeeded one another, with three of them arriving by coup d'état. If thereafter Nguyen Van Thieu and Nguyen Cao Ky, two military men, managed to keep power for the rest of the war, the reason was not their strength but everyone else's weakness. While these things were happening, the government was seriously opposed by a Buddhist movement that was largely independent of the N.L.F. Although American officials unfailingly praised the regime in public, they were rarely less than scathing about it in their private judgments. It was one thing for Senator Mike Mansfield, an opponent of the American involvement, to write to President Johnson in June of 1965 that in Saigon "we are no longer dealing with anyone who represents anybody in a political sense." It was another for the American Ambassador to South Vietnam, Henry Cabot Lodge, to tell President Johnson a month later, "I don't think we ought to take this government seriously. There is simply no one who can do anything"; or for Secretary of Defense Robert McNamara to report to Johnson in December of 1963 that "there is no organized government in South Vietnam"; or for him to call it, in July of 1965, a "non-government"; or for Assistant Secretary of State William Bundy, thinking back to that period later, to characterize Thieu and Ky as brought up from "the bottom of the barrel, absolutely the bottom of the barrel." These expressions were not aberrations; they were thoroughly typical of the opinions of the Americans who had dealings with the Saigon regime. But most galling to the Americans, perhaps, was the seemingly irrepressible inclination of the various regimes that came to power to enter into negotiations with the N.L.F.—a move that the United States regarded as tantamount to capitulation. In the words of General Maxwell Taylor in December of 1964, when he was Ambassador to the South, the South Vietnamese leaders would, if faced with a weakening of American support, "rush to compete with each other in making a deal with the National Liberation Front." Such, he found, were the actual results of any serious attempt to turn things over to "the Vietnamese themselves."

WILL II: THE N.L.F. AND NORTH VIETNAM

"We maintain that the morale factor is the decisive factor in war, more than weapons, tactics, and technique," a resolution of the Central Committee of the N.L.F. stated in October of 1961. The resolution went on: "Politics forms the actual strength of the revolution: politics is the root and war is the continuation of politics." The Communists in both the North and the South kept the question of will uppermost in their minds throughout the war. If the strategy of the Communists was to develop and maintain their will, the specific aim of American policy throughout was to *break* that will. The United States had no military strategy other than to punish the enemy so severely that it would simply give up. In the words of Assistant Secretary of Defense John T. McNaughton, victory would come by "demonstrating to the V.C. that they cannot win." This negative goal, however, ran head on into the requirement for American withdrawal that was built into the war policy. By seeking to "demonstrate" the impossibility of a Communist victory while at the same time promising withdrawal of American forces to the American public, the government turned the war into the waiting game that the Communists felt sure of winning. Once victory was defined in these terms, the clock was set ticking in the war for time, and every day that passed became a strategic gain for the Communists.

The endurance of the Vietnamese revolutionary forces in the face of first the French and then the American military machines is one of the most astounding and mysterious phenomena of its time. As a feat of sustained human will, it inspires awe. The mystery only deepens when certain characteristics of the regime in the North are taken into account. While its passion to achieve independence for Vietnam and to redress deep-seated social wrongs is unquestionable, and certainly was shared by the population at large, the regime's resort to repression and terror at every stage of its career is also unquestionable, and the bitterness created by these practices among large parts of the population is a matter of historical record. When the Communists took power in the North, as many as a million people, most of them Catholics, fled south. Almost immediately, as if to vindicate the wisdom of their flight, the regime launched a campaign of terror against "landlords" in the countryside, killing thousands. In the province of Nghe An, renowned for its anti-French revolutionary fervor, an anti-Communist uprising now broke out, and was ruthlessly suppressed. Later, in a rare and remarkable act of self-criticism, Vo Nguyen Giap said, "We attacked on too large a front, and, seeing enemies everywhere, resorted to terror, which became far too widespread. . . . Instead of recognizing education to be the first essential, we relied exclusively on organizational methods such as disciplinary punishments, expulsion from the party, executions. . . . Worse still, torture came to be regarded as normal practice." In describing the terror as "too widespread" (as opposed, presumably, to just widespread enough) and describing execution as an "organizational method," Giap revealed much about the normal practices of the regime, from which these "excesses" were a departure. Yet even the excesses were repeated. When the revolutionary forces took the city of Hué for several weeks during the Tet offensive in early 1968, they executed, at the very least, hundreds of people; and when the North Vietnamese took control of the South, in 1975, they created conditions such that tens of thousands of people preferred escape into the South China Sea in boats, most of which never arrived at any destination.

THE RELUCTANT EMPEROR

The rise to power of the Communists as the standard-bearer of the fight for national independence is a fact whose causes are rooted in Vietnamese history. What is clear even to the casual observer is that no Vietnamese force ever arose to seriously challenge them in this role. One historical detail is illustrative of the entire story. The French, wishing to find and promote a Vietnamese figure behind whom to rally the Vietnamese against the Vietminh, led by Ho Chi Minh, could find no one better to pick than the former emperor, Bao Dai. His had been a checkered career. Before and during the Second World War, he had served as titular head of the French colonial government. In March of 1945, at the command of the Japanese, who had let the French colonial structure stand during the war but who now learned that the Free French might be planning action against them, Bao Dai resigned and announced Vietnam's independence from France within the Japanese Greater East Asia Co-Prosperity Sphere. In August of that year, the Vietminh seized control of Hanoi while Japanese troops looked on, and declared independence, and now the resilient Bao Dai resigned for the second time in one year and proceeded to serve as "supreme adviser" to the revolutionary government. In 1947, the French entered into negotiations with him, and persuaded him to sign an agreement to be emperor again under what amounted to continued French control. Bao Dai, however, was a reluctant emperor. "A comic scene followed," Stanley Karnow writes in his book *Vietnam*. "Trying to escape his commitment to resume his imperial duties, Bao Dai fled to Europe, where he shifted from one city to another, hiding in cinemas by day and cabarets by night as [French representative] Bollaert chased him like a process server. Bollaert eventually won, and they returned to the Bay of Along on June 8, 1948."

THE REAL WAR

> "You know, you never defeated us on the battlefield," said the American colonel.
> The North Vietnamese colonel pondered this remark a moment. "That may be so," he replied, "but it is also irrelevant."
> —Conversation in Hanoi in April, 1975, quoted in *On Strategy*, by Colonel Harry G. Summers

Throughout the war, the relationship of the fighting in Vietnam to the eventual outcome was unclear. Because the results that mattered were the impact of the fighting on the wills of three peoples, "psychological" gains became more important than tangible ones. In most wars, psychological strategy is a useful adjunct to the actual combat; in Vietnam, the combat was an adjunct to psychological strategy. The fighting was important to whatever extent it influenced the wills of the protagonists; beyond that, it was "irrelevant." That was how the Communists could lose every battle and win the war. For the real war was not military but political, and it was fought in not one country but three. The problem for the United States was how to cash in its military winnings in political coin. In all three of the political theatres, it failed; worse, each military victory seemed to lead to political reverses. In North Vietnam, it appeared, the American bombing only stiffened the will of the country to resist. In South Vietnam, the victories were won at the expense of pulverizing the country physically, providing a poor foundation for the creation of the strong, independent regime in the South that American policy required. The moral absurdity of "destroying" the society we were trying to "save" was often pointed out; the strategic absurdity of the same policy was less often noted. The Americans in Vietnam liked to speak of the "military half" of what they were doing, but the "half" was in reality more like nine-tenths, and the other one-tenth—the contribution to "nation-building"— was often, in the context of the war, pure mockery. For example, it frequently happened that in driving the enemy out of a village the Americans would destroy it. That was the "military half." The "civilian half" then might be to drop thousands of leaflets on the ruins, explaining the evils of the N.L.F., or perhaps introducing the villagers to some hygienic measures that the Americans thought were a good idea. In the United States, where the public awaited with increasing impatience the promised end of the war, each new battle, even when the body count favored the American side, was evidence that the war would continue indefinitely, and here, too, political ground would be lost.

WILL III: THE UNITED STATES

On the morning of July 21, 1965, President Lyndon John-
son held a meeting with his senior advisers to decide how
many additional troops, if any, he should send to Vietnam.
Present among others were Secretary of State Dean Rusk,
Ambassador Henry Cabot Lodge, Secretary of Defense
Robert McNamara, and Adviser for National Security
Affairs McGeorge Bundy, all of whom favored large additional deployments. Almost alone among those present in
opposing the increase was Under-Secretary of State George
Ball. Repeatedly, after Ball had expressed his worries,
Johnson asked him to outline an alternative course. "Tell
me, what other road can I go?" Johnson asked at one point.
"But George, is there another course in the national interest—some course that is better than this one?" he asked
later. At the end of the morning meeting, he called another
for the afternoon, to hear Ball's answer. Ball began that
meeting by predicting an American defeat in Vietnam.
He warned of possible Chinese intervention. He foresaw
a "long war." He argued for a "tactical withdrawal" from
an unfavorable position. "I think we all have underesti-
mated the seriousness of this situation," he said, according
to notes of the meeting. "It is like giving cobalt treatment
to a terminal cancer case. I think a long, protracted war
will disclose our weakness, not our strength. The least
harmful way to cut losses in South Vietnam is to let
the government of South Vietnam decide it doesn't want
us to stay there. Therefore, we should put such pro-
posals to the government of South Vietnam as they can't
accept. Then, it would move to a neutral position. I have
no illusion that after we were asked to leave South
Vietnam that country would soon come under Hanoi
control."

The President did not rebut Ball's drastic prognosis; instead, he described what he saw as the even more drastic consequences of defeat:

> But George, wouldn't all those countries say that Uncle Sam was a paper tiger, wouldn't we lose credibility breaking the word of the three Presidents, if we did as you have proposed? It would seem to be irreparable.

His other advisers agreed. They also did not so much argue with Ball's pessimism (although some did argue that he presented too grim a picture) as articulate an even deeper pessimism about the consequences of an American defeat. McGeorge Bundy regarded the consequences of withdrawal as so utterly "disastrous" that even in the absence of a promising alternative he preferred to "waffle through." Rusk believed that the American commitment in Vietnam made "the U.S. stance with the U.S.S.R. creditable." McNamara agreed.

Today, with South Vietnam and Cambodia under North Vietnamese control, and the United States and the West still intact and strong, it is hard to recall the apocalyptic importance attached by American policy-makers to winning —or, more precisely, to not losing—in Vietnam. Johnson's description of the blow as "irreparable" to the fortunes of American power was characteristic. Nor was this just rhetoric. Johnson paid for his conviction with his presidency. The policy-makers of the Vietnam period were willing to deceive the public about many things (for example, their assessment of the regime in the South), but in this matter the public and the confidential records agree: from the beginning to the end of the Vietnam war, the men in charge of American foreign policy were persuaded that the fall of South Vietnam was a blow that the United States, and even the West as a whole, might well not survive.

In the United States, as in North Vietnam, preservation of the nation's will to fight was of course indispensable to the continuation of the war effort, but in the United States the question of will had, in addition, a global significance that far transcended any result that might occur within the borders of Vietnam. As the comments of the President and his advisers make clear, they believed that the war's chief importance lay in the fact that it was a spectacle on whose outcome the opinion of others around the world about American power depended. The word for the specific commodity they thought was at risk in Vietnam was "credibility," and every president who waged the war, from John F. Kennedy, who in March of 1961 told the columnist James Reston, "Now we have a problem of making our power credible, and Vietnam is the place," to Richard Nixon, who in April of 1970 announced to the public that if he had not just ordered the invasion of Cambodia "the credibility of the United States would be destroyed," asserted its central importance. To the Vietnamese foe, the intangible factor of will was indispensable for winning the war, but the goal of the war effort was the thoroughly concrete one of taking control of South Vietnam and uniting it with the North. American policy, however, was psychological in its ends as well as its means. Our attention was on our will itself, and what the appearance of its strength or weakness, as "demonstrated" in Vietnam, would signify to a watching world.

QUAGMIRE

It has been said that the Vietnam war was a quagmire. If so, it was not a Vietnamese quagmire into which the United

States was sucked but an American quagmire—a quagmire of doubt and confusion regarding its power, its will, and its credibility—into which Vietnam was sucked.

THE ROOTS OF CREDIBILITY

A lesson drawn from history, reasons of strategy, and domestic political pressure all converged to lend the doctrine of credibility its apparently unchallengeable sway over the minds of the policy-makers in the Vietnam period. The lesson of history, of course, was the lesson of Munich, teaching its conclusion that if aggression by a great power is not faced early it will have to be faced later at higher cost. For a generation of policy-makers, this historical analogy, in which communism (variously defined) played the role of Nazi Germany, provided the key to understanding international events. The analogy was not pulled out of thin air. The policy-makers had heard the Soviet Union proclaim that the future of the world was a communist future. They had watched the Soviet Union support and promote communist movements in Europe, Asia, and elsewhere. They had watched the Soviet Union impose its rule on Eastern Europe and back up that rule with the repeated use of military force. They had watched China turn communist, with Soviet support. And they had concluded that in global communism they faced a totalitarian power that, like Nazi Germany before it, was seeking world domination. Turning to Vietnam, they noted that Ho Chi Minh was a dedicated Marxist-Leninist who had lived in Moscow, and they observed him building in the North a single-party communist dictatorship along classic Soviet lines. And they further concluded that the communist movement in Vietnam was in essence an extension of the power of the centralized communist drive for domination of the world.

Yet there were other historical facts, given less importance by the Americans, which led to a different interpretation of events in Vietnam. Vietnam had, of course, been colonized by the French in the nineteenth century, and had been seeking its independence for most of the twentieth. If Ho Chi Minh was an undoubted communist of the old school, he also was an undoubted nationalist, who, more than anyone else, represented his country's longing for independence. The movement for independence, like the communist movement, had a global context: the almost entirely successful anticolonial movements in the former colonial countries, through which dozens of nations were becoming sovereign states. It was, of course, quite possible for Vietnam to become communist and independent at the same time. But it was not possible for Vietnam to become independent and be subjugated by Moscow at the same time: it could not both be a country achieving its independence and be Czechoslovakia in 1938. The key question for American policy was not the virtue of the regime but whether its strength was local or borrowed from a foreign power. If it was the former, then what began locally would end locally; or at any rate, the further spread of communism would depend primarily on local conditions in other countries. If it was the latter, then the further spread of communism could be expected, just as the further spread of Nazism should have been predicted after the fall of Czechoslovakia. If it was the former, the Munich analogy was wrong; if it was the latter, then the Munich analogy was right. The notion that local forces counted more than international ones received further confirmation: the rapidly developing breakup in the nineteen-sixties of the communist movement into a collection of quarreling, and even warring, parties and states, each of which clearly placed its own national or parochial interest ahead of those of the international movement. In this trend, the most dramatic event was the widening Sino-Soviet split. All of these facts, too, were known to the American policy-makers, but they lacked force or influence, and an important reason was the almost hypnotic grip of the Munich analogy upon the policy-makers' minds.

Developments in strategic theory seconded, but also crucially revised, the lesson of history. The chief subject matter of strategic theory was nuclear weapons, and nuclear weapons were much on the minds of the theorists of the Vietnam war. As Ambassador Lodge said in the July meeting with President Johnson, "I feel there is a greater threat to start World War III if we don't go in." And he added, "Can't we see the similarity with Munich?" However, if World War III were in the offing, it almost certainly would involve the use of nuclear weapons, and if they were used, the strategists knew, the outcome would be far different from that of World War II: it would probably not be the victory of one side or the other but the annihilation of both. At the end of the row of falling dominoes there were now two specters: defeat and annihilation. World War II had hardly been a welcome prospect, yet when it came it had been fightable and winnable. World War III, the strategists were coming to agree, would be neither, and any fighting or winning that was to take place had to occur at levels of warfare below the threshold of nuclear war.

"Credibility" first came into vogue as a primary goal of policy in criticisms levelled at the Eisenhower administration's policy of "massive retaliation." For example, in an influential article in 1954, William R. Kaufmann, a professor at Princeton University who later played an important role in the formulation of American nuclear strategy, noted that "we must face the fact that, if we are challenged to fulfill the threat of massive retaliation, we will be likely to suffer costs as great as those we inflict." In other words, both sides would be destroyed. In that situation, the policy of deterrence is "likely to result only in deterring the deterrer." Moreover, the adversary would know this in advance. Hence, "we must immediately face the prospect that the leaders of the Soviet Union and Red China would hardly endow . . . a doctrine [of massive retaliation] with much credibility." The way to shore up the United States' jeopardized credibility, Kaufmann believed, was to "show a willingness and ability to intervene with great conventional power in the peripheral areas, after the manner of Korea." It was through these steps in reasoning taken by Kaufmann and other advocates of limited war that the Vietnam war became entangled in considerations of high nuclear strategy, and came to be fought for the novel goal of maintaining the new holy grail of American policy, credibility.

Reinforcing the lessons of history and strategy were the pressures of domestic politics. Ever since Senator Joseph McCarthy and others on the political right had mounted their highly successful campaign of defamation and intimidation of those who they believed had been instrumental in "losing" China to communism in 1949, it had been an axiom of American politics that to "lose" another country to communism would be a sure path to political ruin. It has been said that the United States was deceived into entering and expanding the Vietnam war by its own overoptimistic propaganda. The record suggests, however, that the policy-makers stayed in Vietnam not so much because of overly optimistic hopes of winning—they could not have heard more pessimistic predictions than Ball's or bleaker assessments of the regime in the South than McNamara's—as because of overly pessimistic assessments of the consequences of losing. President Johnson had every reason to hate the war. Above all, it threatened to jeopardize the social legislation of his Great Society program. But in the event, the historical, strategic, and political wisdom of the day held him fast in Vietnam, and it was not until his own political fortunes crumbled beneath him that he was released.

THE NATURE OF THE WILL

The will of North Vietnam was solid; that of South Vietnam nonexistent. Only the will of the United States was changeable, wavering. It followed that the critical contests of the war would take place in the arena of American public opinion, much as elections, in their last stages, are decided among undecided voters. The choice before the American people, it is important to point out, was not between victory and defeat. Victory required a political victory not in the United States but in Vietnam—it required success in the misbegotten program of nation-building—and the American public was even more helpless to bring about such a thing than the military was in Vietnam. The question before the American public was if and when to liquidate the hopeless venture, if and when to break the stalemate and let the defeat occur.

In trying to understand the contest for the will of the United States, two actions of the will need to be distinguished. The first is the action by which the will decides which goal it wishes to pursue. Using the word in this sense, one can speak of the will of the American people either to remain in Vietnam or to withdraw. The second is the action by which the public, having made up its mind about the goal, backs up its choice with more or less resolve or determination—with more or less willpower.

Under the provisions of the Constitution for waging war, the two actions of the will are deliberately separated. By requiring a declaration of war, the Constitution seeks to ensure that the nation will first decide upon its goal and only then send its troops forth to achieve it—that the nation will debate first and fight later. In Vietnam, not only was there no declaration of war, there was no concerted attempt, until it was too late, to rally the public behind the war. Instead, there was a deliberate effort to evade public scrutiny. Arguing against the proposition that the Vietnam war was lost because of a collapse of American will at home, Harry G. Summers, in his book *On Strategy*, notes that such a collapse was hardly possible, inasmuch as the national will had never been invoked in the first place. By the time the public was brought fully into the discussion, half a million soldiers were in Vietnam and the public was being asked to ratify an accomplished fact. To the policy-makers' shock and dismay, it declined.

The mingling in the Vietnam war of the debating and the fighting sowed bitterness in the field and at home. The soldiers were carrying out their professional obligation to fight a war into which they had been sent by their democratically elected commander-in-chief. The citizens who opposed the war were faithfully carrying out their no less solemn obligation to decide whether it was in the nation's best interest to be in the war. The tragedy was that the two things were going on at the same time. The civilians were stung to hear themselves attacked for want of patriotism, or for lacking the "will" to resist the country's enemies— for being "nervous nellies," in the phrase of President Johnson. The military, for its part, was baffled and humiliated to find that in the arena in which it had been asked to fight, a mere expression of opinion in a debate at home had equal weight with injury and death in battle. That a soldier died capturing a hill in South Vietnam was a supreme sacrifice. That a politician or professor made a nice debating point in a lecture hall was only an expression of opinion. But in the scales in which the fate of the Vietnam venture was being weighed, the latter might outweigh the former. The soldiers were in the unenviable position of knowing that the advance they made in the morning by risking or losing their lives might be unravelled in the evening by a protester holding up a sign in a public demonstration, a columnist turning a clever phrase in his column, or a television interviewer giving a government official a skeptical look.

TET

The turning point in the contest for public opinion, most observers agree, was the Tet offensive, in February and March of 1968, in which the North Vietnamese and the National Liberation Front launched a coordinated attack on more than a hundred cities and other targets throughout South Vietnam. Within days, the attacks were driven back in most of the country; the exception was the city of Hué, which the Communists captured and held for another three weeks. But while the enemy was being driven out of the cities of South Vietnam, public confidence in President Johnson's war policies was being destroyed. Two months after the beginning of the attack, he announced his decision not to run for a second term and his decision to halt the bombing of North Vietnam north of the twentieth parallel. A little more than a month later, on May 10th, peace talks with the North Vietnamese opened in Paris.

Tet was to the United States what the burning of Moscow was to Napoleon's invasion of Russia in 1812: the beginning of the long road out. Henry Kissinger, who arrived in the White House a year later as President Nixon's adviser for national security affairs, remarked later that after Tet, "no matter how effective our actions, the prevalent strategy could no longer achieve its objectives within a period or with force levels politically acceptable to the American people." The protracted, bloody, divisive withdrawal began.

Tet did not in itself end the Vietnam war, but it set in motion a vortex of forces that did. The depth of the political consequences was made clear almost immediately, in the Democratic presidential primary in New Hampshire, in which Johnson was being opposed by Senator Eugene McCarthy, who was running on a platform of opposition to the war. Public-opinion polls showed a mixed reaction to Tet. One showed that the percentage of those who wanted the United States to withdraw from the war had actually declined from forty-five per cent (the figure for the previous November) to twenty-four per cent; but another poll taken during Tet showed the percentage of those who approved President Johnson's handling of the war declining from forty per cent to twenty-six per cent. But the measure of public opinion that counted was none of these; it was the vote in New Hampshire, which McCarthy, who before Tet had not been taken seriously as a political force, fell short of winning by only three hundred votes out of fifty thousand cast. Four days later, Robert Kennedy, a still more formidable opponent of the war and of Johnson, announced his candidacy. The next primary, in Wisconsin, was scheduled for April 2nd, and soundings taken by the Johnson camp showed him losing badly. On March 31st, he announced his decision to withdraw from the race.

Within the administration, in February and March, an equally rapid evolution was taking place. In late March,

Secretary of Defense McNamara, apparently having lost his faith in the war effort, left office, and was replaced by Clark Clifford. Johnson instructed Clifford to prepare a report on the war and to make recommendations for the future. Within a few days, Clifford had decided that the United States had to start to disengage from Vietnam. His thinking at the time, which he described later to Stanley Karnow in the form of a series of questions he put to the top military men, exemplified the rapid erosion of belief in the war in the minds of many men close to Johnson:

> How long would it take to succeed in Vietnam? They didn't know. How many more troops would it take? They couldn't say. Were two hundred thousand the answer? They weren't sure. Might they need more? Yes, they might need more. Could the enemy build up in exchange? Probably. So what was the plan to win the war? Well, the only plan was that attrition would wear out the Communists, and they would have had enough. Was there any indication that we've reached that point? No, there wasn't.

The military vacillated. General William Westmoreland, commander of United States forces in Vietnam, claimed to be heartened by his battlefield successes—in one interview he likened the offensive to the Battle of the Bulge, as if the collapse of the enemy was imminent—but shortly he undercut his optimistic message (which was falling on deaf ears among the members of the public in any case) by joining with Chairman of the Joint Chiefs of Staff Earle G. Wheeler in requesting a global buildup in American forces of 206,000 men, of whom 108,000 would be sent to Vietnam. "I desperately need reinforcements," Westmoreland told the President. On March 10th, the story was leaked to the *New York Times* (which mistakenly reported that all 206,000 men had been requested for dispatch to Vietnam), confirming the growing public impression that the war was out of control. It was two days later that Senator McCarthy achieved his near-victory in New Hampshire.

The 206,000-man troop increase, which was rejected after Clifford's reassessment of policy, would have required mobilization of the reserves—a step that would have sent a particularly strong signal of alarm to the public and that Johnson had rejected several times before. In February, the possible breaching of another important threshold—the most important one of all—became a news story. On February 8th, Senator McCarthy charged that there had been "some demands" in the administration for the use of nuclear weapons in Vietnam. There followed a series of denials from administration spokesmen, culminating in a statement by the President that "so far as I am aware" neither the "Joint Chiefs of Staff, the Secretary of State, nor the Secretary of Defense" had at any time "considered or made a recommendation in any respect to the employment of nuclear weapons." This was true but incomplete. The person conspicuously missing from the list was the President himself, who, alarmed by the course of events in an important battle at the American military base of Khe Sanh in South Vietnam, had queried Westmoreland whether as President he might sometime soon face a decision whether or not the use of nuclear weapons might be required. Westmoreland had replied that their use "should not be required in the present situation," but added that if there were a North Vietnamese invasion across the Demilitarized Zone, then "I visualize that either tactical nuclear weapons or chemical agents would be active candidates for deployment."

As it happened, an economic crisis also was gathering in the crucial months of February and March. The crisis had nothing to do with Tet, but it had everything to do with the Vietnam war. Owing in great measure to a growing imbalance in the federal budget due to the cost of the war, the dollar was losing value in world markets, and a run on purchases of gold had begun. The crisis came to a head in the days just before and after the leak of the troop request and the voting in New Hampshire. On March 11th, there was a run on gold and a flight from the dollar. On March 14th, the Treasury closed the gold market. On March 15th, Johnson wrote a letter to the prime ministers of Europe in which he warned that "these financial disorders—if not promptly and firmly overcome—can profoundly damage the political relations between Europe and America and set in motion forces like those which disintegrated the Western world between 1929 and 1933." The European leaders and financial leaders around the world were worried that a large American troop increase of the kind proposed by Wheeler and Westmoreland would further unbalance the American deficit, further erode the dollar, and spread economic panic. As Gabriel Kolko points out in his book *Anatomy of a War*, anxiety on this score was of crucial importance in the decision by the administration to turn down the troop increase.

In the early nineteen-sixties, Washington planned to fight what in every sense of the word was to be a limited war—limited in casualties, limited in the types of weaponry employed, limited in the number of troops required, limited in its objectives, limited in cost, limited in political impact, and, perhaps most important, limited in time. By March of 1968, every one of these limits had been breached or was in question. The request for mobilization of the reserves, the speculation about the possible need to use nuclear weapons, the economic crisis, and the political collapse formed a tight, interconnected net of forces. When the President led the country into war, his advisers had assured him that the costs could be borne. After Tet, he found himself facing four distinct abysses—the abyss of endless expanding ground war in Asia, the abyss of nuclear escalation, the abyss of global economic catastrophe, and the abyss of his personal political demise in the primaries in New Hampshire and Wisconsin.

MILITARY DEFEAT, "PSYCHOLOGICAL" VICTORY

Tet presented the military paradox at the heart of the Vietnam war in its most acute form: our adversaries' worst military defeat became their greatest victory in the war. They lost their way to victory. Three days after the offensive was launched, President Johnson held a press conference. Defensively, plaintively, he argued that Tet was a defeat for the enemy, and, sounding the theme of self-defeat that was to so occupy President Nixon later, he urged that Americans not, by their own words and actions, transform the real enemy defeat into a "psychological victory." "Now, I am no great sophisticated strategist," he humbly admitted to the reporters. "I know that you are not. But let us assume that the best figures we can have are from our responsible military commanders. They say 10,000 died and we lost 249, and the South Vietnamese lost 500. Now that doesn't look like a communist victory. I can count." Johnson's appeal announced an interpretation of Tet that was to be echoed throughout the war and after. For example, in *Big Story*, a voluminous analysis of the press coverage of Tet, Peter Braestrup argues that distorted press coverage of the offensive turned an actual victory into a seeming defeat. "Rarely," Braestrup writes, "has crisis journalism turned out, in retrospect, to have veered so widely from reality. Essentially, the dominant themes of the words and film from Vietnam, rebroadcast in comments, editorials, and much political rhetoric at home, added up to a portrait of defeat for the allies. Historians, on the contrary, have concluded that the Tet offensive resulted in a military-political setback for Hanoi in the South." This conclusion, in turn, offers support for the conclusion that the war as a whole was a victory won by the soldiers but thrown away by the civilians (though Braestrup himself does not make this broader charge).

The distinction between military results and "psychological" ones became a commonplace at the time of Tet. *Newsweek*, to give just one example, took General Westmoreland to task for judging the offensive in "strictly military—rather than political or psychological—terms," as if to say that the casualty figures and the other results from the battlefield were somehow to be discounted. But what, exactly, was this "psychological" victory in whose name actual military results supposedly lost their meaning? One answer, frequently suggested in the press at the time, was that the offensive disrupted the Pacification Program so badly that it could never recover. Many American officials believed this to be true at the time. However, Braestrup convincingly argues that events in the following years show that the N.L.F., which suffered heavy casualties at Tet, was actually politically weakened by the offensive. The other answer—the principal one offered at the time by the press and by analysts later—is that the "psychological" victory in question was in the United States, in the court of American public opinion. The question then becomes how it could happen that a military victory could bring about a psychological defeat. According to Braestrup, when Robert J. Northshield, a producer for *NBC News,* was once

Robert Kennedy said in a speech, "We have sought to solve by military might a conflict whose issue depends on the will and conviction of the South Vietnamese people. It's like sending a lion to halt an epidemic of jungle rot." And *Newsweek*, in words that foreshadowed the exchange between the American colonel and the Vietnamese colonel at the end of the war, wrote, "Even if the U.S. was to win a clear-cut military victory in South Vietnam—a prospect that now seems remote indeed—it would be a hollow and ephemeral triumph unless the people of South Vietnam demonstrated the will and ability to govern themselves effectively." In the new war, the economic costs were disastrous, the limits on limited war were insecure, and the end was nowhere in sight. The word "stalemate" began to crop up with increasing frequency. In the words of Max Frankel, writing in the *New York Times* in February, Tet "could well create the impression of the stalemate that the Administration has so vigorously denied. If that should ever become the analysis of the American electorate, President Johnson would indeed be vulnerable to the charges of both doves and hawks that he can neither end the war nor win it." The public now understood that the war in its present form would probably last indefinitely and possibly expand greatly, and it had never accepted, or even been asked to accept, such a prospect.

THE FORCES

After the war, Stanley Karnow asked General Tran Do, one of the planners of the offensive, what its goals had been. "In all honesty," he answered, "we didn't achieve our main objective, which was to spur uprisings throughout the South. Still, we inflicted heavy casualties on the Americans and their puppets, and that was a big gain for us. As for making an impact on the United States, it had not been our intention—but it turned out to be a fortunate result." The North Vietnamese had long shown an appreciation for the political dimension of the war, but at Tet it appears that they failed to understand what they had accomplished. They had placed great hopes in a planned uprising in the cities of South Vietnam, and it had failed completely to materialize. They were as dismayed, it seems, by their military reverses and their failed political hopes in South Vietnam as Westmoreland was pleased by them. Insofar as this was the case, none of the principal actors in the Tet offensive were aware of the deeper forces that had been set in motion. But the forces went to work anyway.

GENERAL WESTMORELAND

"In sum, I do not believe Hanoi can hold up under a long war," General Westmoreland said on February 25th at a press conference. It was one of the most spectacular of his many spectacular misjudgments regarding the war he was fighting. Among all the Americans who played a major role in shaping the American war policy, he was perhaps the one who misunderstood it most purely. There was method in his misunderstanding; he misunderstood the war systematically. His eye was fixed rigidly on the measurements for success in a conventional war—on positions taken or defended, on numbers of enemy troops killed—and was blind to the forces that actually were determining the war's outcome. War is not a game, but in war there are certain principles, or rules, which define the pathways to victory or defeat. Westmoreland was following rules, but they were not the ones that applied to Vietnam. Perhaps they were the rules for the Second World War, as his analogy of the Tet offensive with the Battle of the Bulge suggests.

At times, he seemed to live in a world of his own. Events that cast others into despair filled him with elation. Where they saw unbroken gloom, he found the light at the end of the tunnel. In the game that was in his mind, he had made move after move, winning battle after battle, piling up accomplishment after accomplishment, until victory seemed within his grasp. But he was playing checkers, and the game was chess.

VIETNAM AND THE SECOND WORLD WAR

Westmoreland may have been an extreme case, but he was hardly alone in seeking to impose the patterns of the Second World War on Vietnam, as the unshakeable reliance of the policy-makers on the Munich analogy shows. It has to be said in Westmoreland's defense that if the Munich analogy had been the correct one, his conventional strategy would in all likelihood have fit the facts of the case. It was an assumption of the analogy that events in Vietnam were the work of an outside power. If that had been so, two other things would also have been so. First, because the forces opposing the United States would have been outside ones, the American forces probably would have been a suitable and effective instrument for battling them. In that case, American victories in battles would have led to victory in the war, "psychological" factors notwithstanding. Second, there might well have emerged a strong, legitimate political force in South Vietnam which, galvanized into action by the foreign attempt to take away the country's independence, would, with appropriate assistance from the United States (always aiding the local forces, never supplanting them), have been able to build a strong regime based on the support of its own people—thereby providing this crucial element in the American formula

for victory. In short, if Westmoreland's anachronistic operational strategy was at odds at every point with the actual
war he was fighting, it was fully consistent with the war
his civilian superiors had thought they were sending him
to fight.

WIN OR GET OUT

Tet created a consensus of dissatisfaction with President
Johnson's war policy but no similar consensus regarding a
policy to replace it. Some people wanted the United States
to win the war, and others wanted the country to withdraw.
Many—perhaps the majority—professed to prefer either
alternative to current policy, and adopted the opinion that
the United States should "win or get out." Even after the
war ended, this opinion survived as one of the most popular
formulations of what the United States should have done
in Vietnam. Holding this opinion was one of the luxuries
of being a citizen on the sidelines of events rather than a
policy-maker at the center. For while the public supposedly
was broad-mindedly willing to accept either winning or
getting out, it was hardly willing to accept the consequences
that the policy-makers knew ·to be all but inevitable if
either prescription were actually to be followed. The
policy-makers knew that if they tried to "win"—for example, by invading North Vietnam—they would incur
greatly increased casualties and risk a general war, which
could become a nuclear war. And they knew that if they
got the United States out of the war, it would be lost. And
they knew, too, that however pleased the public might be
with its sensible-sounding win-or-get-out formula, it was
likely to be very unhappy either with a wider war or with
losing the war. The public's distaste for a wider war was

demonstrated in the landslide defeat by President Johnson of Senator Barry Goldwater, who had recommended a greater war effort, and it was now being demonstrated again in the public's reaction to Tet. And the public's distaste for losing countries to communism had been demonstrated by the political hue and cry following the "loss" of China in 1949. The public's true counsel was win (but don't wage a wider war) or get out (but don't lose) and neither course corresponded to anything that was possible in the actual world.

THE LEGACY

The defeat in Vietnam left the public with two unsatisfied but contradictory yearnings, which corresponded to its two vain prescriptions for ending the war. On the one hand, feeling humiliated by the defeat, it wanted a victory somewhere. On the other hand, chastened by the terrible price paid in Vietnam, it dreaded paying the cost in money and lives for such a victory. Ideally, the United States would win something somewhere without having to pay any price. Miraculously, just such a victory was provided, in 1983, when the Reagan administration invaded Grenada (population 108,000) and overthrew its leftist government. Grenada was the legacy of Vietnam. A political pollster's dream, it permitted the United States to win *and* get out, the objective that had eluded the policy-makers for more than a decade in Vietnam.

WINNING IN VIETNAM

In his carefully reasoned, strikingly original analysis of Vietnam, *On Strategy*, Colonel Harry G. Summers refights and wins the Vietnam war. Rejecting as he does the notion that the war was lost because of a collapse of national will at home, he becomingly (but in my opinion mistakenly) places the blame for the defeat squarely on the shoulders of his own military profession, whose job it was, he argues, "to judge the true nature of the Vietnam war, communicate those facts to our civilian decision-makers, and to recommend appropriate strategies." Had they done their job right, Summers believes, the war could have been won.

The great mistake of the American military, in his opinion, was to take the Communists at their word when they said that in Vietnam they were fighting a "people's war," or "revolutionary war." In the early years of the war, he grants, the N.L.F. was a force to be reckoned with, but then the war began to change. Around 1965, the North Vietnamese began to send their troops south, and the threat to South Vietnam was transformed into a conventional one. He quotes the pithy Norman Hannah: "In South Vietnam we responded mainly to Hanoi's simulated insurgency rather than to its real but controlled aggression, as a bull charges the toreador's cape, not the toreador." Lunging at the false target, the military became mired in political tasks that were not suitable to it, including nation-building. Summers is as contemptuous of nation-building as any dovish critic of the war. "It is difficult today to recall the depth of our arrogance," he writes, and goes on to quote, and mock, an article written for *Army* magazine in 1962: " 'Although the official U.S. policy is to refrain from injecting Americans into foreign governments under our tutelage and support, the pragmatic approach is to guide the inexperienced and shaky governments of the emerging nations by persuasion and coaxing if possible, and by hard-selling and pressure if the soft methods don't work." And he approvingly quotes an article written in 1976 by General Frederick C. Weyand, who served as commander of the Military Assistance Command, Vietnam:

> The major military error was a failure to communicate to the civilian decision-makers the capabilities and limitations of America military power. There are certain tasks the American military can accomplish on behalf of another nation. They can defeat enemy forces on the battlefield. They can blockade the enemy's coast. They can cut the lines of supply and communication. They can carry the war to the enemy on land, sea, and air. . . . But there are also fundamental limitations of American military power. . . . The Congress and the American people will not permit their military to take total control of another nation's political, economic, and social institutions in order to completely orchestrate the war.

Many critics have suggested that in sending the military to perform political tasks, the American policy-makers misunderstood the political aspects of the war. Summers, equally contemptuous of military meddling in politics, turns the argument around and says that the practice also "obscured the true nature of military force." The price for this loss of clarity was great, in his opinion, for the real task for the United States in Vietnam—stopping the aggression from the North—was one for which the military was excellently suited. Five divisions, withdrawn from their futile mission of supporting the South Vietnamese government with search-and-destroy missions in the south and redeployed in a defensive line just below the Demilitarized Zone and stretching across Laos to the Thai border, could, he thinks, have accomplished the mission.

It's quite possible, of course, that both criticisms of American policy are correct: that the United States misunderstood both the political and the military sides of its endeavor. And while fighting wars in retrospect is no doubt a good deal easier than fighting them at the time, it may be that Summers identifies a military strategy that would have been superior to the one followed by Westmoreland. ("Superior" in this context means superior in relieving the regime in the South from military pressure.) Unanswered and almost unaddressed by Summers' strategy, however, is the political question, which would not have vanished because the American military had prudently withdrawn from the effort to resolve it. Summers and Weyand are surely right in arguing that it is the job of soldiers to defend nations, not to build them. But in South Vietnam it was necessary to create a nation before it could be defended, whether at the Demilitarized Zone or elsewhere. In addressing this unfulfilled but basic need, Summers can only fall back on the old refrain that "the Vietnamese themselves" would have taken care of it: "What the United States could never do was 'solve the internal problems' of South Vietnam. Only the Vietnamese themselves could accomplish this task."

LESSONS OF VIETNAM

A nation can impose its will on another through intervention with military forces, but not after they have been withdrawn.

In our time, the peoples of even the smallest countries are powerfully resolved to choose their own political destinies. Acting within their own borders, they have done more in the last forty years to change the political map of the globe than the superpowers have.

The fact that a people has chosen its own destiny does not mean that it has chosen wisely. (Witness Iran.)

There is abroad in our world a force mightier than force —call it popular will, call it political action. Repeatedly, the possessors of overwhelmingly superior force—the United States in Vietnam, the Shah in Iran, Ferdinand Marcos in the Philippines—have, to their disbelief, found themselves overmatched by it.

The range of circumstances in which the use of force is effective has decreased in our world. The limited-war theory that guided the Vietnam war started with the assumption that nuclear weapons were no longer usable instruments of force. The war was fought in part to "demonstrate" that instruments of force below the threshold of nuclear war were still usable. The demonstration failed. The proposition was disproved. The limited-war forces encountered local forces—of which the most important were political, not military—with which they could not cope. The lion failed to stop the jungle rot. (However, as we now know, the eclipse in many parts of the world of military power, foreign and local, by local political power need not cause the United States to despair. In many countries—Spain, Portugal, Greece, Argentina, the Philippines, among others —the victorious local political forces have brought forth democracies. Not in every case does right-wing dictatorship give way to its left-wing counterpart.)

The government of a democratic country should not go to war without first obtaining the support of its people. Winning this support is not a "problem" for the policymakers to solve after the fact, an ingredient to be added to the mixture once the war is under way. It is the foundation of the war effort, and when it is not present the war should not be fought at all.

When popular support is lacking, wars fought to secure liberty abroad undermine liberty at home.

The power and prestige of the United States are based on more substantial stuff than our image-conscious policy-makers have believed in recent years. They are prone to a drastically pessimistic view according to which the failure of American power anywhere must lead to its collapse everywhere. It was this pessimistic view of the global situation—compounded of the lesson of Munich and nuclear strategic theory of the late nineteen-fifties and early sixties, and summed up in the obsessive concern with the "credibility" of American power—and not mistaken optimisism about the situation in Vietnam, that pinned the United States in Vietnam for more than a decade. Events have shown this view to be false. South Vietnam fell, but the United States still stands.

THE LAST DAYS

Colonel Summers discovers within the "people's war" in Vietnam a conventional war that he thinks could have been won, and in this conventional war he believes he has identified "the true nature of the war." As conclusive proof, he offers the postmortem on North Vietnam's final victorious offensive against the South written by General Van Tien Dung, the North Vietnamese Army's field commander at the time. In this document, called *Our Great Spring Victory*, Summers finds the classic, Clausewitzian essence of the war finally revealed, stripped bare of any cant about "people's war." "General Dung's account of the North Vietnamese final offensive reads like a Leavenworth practical exercise on offensive operations," Summers writes. He continues, with unconcealed admiration, "Like the plaque at the entrance to our own Command and Staff College—'Audace, audace, toujours audace'—the North Vietnamese General Staff charged with planning the endeavor of Dung's four Army corps worked beside a large poster which read, 'Lightning speed, more lightning speed; boldness, more boldness.' They put the motto into practice." Here was no vague thinking about the primacy of the "political" over the "military," of "psychological" victories over battlefield ones. Instead, as Summers shows, there is only a cool and rational appraisal of the opposing armed forces, and a carefully thought-through plan for military victory. For example:

> The question was to determine the correct direction for developing the operations of the Central Highlands forces in the most continuous, rapid and effective manner in order to make full use of their might in the least possible time. Such a direction must be aimed at destroying as many vital forces of the enemy as possible and strategically dividing both militarily and administratively the territory under the Thieu administration's temporary control of the south in order to upset the arrangement of the strategic positions and the strategic situation of the enemy.

In Dung's account, the principles of classical warfare seem suddenly to come to life. Here are forces "massing" to overwhelm the foe; here are feints and diversions; here are attacks "developing" according to sound strategic principles. And all of it is proceeding like clockwork, or even better, for, as Dung notes, the cadres "could not draw maps

quickly enough to catch up with the advance of our forces."
The ironies inherent in Summers' picture are rich: the
mighty United States Army is mired in woolly-headed,
"fashionable" strategies of "people's war" put forward by
Communist propaganda, while Communist generals, entirely unburdened by any such nonsense, are applying our
traditional military principles to defeat us.

If General Dung's account in *Our Great Spring Victory*
were all we knew of the fall of South Vietnam, it would
indeed appear as if the real war in Vietnam was a conventional one, and that the North Vietnamese won it by
outstrategizing (though not outfighting) us. But we know
more, and in the full historical record something much
stranger than the rational and orderly victory described by
General Dung emerges. When the North Vietnamese
struck, in March of 1975, a sort of shudder ran through
South Vietnamese society from top to bottom. Like a building that hangs suspended in midair for a split second after
its foundations have been dynamited, the government of
South Vietnam remained standing briefly, and began to go
through motions of responding; then it flew to pieces.
"The military fate of South Vietnam really was sealed in
about twenty days," write Stephen T. Hosmer, Konrad
Kellen, and Brian M. Jenkins in *The Fall of South Vietnam*, which was written for the Historian, Office of the
Secretary of Defense. It was, in the words of one South
Vietnamese officer who spoke to Hosmer, a rout "unique
in the annals of military history." At the top of the government, the authors write, there was "irresolution and
violent reversal of strategy." Within a few days of the
attack, President Thieu made a ruinous decision to in
effect abandon large portions of the northern section of
South Vietnam by withdrawing the troops there farther

south. These troops, judged unable to defend their territory by their commander, soon proved incapable even of
retreating. Instead, they disintegrated as a military force.
Scenes of pointless horror began to unfold along the route
of abortive withdrawal. In the words of a South Vietnamese colonel:

> I saw old people and babies fall down on the
> road and tanks and trucks would go over
> them. . . . Nobody could control anything.
> No order. The troops were mixed with the
> dependents and civilians and were trying to
> take care of all the children and wives. You
> can't imagine it.

And according to another officer:

> The soldiers kept shouting insults at Thieu
> for this impossible and terrible retreat. Some
> reached the limit of despair and killed their
> officers. An artillery commander was shot to
> death by some Rangers who wanted his beauti-
> ful wristwatch. The despair was so great that
> at one point two or three guerillas arriving
> at the scene could make prisoners of a hun-
> dred Rangers.

Soon, the pandemonium of the retreat spread to the society
at large. The phrase "disintegration of society" is given
concrete meaning by what now occurred. South Vietnamese
soldiers, far from fighting the enemy, began to battle one
another and shoot civilians. They went on rampages of
looting. A South Vietnamese officer described the scene in
Danang:

Bands of children, hungry and thirsty, wan-
dered aimlessly on the streets, demolishing
everything which happened to fall into their
hands. Danang was seized by convulsions of
collective hysteria.

And an American reporter on the scene wrote:

People are jogging pointlessly and crazily
down the streets. Others are taking houses
apart, piece by piece. A young man walks outside carrying a wooden door, wrenched from
its hinges, atop his head. Another is carrying bits of broken glass in his hands.

As for fighting between the opposing armies, it was rare.
In the words of one American official on the scene, there
was "no war." In the city of Nha Trang, there was "no
fighting at all," a South Vietnamese colonel recalled. The
same was true at Hué and Danang. In I Corps, there was
no large battle. With the exception of a few engagements,
in which units of the South Vietnamese Army stood and
fought, the same pattern repeated itself throughout the
country. The officers deserted the men, and the men fled or
went on rampages. A colonel recalled the scene at Nha
Trang:

No one in charge of the whole area. So everyone is thinking about running. That is all.
Each province chief is in charge of a big sum
of money, so everyone tries to get it out from
the treasury and run with it.

Something other than a military defeat was occurring. A
society was tearing itself to shreds, and it was the action of

this dissolution, not North Vietnamese shells and bullets, that was the specific process by which South Vietnam fell. In the words of more than one South Vietnamese official to Hosmer, "We defeated ourselves."

The collapse of South Vietnam revealed its true nature, and with it, the true nature of the war. It was a society entirely without inner cohesion, held together only by foreign arms, foreign money, foreign political will. When, deprived of that support, it faced its foe alone and the mirage evaporated, it was revealed for what it was—a loose collection of individuals. In their bones, the officials of the Saigon regime knew that by itself South Vietnam had no powers of resistance. Their real "plan" for defeating the North Vietnamese, as they told Hosmer, was American reintervention in the war. They wanted the United States to "do something." When it became clear that it wouldn't, they gave up. So great was the habit of relying on the United States that as the government was falling rumors became widespread that a "deal" had been struck between the Americans and the North Vietnamese to let them have the country. Having depended on the United States' support for several decades, the South Vietnamese apparently could not conceive of a fate that might befall them other than by American arrangement.

The record of the fall of the South does not, strictly speaking, contradict General Dung's version of it, but it places it in a completely different light. There is no reason to doubt that everything he says happened happened—that, in best Clausewitzian fashion, he executed plans that, for example, involved "simultaneously and actively carrying out diversionary tactics to attract the enemy to the northwestern part of the Central Highlands in order to enable our side to maintain secrecy and surprise in the south until we opened fire on Ban Me Thout," or that he fashioned things in such a way that in spite of overall equality of his infantry with South Vietnamese infantry, the ratio of troop strength in I Corps was "5.5 of our troops for each enemy soldier," and "the ratio of tanks 1.2 to 1." Nor is there any reason to doubt that all this planning was just as brilliant as Colonel Summers believes it was. But there is every reason to doubt that it caused the North Vietnamese victory, or that it revealed "the true nature of the war." For in actuality "there was no war."

The North Vietnamese, victors over the French, and acknowledged even by their foes to be masters of the military art, never did win any battles in the war against the United States. When they faced a force mightier than theirs—the American military machine—they lost every time. When they faced a foe they could beat—the South Vietnamese—he ran away so fast that he could not be engaged. In neither case did it make any difference. The Communists' defeats at the hands of the Americans led to victory over them, and the failure to engage the South Vietnamese led to the same result. The reason in both cases was the primacy of politics in all phases of the Vietnam war and in all theatres of the conflict. In the first case, even as the United States was winning battles, the American people were turning against the war. In the second case, the political collapse of the South everywhere outran the attack by the North. General Dung's feints and diversions played to an empty theatre, his traps closed on a vacuum. The motto of the North Vietnamese forces might be "Lightning speed, more lightning speed," but the political forces fuelling the collapse of the South were faster still. The North Vietnamese Army was moving so fast that its cadres could not keep it supplied with maps, but History, racing in the same direction, arrived at the goal first, snatching victory from the jaws of victory.

It fell to one Bui Tinh, a colonel in the North Vietnamese Army, to take the surrender of the Saigon regime.

"I have been waiting since early this morning to transfer power to you," General Minh, who had been head of state for only the last two days, told Bui Tinh when he met him.

"There is no question of your transferring power," Bui Tinh answered. "Your power has crumbled. You cannot give up what you do not have." Bui Tinh meant that the collapse of South Vietnam was already complete and that General Minh now represented nobody, but his words were also true in a broader sense. The power of the South Vietnamese had never been truly theirs, whether to keep or to hand over. It had belonged to the Americans, and the Americans were gone.

THE
VILLAGE
OF
BEN SUC

I DEDICATE this book,
with love, to my parents

UP TO A FEW months ago, Ben Suc was a prosperous village of some thirty-five hundred people. It had a recorded history going back to the late eighteenth century, when the Nguyen Dynasty, which ruled the southern part of Vietnam, fortified it and used it as a base in its campaign to subjugate the natives of the middle region of the country. In recent years, most of the inhabitants of Ben Suc, which lay inside a small loop of the slowly meandering Saigon River, in Binh Duong Province, about thirty miles from the city of Saigon, were engaged in tilling the exceptionally fertile paddies bordering the river and in tending the extensive orchards of mangoes, jackfruit, and an unusual strain of large grapefruit that is a famous product of the Saigon River region. The village also supported a small group of merchants, most of them of Chinese descent, who ran shops in the marketplace, including a pharmacy that sold a few modern medicines to supplement traditional folk cures of herbs and roots; a bicycle shop that also sold second-hand motor scooters; a hair-dresser's; and a few small restaurants, which sold mainly noodles. These merchants were far wealthier than the other villagers; some of them even owned second-hand cars for their businesses. The village had no electricity and little machinery of any kind. Most families kept pigs, chickens, ducks, one or two cows for milk, and a team of water buffaloes for labor, and harvested enough rice and vegetables to sell some in the market every year. Since Ben Suc was a rich village, the market was held daily, and it attracted farmers from neighboring villages as well as the Ben Suc farmers. Among the people of Ben Suc, Buddhists were more numerous than Confucianists, but in practice the two religions tended to resemble each other more than they differed, both conforming more to locally developed village customs practiced by everyone than to the requirements of the two doctrines. The Confucianists prayed to Confucius as a Buddha-like god, the Buddhists regarded their ancestors as highly as any Confucianist did, and everyone celebrated roughly the same main holidays. In 1963, Christian missionary teams, including both Vietnamese and Americans, paid several visits to the village. One of these groups began its missionary work by slowly driving its car down the narrow main streets of the village, preaching through a loudspeaker mounted on the top of the car, and singing hymns accompanied by an accordion. Then, in the center of the village, a Vietnamese minister gave a sermon. He argued for the existence of God by pointing out that Vietnamese spontaneously cry out *"Troi oi!"* ("Oh God!") when they fall or get hurt, and told the villagers that their sins were as numerous as the particles of red dust that covered the leaves of the trees in the dry season. (The soil around Ben Suc is of a reddish hue.) Just as only God could wash every leaf clean by sending down a rainstorm, only God could wash away their countless sins. At the end of the sermon, he asked the villagers to kneel and pray, but none did. When he asked for questions, or even for arguments against what he had said, only the old village fool stepped forward to challenge him, to the amusement of the small group of villagers who had assembled to listen. Ordinarily, to entertain themselves, small groups of men would get together in the evening every two weeks or so to drink the local liquor—sometimes until dawn—and occasionally they would go fishing in the river and fry their catch together at night. Some of the marriages in the village were arranged and some were love matches. Although parents—particularly the girls' parents— didn't like it, couples often sneaked off in the evenings for secret rendezvous in the tall bamboo groves or in glades of banana trees. At times, there were stormy, jealous love affairs, and occasionally these resulted in fights between the young men. Parents complained that the younger generation was rebellious and lazy, and sometimes called their children *hu gao*—rice pots— who did nothing but eat.

Troops of the Army of the Republic of Vietnam (usually written "ARVN" and pronounced "Arvin" by the Americans) maintained an outpost in Ben Suc from 1955 until late 1964, when it was routed in an attack by the National Liberation Front (or N.L.F., or Vietcong, or V.C.), which kidnapped and later executed the government-appointed village chief and set up a full governing apparatus of its own. The Front demanded—and got—not just the passive support of the Ben Suc villagers but their active participation both in the governing of their own village and in the war effort. In the first months, the Front called several village-wide meetings. These began with impassioned speeches by leaders of the Front, who usually opened with a report of victories over the Americans and the "puppet troops" of the government, emphasizing in particular the downing of helicopters or planes and the disabling of tanks. Two months after the "liberation" of the village, the Front repelled an attack by ARVN troops, who abandoned three American M-113 armored personnel-carriers on a road leading into the village when they fled. The disabled hulks of these carriers served the speakers at the village meetings as tangible proof of their claimed superiority over the Americans, despite all the formidable and sophisticated weaponry of the intruders. Occasionally, a badly burned victim of an American napalm attack or an ex-prisoner of the government who had been tortured by ARVN troops was brought to Ben Suc to offer testimony and show his wounds to the villagers, giving the speakers an opportunity to condemn American and South Vietnamese-government atrocities. They painted a monstrous picture of the giant Americans, accusing them not only of bombing villages but also of practicing cannibalism and slitting the bellies of pregnant women. The speeches usually came to a close with a stirring call for support in the struggle and for what was sometimes called "the full coöperation and solidarity among the people to beat the American aggressors and the puppet troops." The speeches were often followed by singing and dancing, particularly on important National Liberation Front holidays, such as the founding day of the Front, December 20th, and Ho Chi Minh's birthday, May 19th. At one meeting, the dancers represented the defeat of a nearby "strategic hamlet." Usually, some of the women from Ben Suc itself danced, after being instructed by dancers from the Front. During the first year of Front government, a group of village teen-agers formed a small band, including a guitar, a trumpet, and various traditional Vietnamese instruments, and played for the meetings, but toward the end of 1965 they were replaced by a professional itinerant band. In all its meetings to boost morale and rally the villagers, the Front attempted to create an atmosphere combining impassioned seriousness with an optimistic, energetic, improvised gaiety that drew the villagers into participation. At every opportunity, it attempted to make the villagers aware of their own collective power and of the critical necessity of their support in winning the war.

The Front organized the entire village into a variety of "associations" for the support of the war effort. The largest were the Youth Liberation Association, the Farmers' Liberation Association, and the Women's Liberation Association. Each of these three associations met twice a month, and in times of emergency they met more often. At the meetings, leaders again reported news of recent victories and also delivered instructions from higher authorities for the coming month. The Youth Liberation Association exacted dues of one piastre (about three-quarters of a cent) a month. The usual duties of its members were to carry supplies and rice for the troops, build blockades to make the roads impassable to jeeps and slow for armored personnel-carriers, and dig tunnels, usually as bomb shelters for the village but sometimes as hideouts or hospitals for the Front's troops. Every once in a while, the members were called to the scene of a battle to remove the dead and wounded. The Farmers' Liberation Association asked for dues of two piastres a month. The farmers also had to pay the Front a tax of up to ten per cent of their harvest. Taxes were assessed on a graduated scale, with the richest farmers paying the most and the poorest paying nothing, or even receiving a welfare allotment. In its propaganda, the Front emphasized the fact that rich peasants, who had the most to lose from the Front's policy of favoring the poor as a "priority class," would not be allowed to slip out of their obligations to the war effort or to play a merely passive role in it. Soldiers were recruited from both the Youth Association and the Farmers' Association, with members of the priority class most often entrusted with positions as officers and leaders. In one case, the Front supported a young orphan on welfare until he became established as a farmer, and then made him a soldier and promoted him to the rank of squad commander within a few months. Generally speaking, rich families and families with relatives in ARVN were mistrusted and kept under close watch. The duties of members of the Women's Liberation Association were not fixed. They supported the war effort through a number of miscellaneous jobs, among them making clothes. A few young women served as nurses, helping roving Front doctors at a large underground hospital in the jungle, only a few miles from the village. On the non-military side, the Women's Association took a strong stand on the need to break the bonds imposed on women by the "dark feudal society" and to raise women to an equal position with men. There was no Front organization for old people— formerly the most influential group in village life. As an ex-member of the Farmers' Association has put it, the Front's policy toward old people was to "recruit them if they were smart" and otherwise leave them alone with their old ways. The activities of the three large associations were coordinated by the Village Committee, a group of three men in close contact with higher officials of the Front. The three men on the Village Committee were the village chief, who dealt with military and political matters; the village secretary, who dealt with taxes and supplies; and the education officer, who was responsible for the schools and the propaganda meetings. The Front was particularly diligent in establishing schools where the children, along with reading and their multiplication tables, learned anti-American slogans. In short, to the villagers of Ben Suc the National Liberation Front was not a band of roving guerrillas but the full government of their village.

In the two years between the Front's victory at Ben Suc and the beginning of 1967, both the war on the ground and what the Americans call the "air war" escalated rapidly throughout the area of Binh Duong Province bordering on the Saigon River. This was the period of the extensive American buildup in Vietnam, and at the villages of Di An, Lai Khé, Ben Cat, and Dau Tieng—all in the vicinity of Ben Suc—American and ARVN bases were either established or greatly expanded. Following its initial failure to retake Ben Suc, ARVN ran several more campaigns in the area, but in these it either failed to make contact with the enemy or was beaten back. A push by the American 173rd Airborne Brigade in October, 1965, failed to engage the enemy significantly. In late 1965, the Front permitted a team of ARVN troops to come into Ben Suc and attempt their own version of the Front's village meetings. This kind of ARVN meeting, which the Americans call a Hamlet Festival, is, like so many of the techniques employed by the South Vietnamese government and the United States Army, a conscious imitation of the Front's programs. (In a full-scale Hamlet Festival, troops will surround a village and order everyone into the center. Then, while intelligence men set up a temporary headquarters to interrogate the males caught in the roundup, searching for draft dodgers as well as for the enemy, a special team of entertainers will put on a program of propaganda songs and popular love songs for the women and children. Sometimes a medical team will give shots, hand out pills, and offer medical advice. Lunch is usually served from a mess tent. In the most abbreviated version of the Hamlet Festival, only a medical team will go into a village.) The fact that the Front allowed an ARVN medical team to enter the village in 1965 was quite consistent with the Front's continuing policy of deriving whatever benefit it can from government programs and facilities. One American official has noted, "If they don't try to blow up a certain power station, it usually means they're drawing power off it for themselves."

Between 1965 and 1967, American bombing of every kind increased tremendously throughout the Saigon River area. There were strikes with napalm and phosphorus, and strikes by B-52s, whose bombs usually leave a mile-long path of evenly spaced craters. As the

American bases grew, the amount of large artillery also increased. There is apparently a policy in Vietnam of never letting any big gun remain silent for more than twenty-four hours, and the artillery on many bases fires a certain number of rounds every evening. Ordinarily, before bombing or shelling, an American pilot or artillery man must obtain permission from the province chief, or district chief, who, as a Vietnamese, is presumed to be more familiar with the surroundings than the Americans and able to restrain them from destroying populated areas. However, in the case of Binh Duong Province in January of 1967 the province chief, himself a colonel in ARVN, who was from outside the province, had taken his post only three months before, and had never controlled most of the areas being bombed, so he knew less about the area than most of the Americans. In South Vietnam, certain areas have been designated Free Strike Zones, which means that no permission is needed to fire into them. These are usually unpopulated jungle areas in which the Front is suspected of operating at night. Most of the routine nightly fire is lobbed into these zones, where it blows up jungle trees and—the Americans hope—the caves and bunkers of the Front. As there was at least one Free Zone within a few miles of Ben Suc, the thump of incoming artillery shells jarring the ground became a regular feature of life in the village.

In the daytime, pilots of fighter-bombers are shown their targets by troops on the ground or by small pro-

peller planes called bird dogs, which spot promising
targets from the air. The fliers adhere to a policy of
bombing populated areas as little as possible, but sometimes beleaguered ground troops will call in planes or
artillery fire to destroy a village that is being defended
by the Front. In such cases, if there is time, an attempt
is made to warn the villagers, either by airborne loudspeakers or by leaflets dropped on the village. The
United States Army's Psychological Warfare Office has
many hundreds of different leaflets, designed for subtly
different situations. On one side of Leaflet No. APO-
6227, for instance, a cartoon drawing represents the
long trajectory of a large shell from a ship at sea to an
inland village, where a human figure has been blown
into the air and a grass-roofed house is bursting into
pieces under the impact of the explosion. On the other
side is a message in Vietnamese, reading, "Artillery
from our ships will soon hit your village. You must look
for cover immediately. From now on, chase the Vietcong away from your village, so the government won't
have to shell your area again."

The center of Ben Suc was bombed one morning in
mid-1965. The bombs destroyed several two-story brick-
and-mortar houses and wounded or killed more than
twenty people, including several children. Some
months before the bombing, the Front, to protect the
center of the village, had made a mocking use of a new
policy of the South Vietnamese government. Around
that time, the government had publicly offered a guar-

antee that Allied troops would refrain from attacking any building or vehicle showing the government flag of three red stripes on a yellow ground. The purpose, as an American officer explained it, was to encourage the people to "associate safety with the national flag," for "it means something when everybody's going around carrying the national flag." In Ben Suc, however, the Front, moved by a spirit of irreverent humor quite typical of it at times, raised the government flag over a rice-storage house—more as a prank than as a serious preventive measure against bombings. For several months, it fluttered at the top of the storehouse—a bold joke, known through the whole village, and a brazen taunt to the government. The joke had a bitter ending when the center of the village was bombed and the rice storehouse destroyed. After this bombing, the Front government in Ben Suc moved about a hundred people from the center of the village to the outskirts, where they lived with relatives. It also laid explosive booby traps in various spots outside the village. The job of warning villagers away from these spots was entrusted to teams of teen-age girls. In addition, the Front encouraged families to dig out rooms beneath their houses as bomb shelters. Later, there were many bombings, and many casualties, in the fields outside the village—particularly near the river, where the bombing was most frequent. From Ben Suc halfway to the provincial capital of Phu Cuong, about fifteen miles down the river, the riverside fields were polka-dotted with

craters of every size. At least a third of the small fields
had been hit at least once, and some of the craters had
turned entire fields into ponds. The bombing and the
artillery fire were at their most intense in the early
morning, when the Americans considered anything that
moved highly suspicious, so the farmers took to starting
work in the fields around eight or nine o'clock instead
of at seven, as their custom had been. Not only the
destruction but the crashing of bombs and shells nearby and in the distance made life continuously nerve-
racking, with everyone tensely ready to run to a bomb
shelter at a second's notice. The Psychological Warfare
Office sought to make the most of the fear and tension
by stepping up the volume of the leaflets dropped on
the area. In a booklet describing the leaflets available
for these purposes, Leaflet No. AVIB-246, whose
"theme" is listed as "scare," has a cartoon drawing on
one side showing a soldier of the Front dying, his hands
futilely clutching the air in front of him and his face in
the dirt, while jet planes fly overhead, dropping bombs.
The message on the other side reads, "Each day, each
week, each month, more and more of your comrades,
base camps, and tunnels are found and destroyed. You
are shelled more often, you are bombed more often.
You are forced to move very often, you are forced to
dig deeper, you are forced to carry more loads away.
You are tired, you are sick. Your leaders tell you victory
is near. They are wrong. Only DEATH is near. Do you
hear the planes? Do you hear the bombs? These are the

sounds of DEATH: your DEATH. Rally now to survive."
Another leaflet shows a photograph of the mutilated
corpse of a young man. His stomach and intestines are
flowing out of him onto the ground. The message on the
other side reads, "If you continue to follow the Vietcong, and destroy villages and hamlets, sooner or later
you will be killed, like Colonel Tran Thuoc Quong.
Colonel Quong will never need his belt again. He is
DEAD." The word "dead" is written in large block letters
that drip with blood. Some leaflets depict American
weapons with the teeth and claws of beasts, killing or
torturing people in the manner of the fantastic devils in
medieval paintings of Hell. The drawing on one leaflet
shows a tank with evil, slitted eyes, fangs, and long
mechanical arms with metal talons that reach out toward the viewer. The tank crushes one man under its
treads, squeezes drops of blood from a screaming
second man in its talons, and engulfs a third man in a
column of flame that spurts from between its dragon-
like fangs.

People from many villages around Ben Suc who had
been left homeless after ground battles, bombing, and
shelling migrated to the comparative safety of other
villages, to live with relatives or just fend for themselves. When the small village of Mi Hung, across the
river from Ben Suc, was heavily bombed, at least a
hundred of its people moved into Ben Suc. During
1966, a scattering of refugees from other bombed villages had also found their way there. Then, in the

second week of the month of January, 1967—when the population of Ben Suc was further swollen by relatives and friends from neighboring villages who had come to help with the harvest, which was exceptionally abundant that season, despite the war—the Americans launched in Binh Duong Province what they called Operation Cedar Falls. It was the largest operation of the war up to that time.

For the Americans, the entire Saigon River area around Ben Suc, including particularly a notorious forty-square-mile stretch of jungle known as the Iron Triangle, had been a source of nagging setbacks. Small operations there were defeated; large operations conducted there turned up nothing. The big guns shelled and bombed around the clock but produced no tangible results. The enemy "body count" was very low, and the count of "pacified" villages stood at zero. In fact, a number of villages that had been converted into "strategic hamlets" in Operation Sunrise, launched three years earlier, had run their government protectors out of town and reverted to Front control. Late in 1966, the American high command designed the Cedar Falls operation as a drastic method of reducing the stubborn resistance throughout the Iron Triangle area. Named after the home town, in Iowa, of a 1st Division lieutenant who had been posthumously awarded the Medal of Honor, Operation Cedar Falls involved thirty thousand men, including logistical support, and it was

planned and executed entirely by the Americans, without the advance knowledge of a single Vietnamese in
the province. The decision that *no* Vietnamese was a
good enough security risk was based on previous experiences, in which the enemy had learned about operations ahead of time and had laid traps for the at-
tackers or simply disappeared. It also reflected the
Army's growing tendency to mistrust all Vietnamese,
regardless of their politics. On several American bases,
entrance is forbidden to all Vietnamese, including
ARVN soldiers, after a certain hour in the evening.
During Cedar Falls, security was particularly tight.

A plan was made to attack Ben Suc, but Ben Suc
was regarded as an objective quite separate from the
operation's principal target—the Iron Triangle. The
Iron Triangle is a patch of jungle bounded on the west,
for about thirteen miles, by the Saigon River; on the
east, also for about thirteen miles, by National Route
No. 13; and on the north, for six miles, by a nameless
smaller road. Ben Suc lay just beyond the northwest
corner of the Triangle. Until the Cedar Falls operation,
the Triangle long had a reputation as an enemy stronghold impenetrable to government troops, and had been
said to shelter a full division of enemy troops and also a
vast system of bunkers and tunnels used by the Front as
headquarters for its Military Region IV, which sur-
rounds the city of Saigon. American intelligence had
also received reports of a twelve-mile tunnel running
the length of the Triangle from north to south. The

operation was the first move in a newly devised long-term war strategy in which large American forces would aim primarily at engaging the main forces of the enemy and destroying their jungle bases one by one, while ARVN troops would aim primarily at providing security for the villages thus freed from Front control. General Earle G. Wheeler, Chairman of the Joint Chiefs of Staff, who visited the area later, said, in an interview, "We must continue to seek out the enemy in South Vietnam—in particular, destroy his base areas where the enemy can rest, retrain, recuperate, resupply, and pull up his socks for his next military operation. . . . Primarily, the American units are engaged in search-and-destroy operations. In other words, they don't stay permanently in any given locale. . . . The Vietnamese military and paramilitary units are the ones which are used in the permanent security operations. The situation being what it is, General Westmoreland's first effort is to engage the Viet Cong main-force units and the North Vietnamese Army units and defeat them." He added, "The South Vietnamese forces are not ample enough to cope with the main-force units throughout the country. . . . I don't wish to imply that the South Vietnamese are not going to participate in the operations there. Of course they will. . . . This does not mean that all of the Vietnamese forces are going to be devoted to pacification. They can't be. And there's no intent for them to be. I just said a substantial portion."

According to the Cedar Falls plan, the Triangle was to be bombed and shelled heavily for several days both by B-52s and by fighter-bombers, and then blocked off around its entire thirty-two-mile perimeter with elements of the 1st Infantry Division along the northern edge, elements of the 196th Light Infantry Brigade along the river, on the west side, and elements of the 173rd Airborne Brigade along Route 13, on the east side. Together, these troops would man a hundred and sixty pieces of artillery. After the jungle had been heavily shelled and bombed, the 1st Division troops were to flatten the jungle in fifty-yard swaths on both sides of the road, using sixty bulldozers airlifted in by the huge, two-rotor Chinook helicopters. Then they were simultaneously to destroy the villages of Rach Bap, Bung Cong, and Rach Kien, evacuate the villagers, and start cutting broad avenues in the jungle with special sixty-ton bulldozers nicknamed hogjaws. These drives would be supported by air strikes and artillery barrages against the jungle. American troops would enter the Triangle behind the bulldozers, in an attempt to engage the enemy division that was rumored to be there and destroy the enemy headquarters.

The attack on Ben Suc was planned for January 8th—the day before the thrust into the Triangle. I joined a group of six newsmen outside a field tent on the newly constructed base at the village of Lai Khé, to hear Major Allen C. Dixon, of the 173rd Airborne Brigade, outline the plan and purpose of this part of the operation. "We have two targets, actually," he explained, pointing to a map propped on a pile of sandbags. "There's the Iron Triangle, and then there's the village of Ben Suc. This village is a political center, as far as the V.C. is concerned, and it's been solid V.C. since the French pulled out in '56. We haven't even been able to get a census taken in there to find out who's there." Most of the American officers who led the operation were not aware that ARVN had had an outpost in Ben Suc for the nine years preceding 1964. They saw the village as "solid V.C. as long as we can remember." Major Dixon continued, "Now, we can't tell you whether A, B, and C are at their desks or not, but we *know* that there's important infrastructure there—what we're really after here is the infrastructure of the V.C. We've run several operations in this area before with ARVN, but it's always been hit and run—you go in there, leave the same day, and the V.C. is back that night. Now, we realize that you can't go in and then just abandon the people to the V.C. This time we're really going to do a thorough job of it: we're going to clean out the place completely. The people are all going to be resettled in a temporary camp near Phu Cuong, the provincial capital down the river, and then we're going to move *everything* out—livestock, furniture, and all of their possessions. The purpose here is to deprive the V.C. of this area for good. The people are going to Phu Cuong by barge and by truck, and when they get there the provincial government takes over—it has its own

Revolutionary Development people to handle that, and U.S. AID is going to help."

A reporter asked what would happen to the evacuated village.

"Well, we don't have a certain decision or information on that at this date, but the village may be levelled," Major Dixon answered, and went on to say, "The attack is going to go tomorrow morning and it's going to be a complete surprise. Five hundred men of the 1st Infantry Division's 2nd Brigade are going to be lifted *right into* the village itself in sixty choppers, with Zero Hour at zero eight hundred hours. From some really excellent intelligence from that area, we have learned that the perimeter of the village is heavily mined, and that's why we'll be going into the village itself. Sixty choppers is as large a number as we've ever used in an attack of this nature. Simultaneous with the attack, choppers with speakers on them are going to start circling over the village, telling the villagers to assemble in the center of the town or they will be considered V.C.s. It's going to be hard to get the pilots on those choppers to go in low to make those announcements audible, but everything depends on that. Also, we're going to drop leaflets to the villagers." (Later, I picked up one of these leaflets. On one side, the flags of the Republic of Vietnam, the United States, the Republic of Korea, New Zealand, and Australia were represented in color; on the other side was a drawing of a smiling ARVN soldier with his arm around a smiling soldier of the National Liberation Front. The text, written in English, Vietnamese, and Korean, read, "Safe conduct pass to be honored by all Vietnamese Government Agencies and Allied Forces." I learned that the Chieu Hoi, or Open Arms, program would be in operation during the attack. In an attempt to encourage defections from the Front, the government was opening its arms to all *hoi chanh,* or returnees who turned themselves in. Hence the unusually friendly tone of the leaflets.)

About the encirclement of the village, Major Dixon said, "There are going to be three landing zones for the choppers. Then the men will take up positions to prevent people from escaping from the village. Five minutes after the landing, we're going to bring artillery fire and air strikes into the whole area in the woods to the north of the village to prevent people from escaping by that route. At zero eight thirty hours, we're going to lift in men from the 2nd Brigade below the woods to the south to block off that route. After the landing is completed, some of our gunships are going to patrol the area at treetop level to help keep the people inside there from getting out. After the area is secure, we're lifting a crew of ARVN soldiers into the center of the village to help us with the work there. We want to get the Vietnamese dealing with their own people as much as we can here. Now, we're hoping that opposition is going to be light, that we're going to be able to get this thing over in one lightning blow, but if they've got intelligence on this, the way they did on some of our other operations, they could have something ready for us and this *could* be a hot landing. It could be pretty hairy."

For several reasons, the plan itself was an object of keen professional satisfaction to the men who devised and executed it. In a sense, it reversed the search-and-destroy method. This time, they would destroy first and search later—at their leisure, in the interrogation rooms. After all the small skirmishes and ambushes, after months of lobbing tons of bombs and shells on vague targes in Free Strike Zones, the size, complexity, and careful coördination of the Cedar Falls operation satisfied the military men's taste for careful large-scale planning. Every troop movement was precisely timed, and there would be full use of air support and artillery, in a design that would unfold over a wide terrain and, no matter what the opposition might be, would almost certainly produce the tangible result of evacuating several thousand hostile civilians, thereby depriving the V.C. of hundreds of "structures," even if the "infrastructure" was not present. This time, unless the entire village sneaked off into the forest, the objective of the operation could not wholly elude the troops, as it had in previous campaigns. Thus, a measure of success was assured from the start. In concluding his briefing to the newsmen, Major Dixon remarked, "I think this really ought to be quite fascinating. There's this new element of surprise, of going right into the enemy vil-

lage with our choppers and then bringing in our tremendous firepower. Anyway, it ought to be something
to see."

That evening, I was sent by helicopter to a newly
constructed base ten miles north of Ben Suc, at Dau
Tieng, where Colonel James A. Grimsley, commanding
officer of the 2nd Brigade, 1st Infantry Division, was
winding up his briefing of his officers on the next morning's attack on Ben Suc. The officers were assembled in
a tent, in which a single light bulb hung from the
ceiling. "The purpose of this operation is to move in
there absolutely as fast as we can get control of the
situation," Colonel Grimsley said. "I want to emphasize
that you're going to have only about ten seconds to
empty each chopper, because another chopper will be
coming right in after it. A last word to men landing
below the southwest woods: Your job is to keep anyone
from escaping down that way. Now, of course, if it's
just a bunch of women and children wandering down
through the woods, who obviously don't know what
they're doing, don't fire, but otherwise you'll have to
take them under fire. The choppers will be taking off at
zero seven twenty-three hours tomorrow morning. Are
there any questions?" There were no questions, and the
officers filed out of the tent into the darkness.

The men of the 1st Division's 2nd Brigade spent the
day before the battle quietly, engaging in few pep talks
or discussions among themselves about the dangers

ahead. Each man seemed to want to be alone with his thoughts. They spent the night before the attack in individual tents on the dusty ground of a French rubber plantation, now the Americans' new base at Dau Tieng. The airstrip was complete, but not many buildings were up yet, and construction materials lay in piles alongside freshly bulldozed roads. The men were brought in by helicopter in the afternoon from their own base and were led to their sleeping area among the rubber trees. Most of the transporting of American troops in Vietnam is done by helicopter or plane. So the men, hopping from American base to American base, view rural Vietnam only from the air until they see it through gunsights on a patrol or a search-and-destroy mission.

Darkness fell at about six-thirty. Thanks to a cloudy sky over the high canopy of rubber leaves, the area was soon in perfect blackness. A few men talked quietly in small groups for an hour or so. Others turned to their radios for company, listening to rock-'n'-roll and country-and-Western music broadcast by the American armed-services radio station in Saigon. The great majority simply went to sleep. Sleep that night, however, was difficult. Artillery fire from the big guns on the base began at around eleven o'clock and continued until about three o'clock, at a rate of four or five rounds every ten minutes. Later in the night, along with the sharp crack and whine of outgoing artillery the men heard the smothered thumping of bombing, including the rapid series of deep explosions that indicates a B-52 raid. Yet if the outgoing artillery fire had not been unusually near—so near that it sent little shocks of air against the walls of the tents—the sleepers would probably not have been disturbed very much. Because artillery fire is a routine occurrence at night on almost every American base in Vietnam, and because everyone knows that it is all American or Allied, it arouses no alarm, and no curiosity. Furthermore, because most of it is harassment and interdiction fire, lobbed into Free Strike Zones, it does not ordinarily indicate a clash with the enemy. It does make some men edgy when they first arrive, but soon it becomes no more than a half-noticed dull crashing in the distance. Only the distinctive sound of mortar fire—a popping that sounds like a champagne cork leaving a bottle—can make conversations suddenly halt in readiness for a dash into a ditch or bunker. Throughout that night of January 7th, the roaring of one of the diesel generators at the base served as a reminder to the men that they were sleeping on a little island of safety, encircled by coils of barbed wire and minefields, in a hostile countryside.

The men got up at five-thirty in the morning and were guided in the dark to a mess tent in a different part of the rubber grove, where they had a breakfast of grapefruit juice, hot cereal, scrambled eggs, bacon, toast, and coffee. At about six-thirty, the sky began to grow light, and they were led back to the airstrip. Strings of nine and ten helicopters with tapered bodies could be seen through the treetops, filing across the gray early-morning sky like little schools of minnows. In the distance, the slow beat of their engines sounded soft and almost peaceful, but when they rushed past overhead the noise was fearful and deafening. By seven o'clock, sixty helicopters were perched in formation on the airstrip, with seven men assembled in a silent group beside each one. When I arrived at the helicopter assigned to me—No. 47—three engineers and three infantrymen were already there, five of them standing or kneeling in the dust checking their weapons. One of them, a sergeant, was a small, wiry American Indian, who spoke in short, clipped syllables. The sixth man, a stocky infantryman with blond hair and a red face, who looked to be about twenty and was going into action for the first time, lay back against an earth embankment with his eyes closed, wearing an expression of boredom, as though he wanted to put these wasted minutes of waiting to some good use by catching up on his sleep. Two of the other six men in the team were also going into combat for the first time. The men did not speak to each other.

At seven-fifteen, our group of seven climbed up into its helicopter, a UH-1 (called Huey), and the pilot, a man with a German accent, told us that four of us should sit on the seat and three on the floor in front, to balance the craft. He also warned us that the flight might be rough, since we would be flying in the turbulent wake of the helicopter in front of us. At seven-twenty, the engines of the sixty helicopters started simultaneously, with a thunderous roar and a storm of dust. After idling his engine for three minutes on the airstrip, our pilot raised his right hand in the air, forming a circle with the forefinger and thumb, to show that he hoped everything would proceed perfectly from then on. The helicopter rose slowly from the airstrip right after the helicopter in front of it had risen. The pilot's gesture was the only indication that the seven men were on their way to something more than a nine-o'clock job. Rising, one after another, in two parallel lines of thirty, the fleet of sixty helicopters circled the base twice, gaining altitude and tightening their formation as they did so, until each machine was not more than twenty yards from the one immediately in front of it. Then the fleet, straightening out the two lines, headed south, toward Ben Suc.

In Helicopter No. 47, one of the men shouted a joke, which only one other man could hear, and they both laughed. The soldier who had earlier been trying to catch a nap on the runway wanted to get a picture of the sixty helicopters with a Minolta camera he had hanging from a strap around his neck. He was sitting on the floor, facing backward, so he asked one of the men on the seat to try to get a couple of shots. "There are sixty choppers here," he shouted, "and every one of them costs a quarter of a million bucks!" The Huey flies with its doors open, so the men who sat on the outside seats were perched right next to the drop. They held tightly to ceiling straps as the helicopter rolled and pitched through the sky like a ship plunging through a heavy sea. Wind from the rotors and from the forward motion blasted into the men's faces, making them squint. At five minutes to eight, the two lines of the fleet suddenly dived, bobbing and swaying from the cruising altitude of twenty-five hundred feet down to treetop level, at a point about seven miles from Ben Suc but heading away from it, to confuse enemy observers on the ground. Once at an altitude of fifty or sixty feet, the fleet made a wide U turn and headed directly for Ben Suc at a hundred miles an hour, the helicopters' tails raised slightly in forward flight. Below, the faces of scattered peasants were clearly visible as they looked up from their water buffalo at the sudden, earsplitting incursion of sixty helicopters charging low over their fields.

All at once, Helicopter No. 47 landed, and from both sides of it the men jumped out on the run into a freshly turned vegetable plot in the village of Ben Suc—the first Vietnamese village that several of them had ever set foot in. The helicopter took off immediately, and another settled in its place. Keeping low, the men I was with ran single file out into the center of the little plot, and then, spotting a low wall of bushes on the side of the plot they had just left, ran back there for cover and filed along the edges of the bushes toward several soldiers who had landed a little while before them. For a minute, there was silence. Suddenly a single helicopter came clattering overhead at about a hundred and fifty feet, squawking Vietnamese from two stubby speakers that stuck out, winglike, from the thinnest part of the fuselage, near the tail. The message, which the American soldiers could not understand, went, "Attention, people of Ben Suc! You are surrounded by Republic of South Vietnam and Allied Forces. Do not run away or you will be shot as V.C. Stay in your homes and wait for further instructions." The metallic voice, floating down over the fields, huts, and trees, was as calm as if it were announcing a flight departure at an air terminal. It was gone in ten seconds, and the soldiers again moved on in silence. Within two minutes, the young men from No. 47 reached a little dirt road marking the village perimeter, which they were to hold, but there were no people in sight except American soldiers. The young men lay down on the sides of embankments and in little hollows in the small area it had fallen to them to control. There was no sign of an enemy.

For the next hour and a half, the six men from No. 47 were to be the masters of a small stretch of vegetable fields which was divided down the center by about fifty yards of narrow dirt road—almost a path— and bounded on the front and two sides (as they faced the road and, beyond it, the center of the village) by several small houses behind copses of low palm trees and hedges and in back by a small graveyard giving onto a larger cultivated field. The vegetable fields, most of them not more than fifty feet square and of irregular shape, were separated by neatly constructed grass-covered ridges, each with a path running along its top. The houses were small and trim, most of them with one side open to the weather but protected from the rain by the deep eaves of a thatch-grass roof. The houses were usually set apart by hedges and low trees, so that one house was only half visible from another and difficult to see from the road; they were not unlike a wealthy American suburb in the logic of their layout. An orderly small yard, containing low-walled coops for chickens and a shed with stalls for cows, adjoined each house. Here and there, between the fields and in the copses, stood the whitewashed waist-high columns and brick walls of Vietnamese tombs, which look like small models of the ruins of once-splendid palaces. It was a tidy, delicately wrought small-scale landscape with short views—not overcrowded but with every square foot of land carefully attended to.

Four minutes after the landing, the heavy crackle of several automatic weapons firing issued from a point out of sight, perhaps five hundred yards away. The men, who had been sitting or kneeling, went down on their bellies, their eyes trained on the confusion of hedges, trees, and houses ahead. A report that Mike Company had made light contact came over their field radio. At about eight-ten, the shock of tremendous explosions shattered the air and rocked the ground. The men hit the dirt again. Artillery shells crashed somewhere in the woods, and rockets from helicopters thumped into the ground. When a jet came screaming low overhead, one of the men shouted, "They're bringing in air strikes!" Heavy percussions shook the ground under the men, who were now lying flat, and shock waves beat against their faces. Helicopter patrols began to wheel low over the treetops outside the perimeter defended by the infantry, spraying the landscape with long bursts of machine-gun fire. After about five minutes, the explosions became less frequent, and the men from the helicopters, realizing that this was the planned bombing and shelling of the northern woods, picked themselves up, and two of them, joined by three soldiers from another helicopter, set about exploring their area.

Three or four soldiers began to search the houses behind a nearby copse. Stepping through the doorway of one house with his rifle in firing position at his hip, a solidly build six-foot-two Negro private came upon a young woman standing with a baby in one arm and a little girl of three or four holding her other hand. The woman was barefoot and was dressed in a white shirt and rolled-up black trousers; a bandanna held her long hair in a coil at the back of her head. She and her children intently watched each of the soldier's movements. In English, he asked, "Where's your husband?" Without taking her eyes off the soldier, the woman said something in Vietnamese, in an explanatory tone. The soldier looked around the inside of the one-room house

and, pointing to his rifle, asked, "You have same-same?"
The woman shrugged and said something else in Vietnamese. The soldier shook his head and poked his hand
into a basket of laundry on a table between him and the
woman. She immediately took all the laundry out of the
basket and shrugged again, with a hint of impatience,
as though to say, "It's just laundry!" The soldier nodded
and looked around, appearing unsure of what to do
next in this situation. Then, on a peg on one wall, he
spotted a pair of men's pants and a shirt hanging up to
dry. "Where's *he*?" he asked, pointing to the clothes.
The woman spoke in Vietnamese. The soldier took the
damp clothing down and, for some reason, carried it
outside, where he laid it on the ground.

The house was clean, light, and airy, with doors on
two sides and the top half of one whole side opening
out onto a grassy yard. On the table, a half-eaten bowl
of rice stood next to the laundry basket. A tiny ham-
mock, not more than three feet long, hung in one
corner. At one side of the house, a small, separate
wooden roof stood over a fireplace with cooking utensils hanging around it. On the window ledge was a row
of barley sprouting plants, in little clods of earth
wrapped in palm leaves. Inside the room, a kilnlike
structure, its walls and top made of mud, logs, and large
stones, stood over the family's bedding. At the rear of
the house, a square opening in the ground led to an
underground bomb shelter large enough for several
people to stand in. In the yard, a cow stood inside a

third bomb shelter, made of tile walls about a foot thick.

After a minute, the private came back in with a bared machete at his side and a field radio on his back. "Where's your husband, huh?" he asked again. This time, the woman gave a long answer in a complaining tone, in which she pointed several times at the sky and several times at her children. The soldier looked at her blankly. "What do I do with her?" he called to some fellow-soldiers outside. There was no answer. Turning back to the young woman, who had not moved since his first entrance, he said, "O.K., lady, you stay here," and left the house.

Several other houses were searched, but no other Vietnamese were found, and for twenty minutes the men on that particular stretch of road encountered no one else, although they heard sporadic machine-gun fire down the road. The sky, which had been overcast, began to show streaks of blue, and a light wind stirred the trees. The bombing, the machine-gunning from helicopters, the shelling, and the rocket firing continued steadily. Suddenly a Vietnamese man on a bicycle appeared, pedalling rapidly along the road from the direction of the village. He was wearing the collarless, pajamalike black garment that is both the customary dress of the Vietnamese peasant and the uniform of the National Liberation Front, and although he was riding away from the center of the village—a move forbidden by the voices from the helicopters—he had, it appeared, already run a long gantlet of American soldiers without being stopped. But when he had ridden about twenty yards past the point where he first came in sight, there was a burst of machine-gun fire from a copse thirty yards in front of him, joined immediately by a burst from a vegetable field to one side, and he was hurled off his bicycle into a ditch a yard from the road. The bicycle crashed into a side embankment. The man with the Minolta camera, who had done the firing from the vegetable patch, stood up after about a minute and walked over to the ditch, followed by one of the engineers. The Vietnamese in the ditch appeared to be about twenty, and he lay on his side without moving, blood flowing from his face, which, with the eyes open, was half buried in the dirt at the bottom of the ditch. The engineer leaned down, felt the man's wrist, and said, "He's dead." The two men—both companions of mine on No. 47—stood still for a while, with folded arms, and stared down at the dead man's face, as though they were giving him a chance to say something. Then the engineer said, with a tone of finality, "That's a V.C. for you. He's a V.C., all right. That's what they wear. He was leaving town. He had to have some reason."

The two men walked back to a ridge in the vegetable field and sat down on it, looking off into the distance in a puzzled way and no longer bothering to keep low. The man who had fired spoke suddenly, as though coming out of deep thought. "I saw this guy coming down the road on a bicycle," he said. "And I thought, you know, Is this it? Do I shoot? Then some guy over there in the bushes opened up, so I cut loose."

The engineer raised his eyes in the manner of someone who has made a strange discovery and said, "I'm not worried. You know, that's the first time I've ever seen a dead guy, and I don't feel bad. I just don't, that's all." Then, with a hard edge of defiance in his voice, he added, "Actually, I'm glad. I'm glad we killed the little V.C."

Over near the copse, the man who had fired first, also a young soldier, had turned his back to the road. Clenching a cigar in his teeth, he stared with determination over his gun barrel across the wide field, where several water buffaloes were grazing but no human beings had yet been seen. Upon being asked what had happened, he said, "Yeah, he's dead. Ah shot him. He was a fuckin' V.C."

At about nine o'clock, people from outlying areas of the village began to appear on the road, walking toward the village center and bringing with them as many pieces of furniture, bicycles, pots, chickens, pigs, cows, ducks, and water buffalo as they could carry or herd along. At this point, the young mother also left her house, with her children, and started along the road. But about five minutes later she reappeared, with only the baby. She was walking in the forbidden direction, and several soldiers who saw her looked at each other questioningly as she passed. Arriving at her house, she encountered the tall soldier she had first met, and began a long explanation in Vietnamese, in a highly irritated tone. Then, rummaging in the laundry bag, she pulled out a woman's light-blue wallet and produced identification papers to show the soldier. She had returned for these. Still talking in an explanatory tone, in a loud voice, she returned to the line of villagers. Particularly at first, women and children predominated in the line. One woman carried a shoulder pole with her belongings balanced in a basket hanging on one end and a baby sitting in a basket on the other end. The villagers walked with slow, careful steps, looking straight in front of them. Some slowed their pace and turned their heads slightly when they passed the open-eyed corpse in the ditch, but none stopped and none showed any emotion. This procession, like the appearance of the houses, made it plain that Ben Suc was a wealthy village. Most of the villagers wore clean, unpatched clothing. The children had rosy cheeks and stout limbs. The cows were fat and sleek, and a great number of pigs and chickens were left rooting and pecking in deserted yards.

As the villagers passed, machine-gun fire rang out across the vegetable fields once more, this time accompanied by shouting. A few feet from where the cyclist had fallen, a soldier stood firing from the hip into a cluster of houses and trees. Twenty yards away, the sergeant of his unit, enraged, was yelling at him, "Git on back here! Git on back here! Do you hear? Killin' the fuckin' water buffalo! Fartin' around killin' the fuckin' water buffalo!" But the soldier did not look back or move. Again he fired, and a water buffalo in a small yard twenty feet away sank silently to its knees, then rolled over on its side. The sergeant swore and again shouted several times for the soldier to come back, but the soldier continued to peer toward the cluster of houses, holding his gun ready, in a challenging stance, as though there still might be something threatening there. After twenty seconds, he walked back to the furious sergeant. During this episode, the villagers did not break step but allowed themselves to turn their heads just enough to observe the proceedings. A few minutes later, a thin middle-aged man dressed in black, with long, straight hair that stuck out from his head at a number of angles, came down the road, looking freely from side to side and walking with a jauntier step than the other villagers. He was headed toward the center of the village. At one point, he stopped in the road to look directly at a group of Americans. The soldier with the cigar, who had first fired on the cyclist, told the man next to him, "That bastard better watch out. If he starts to run, he's going to get it in the head." At nine-thirty, new orders came, and the men abandoned their road to defend a wider perimeter around the village.

Following the villagers in toward the schoolhouse, I observed that all the houses had newly constructed bomb shelters both inside and outside—for animals as well as people. Noticing these, one American officer remarked that he wished ARVN would construct its bunkers as strongly. In back of a small temporary schoolhouse was a whole maze of trenches—presumably enough to hold the entire student body. In front of the school, a wooden signboard posted on a large tree bore the hand-lettered legend, in both Vietnamese and English, "If anyone aggresses your fatherland, enslaves you, what will you say to it?" Later in the morning, after hesitating a moment for fear the sign might be booby-trapped to explode if he touched it, a soldier took it down, asking a companion, "Hey, do you think this will make a good souvenir?"

At the center of the village was a small square, where three narrow roads intersected. Around it were eight or ten two-story brick houses, but most of them were in disrepair and had obviously been abandoned a long time ago. The first floor of one building, which had a sign on it in Vietnamese reading "Pharmacy," had no front, and the floor inside the single room was covered with debris. In several places, charred wrecks of buildings rose only slightly above their foundations. The roads in this area were blocked at regular intervals by low mounds of earth that would prevent a car but not a bicycle from passing. A sign posted on a tree exhorted in Vietnamese, "1. Battle vigorously against the American aggressors. 2. Develop the revolutionary force. 3. Develop solidarity among the people to win freedom and independence."

By ten o'clock, about a thousand villagers had assembled in an L formed by two fifty-foot-long roofless and half-ruined masonry buildings, near the center of the village, that had once been used as a school. The buildings faced a large pasture, which was now serving as a landing pad for a continuous stream of helicopters. The sky was clear and blue except for a few cottony clouds sailing low on the horizon in a strong, warm wind from the north. Bombs continued to crash in the jungle, sometimes no more than a half mile away, and they sent up large puffs of smoke—white for phosphorus, black for napalm. The soldiers watched with fascination as three jets, evenly spaced, made a wide circle and took turns at dive-bombing the forest to the southwest with napalm. Each came right over the village at the beginning of its dive, and the canisters of napalm were clearly visible as they sped earthward from the bellies of the dart-shaped planes.

Vietnamese soldiers, who had been lifted in by United States helicopters after the center of the village had been made secure, were directing still more villagers to the gathering point in front of the schoolhouse. Throughout Operation Cedar Falls, the pattern was to fly in ARVN troops after the initial fighting was over, so that they might search the villages, perform manual labor such as loading captured rice into bags, and carry on the administrative work of organizing the villagers. It was felt that the presence of ARVN troops would divert the villagers' feelings of awe at the operation from the American troops and toward its proper object, the government of South Vietnam. Perhaps the most important role of the ARVN troops, however, was to serve as a link between the Americans and the villagers. The task of crossing the language barrier between Vietnamese and English devolves squarely on ARVN troops. A number of American officers have undergone an intensive Army six-week language-training program, but—if only because of the exceptional difficulties of learning a language whose vocabulary has no common root with English and, furthermore, is pronounced "tonally," so that the same syllable can have many, often hilariously unrelated, meanings, according to its inflection and pitch—even the most linguistically talented students learn only basic constructions, adequate for dealing with only very simple situations. Every once in a while, with a display of uneasy shyness, an officer brings out a few words of Vietnamese, but if these ask a question, he more often than not listens to the answer in blank incomprehension. As the tour of duty in Vietnam is ordinarily no more than one year, very few Americans become fluent in Vietnamese. At Ben Suc, I found just one who was able to put his Vietnamese to practical use. For the most part, the Americans dealt with the Vietnamese soldiers, and the Vietnamese soldiers dealt with the people.

Except at the temporary headquarters, the American soldiers, the Vietnamese soldiers, and the villagers remained in almost entirely separate groups throughout the day of the attack. The villagers sat waiting, with nothing to do, among their kitchen utensils, hastily wrapped bundles, and animals. Beaks, legs, and wings of chickens protruded from the open mesh of large baskets into which they had been thrust. In accordance with village custom, children under about three years old wore nothing below the waist. Children from about seven up were used to working along with the adults. Now they carried heavy loads on shoulder poles, or held strings tied to the front legs of pigs. The women went barefoot, walked with a practical, flat-footed stride, and tied their bundles with the deft, unhesitating movements of people for whom physical labor is second nature. Standing in the schoolyard, each mother seemed wholly engrossed in keeping her children near her and looking after her animals and possessions, and carefully avoided turning her eyes toward her captors. The men were less concerned with the children, and their eyes moved behind sullen, cold masks, observing the Americans and the fate of their village, but they said nothing. To the untrained American eye, Vietnamese men, being slight and often beardless, appear younger than they are. A man in his late twenties may look like a teen-ager. This is particularly true in the villages, where the men usually wear their hair in a long, straight shock that looks boyish to Americans.

Whenever an American soldier or a Vietnamese soldier approached the throng of villagers, several of the older people smiled, folded their arms, and bowed, displaying what seemed an almost automatic deference toward these new authorities. The younger people never bowed or smiled. Some of the Americans had continued to guard the perimeter, but another group had set up tents in the pasture across the road from the old schoolhouse. Throughout the morning and the early afternoon, a special team of Americans detonated numerous booby traps and land mines that had been found around the village, with the result that there were no American casualties at Ben Suc. After digging trenches as a precaution against a mortar attack, the men mostly went to sleep in the sun or inside their tents. A few, who had been lifted in later in the morning, listened to popular songs on transistor radios or read their mail. Another part of the pasture was a busy helicopter landing pad. All day, enormous Chinook helicopters landed with supplies and took off again, blasting everyone with a gale of leaves, pebbles, and dust.

Having completed an initial search of the village, most of the Vietnamese soldiers had few immediate tasks to perform. Some simply lay on the ground and laughed, and others engaged in playfully aggressive games. Soldiers sparred with each other, and there was one loudly cheered wrestling match. At lunchtime, several of the ARVN soldiers gravitated to the center of the village, where they took a teapot and some food from one of the houses and cooked themselves a quick snack. One brought an old guitar out of a house and strummed the instrument clumsily, to the amusement of his friends. Two other soldiers got a fit of the giggles giving each other rides in a rickety wheelbarrow. One of the few unofficial contacts between American and Vietnamese soldiers took place when an American with a camera had the two pose with their wheelbarrow. One sat in the wheelbarrow and the other held the handles, and both momentarily put on fierce, stern expressions for the photograph.

In the middle of this relaxed, almost drowsy scene, the temporary command post was humming with activity. On the field radio, between bursts of static, calm, slow voices brought fresh orders and news of the rest of the operation. Though bombs continued to crash in the woods and smoke to rise on the horizon, they no longer created an impression of urgency but seemed wholly routine. The American soldiers showed only a technical interest in identifying the planes that passed overhead and guessing the kind of explosive used from the sound of the explosion and color of the smoke. The American arsenal is so varied that this game requires a subtle ear and considerable experience. "There goes a B-52 raid," a soldier would say. Or "That's outgoing artillery." Or "That's napalm."

With most of the populace assembled in one place, the Americans launched two projects that were a source of intense pride to the men in the field—a mess tent and a field hospital, both for the villagers. It is a cliché among the American military in Vietnam that "there are two wars in Vietnam": the military war, to provide security against the enemy, and what is usually called "the other war"—the war to "win the hearts and minds of the people." On the one hand, resolutely destroy the enemy; on the other hand, rebuild and reform. To the soldiers at Ben Suc, the hospital and the mess tent represented an essential counterweight to the killing and destruction. They saw the two installations as "the other half" of what they had done that morning. As one soldier put it, with astonishment, as if he were wondering whether this wasn't carrying benevolence to the enemy *too* far, "Our hospitals are full of V.C. at forty dollars a day. Just this morning, there was a woman who got shot up real bad. Both her legs were broken. A real mess. And they dusted her off in a chopper to the military hospital. We dusted off another little V.C. this morning." He shook his head and smiled at the idea of an army that tried to save the lives of an enemy it had just been trying to kill.

The hospital tent and the mess tent were set up side by side at one edge of the pasture. An officer explained to me that treatment was available not only to those wounded during the attack but to anyone, whatever his ailment. A team of Vietnamese doctors was to be lifted in later in the day to treat the patients—again in order to give the villagers the impression that this was a

Vietnamese project, not an American one. Meanwhile, in the hot morning sun, the tent walls of the hospital were open on all sides, and a young man who had been shot in one leg lay quietly on a cot, his eyes glassy and still. A young American medic in his shirtsleeves said that between ten and twenty villagers had been brought in for treatment—most of them children with minor skin diseases. He remarked on the exceptional good health of the Ben Suc villagers, but he went on to say that earlier that morning a distraught woman had brought a sick baby to a Vietnamese Army doctor, who had diagnosed the disease as malaria and had immediately administered an anti-malaria shot. The baby's condition had declined rapidly, and within two hours it had died. The American medic speculated that the baby had been allergic to the shot, and concluded that this incident helped to explain a subsequent reluctance among the villagers to come to the hospital tent. The mess tent was operated entirely by Americans. At noon, the villagers were offered a lunch of hot dogs, Spam, and crackers, served with a fruit-flavored beverage called Keen. Keen, a sweet drink made by dissolving a colored powder in water, is served on many American bases in Vietnam. Again, however, the turnout was less than a hundred; perhaps there had been propaganda from the Front warning that the Americans would try to poison the villagers, or perhaps the villagers were seeking to keep all involvement with their captors to a minimum. In the late morning, one American infantryman offered sticks of gum to a few of the assembled children, and it was several minutes before the children overcame their fear sufficiently to dart forward for the gift.

With the attack over, the tricky task of distinguishing V.C.s from the civilians moved from the battlefield into the interrogation room. First, under the direction of the Americans, ARVN soldiers segregated the villagers by age level, sex, and degree of suspiciousness. All males between the ages of fifteen and forty-five were slated to be evacuated to the Provincial Police Headquarters in the afternoon. From among them, all who were suspected of being Vietcong and a smaller group of "confirmed V.C.s" were singled out. Some of these men were bound and blindfolded, and sat cross-legged on the ground just a few yards from the large assemblage of women, children, and aged. They were men who had been caught hiding in their bomb shelters or had otherwise come under suspicion. One group, for example, was unusually well dressed and well groomed. Instead of bare feet and pajamalike garb, these men wore Japanese foam-rubber slippers and short-sleeved cotton shirts. Standing over them, his arms akimbo, an American officer remarked, "No question about these fellas. Anyone in this village with clothes like that is a V.C. They're V.C.s, all right." A group of about a dozen men categorized as defectors were singled out to be taken to the special Open Arms center near Phu Cuong.

The Americans interrogated only the prisoners they themselves had taken, leaving the prisoners taken by the Vietnamese to the Vietnamese interrogators. The American interrogations were held in a large, debris-strewn room of the roofless schoolhouse. Four interrogating teams worked at the same time, each consisting of one American and an interpreter from the Vietnamese Army. The teams sat on low piles of bricks, and the suspects sat on the floor, or on one brick. These sessions did not uncover very much about the enemy or about the village of Ben Suc, but I felt that, as the only extensive spoken contact between Americans and the Ben Suc villagers throughout the Cedar Falls operation, they had a certain significance. Approximately forty people were questioned the first day.

In one session, a stout American named Martinez questioned, in a straightforward, businesslike manner, a small, barefoot, gray-haired man with a neat little gray mustache, who wore a spotlessly clean, pure-white loose-fitting, collarless shirt and baggy black trousers. First, Martinez asked to see the old man's identification card. By law, all South Vietnamese citizens are required to carry an identification card issued by the government and listing their name, date and place of birth, and occupation. (The Americans considered anyone who lacked this card suspicious, and a man who last registered in another village would have to supply a reason.) This suspect produced an I.D. card that showed him to be sixty years old and born in a village across the river. A search of his pockets also revealed an empty tobacco pouch and a small amount of money.

"Why did he come to Ben Suc?" Throughout the session, Martinez, who held a clipboard in one hand, spoke to the interpreter, who then spoke to the suspect, listened to his reply, and answered Martinez.

"He says he came to join relatives."

"Has he ever seen any V.C.?"

"Yes, sometimes he sees V.C."

"Where?"

"Out walking in the fields two weeks ago, he says."

"Where were they going?"

"He says he doesn't know, because he lives far from the center of the village. He doesn't know what they were doing."

"Does he pay any taxes?"

"Yes. The V.C. collect two piastres a month."

"What's his occupation?"

"He says he is a farmer."

"Let's see his hands."

Martinez had the man stand up and hold out his hands, palms up. By feeling the calluses on the palms, Martinez explained, he could tell whether the man had been working the fields recently. Aside from asking questions, Martinez employed only this one test, but he employed it on the majority of his suspects. He squeezed the old man's palms, rubbed the calves of his legs, then pulled up his shirt and felt his stomach. The old man looked down uneasily at Martinez's big hands on his stomach. "He's not a farmer," Martinez announced, and then, with a touch of impatience and severity, he said, "Ask him what he does."

The interpreter talked with the suspect for about half a minute, then reported, "He says that recently he works repairing bicycles."

"Why did he say he was a farmer?"

"He says he has repaired bicycles only since he finished harvesting."

Deliberately accelerating the intensity of the interrogation, Martinez narrowed his eyes, looked straight at the suspect crouching below him, and, in a suddenly loud voice, snapped, "Is he a V.C.?"

"No, he says he's not," the interpreter announced, with an apologetic shrug.

Martinez relaxed and put his clipboard down on a table. A weary smile took the place of his aggressive posture. "O.K. He can go now," he told the interpreter.

The interpreter, a thin young man with sunglasses, who had spoken to the suspect in a courteous, cajoling manner throughout the questioning, seemed pleased that the interrogation was to involve nothing more unpleasant than this. He gave the old man a smile that said, "You see how nice the Americans are!" and then patted him on the shoulder and delivered him into the hands of a guard.

After the old man had gone, Martinez turned to me with the smile of a man who has some inside information and said confidentially, "He was a V.C. He was probably a tax collector for the V.C." After a moment, he added, "I mean, that's my supposition, anyway."

The other interrogations were very similar. Martinez asked the same questions, with little variation: "Where does he live?" "Is he a farmer?" (Then came the touch test.) "Has he seen any V.C.?" And, finally, "Is *he* a V.C.?" And the suspects, instead of insisting that the National Liberation Front actually governed the village and involved the entire population in its programs, supported him in his apparent impression that the Front was only a roving band of guerrillas. To judge by their testimony to Martinez, the villagers of Ben Suc knew the Front as a ghostly troop of soldiers that appeared once a fortnight in the evening on the edge of the forest and then disappeared for another fortnight. When one young suspect was asked if he had "ever seen any V.C.s in the area," he answered that he had seen "fifty armed men disappearing into the forest two weeks ago." Another man, asked if he knew "any V.C.s in the village," answered in a whisper that he knew of *one*—a dark-complexioned man about forty-five years old named Thang. Still another man said that he had been "taken into the jungle to build a tunnel a year ago" but couldn't remember where it was. I had the impression that the suspects were all veterans of the interrogation room. For one thing, they were able to switch immediately from the vocabulary of the Front to the vocabulary of the American and South Vietnamese-government troops. It is a measure of the deep penetration of propaganda into every medium of expression in wartime Vietnam that few proper names serve merely as names. Most have an added propagandistic import. Thus, to the Americans the actual *name* of the National Liberation Front is "Vietcong" (literally, "Vietnamese Communists")—a term that the Front rejects on the ground that it represents many factions besides the Communists. Likewise, to the Front the actual *name* of the Army of the Republic of Vietnam is "Puppet Troops." Even the names of the provinces are different in the two vocabularies. The Front refuses to comply with a presidential decree of 1956 renaming the provinces, and insists on using the old names—calling Binh Duong, for instance, by its old name of Thu Dau Mot. There is no middle ground in the semantic war. You choose sides by the words you use. The suspects made the necessary transitions effortlessly. (Confronted with this problem myself, I have tried in this article to use for each organization the name that its own side has chosen for it.)

Several women were brought into the schoolhouse for interrogation, sometimes carrying a naked child balanced astride one hip. Unlike the men, they occasionally showed extreme annoyance. One young woman only complained loudly, and did not answer any of the questions put to her. Her baby fixed the interrogator with an unwavering, openmouthed stare, and an old woman, squatting next to the suspect, looked at the ground in front of her and nodded in agreement as the young mother complained.

"Do you know any V.C.s in this village?" the interrogator, a young man, asked.

The interpreter, having tried to interrupt the woman's complaining, answered, "She says she can't remember anything. She doesn't know anything, because the bombs were falling everywhere."

"Tell her to just answer the question."

"She says she couldn't bring her belongings and her pig and cow here." The interpreter shook his head and added, "She is very angry."

The interrogator's face grew tense for a moment, and he looked away, uncertain of what to do next. Finally, he dismissed the woman and impatiently turned his pad to a fresh sheet.

The Vietnamese troops had their own style of interrogation. At eleven o'clock that morning, an ARVN officer stood a young prisoner, bound and blindfolded, up against a wall. He asked the prisoner several questions, and, when the prisoner failed to answer, beat him repeatedly. An American observer who saw the beating reported that the officer "really worked him over." After the beating, the prisoner was forced to remain standing against the wall for several hours. Most of the ARVN interrogations took place in a one-room hut behind the school where the Americans were carrying on their interrogations. The suspects, bound and blindfolded, were led one by one into the hut. A group of ten or twelve fatherless families sitting under the shade of a tree nearby heard the sound of bodies being struck, but there were no cries from the prisoners.

As one young man was being led by one arm toward the dark doorway of the interrogation hut, a small boy who was watching intently burst into loud crying. I went inside after the suspect, and found that three tall, slender, boyish Vietnamese lieutenants, wearing crisp, clean American-style uniforms crisscrossed with ammunition belts, and carrying heavy new black pistols at their hips, had sat the young man against the wall, removed his blindfold, and spread a map on the floor in front of him. Pointing to the map, they asked about Vietcong troop movements in the area. When he replied that he didn't have the answers they wanted, one lieutenant beat him in the face with a rolled-up sheet of vinyl that had covered the map, then jabbed him hard in the ribs. The prisoner sat wooden and silent. A very fat American with a red face and an expression of perfect boredom sat in a tiny chair at a tiny table near the door, looking dully at his hands. The three lieutenants laughed and joked among themselves, clearly enjoying what seemed to them an amusing contest of will and wits between them and the silent, unmoving figure on the floor in front of them. Looking at the prisoner with a challenging smile, the lieutenant with the map cover struck him again, then asked him more questions.

The prisoner again said he couldn't answer. Suddenly noticing my presence, all three lieutenants turned to me with the wide, self-deprecating grins that are perhaps the Vietnamese soldiers' most common response to the appearance of an American in any situation. Realizing that I could not speak Vietnamese, they called in an American Intelligence officer—Captain Ted L. Shipman, who was their adviser, and who could speak Vietnamese fluently. They asked him who I was, and, upon learning that I was not a soldier but a reporter, they looked at each other knowingly, saluted me, and continued their interrogation, this time without beatings. A few minutes later, however, Captain Shipman, who had been standing beside me, said that he was extremely sorry but they wanted me to leave. When we were outside, Captain Shipman, a short man with small, worried eyes behind pale-rimmed glasses, drew me aside and, shaking his head, spoke with considerable agitation. "You see, they *do* have some—well, methods and practices that *we* are not accustomed to, that we wouldn't use if we were doing it, but the thing you've got to understand is that this is an Asian country, and their first impulse is force," he said. "Only the fear of force gets results. It's the Asian mind. It's completely different from what we know as the Western mind, and it's hard for us to understand. Look—they're a thousand years behind us in this place, and we're trying to educate them up to our level. We can't just do everything for them ourselves. Now, take the Koreans—

they've got the Asian mind, and they really get excellent results here. Of course, we believe that that's not the best way to operate, so we try to introduce some changes, but it's very slow. You see, we know that the kind of information you get with these techniques isn't always accurate. Recently, we've been trying to get them to use some lie detectors we've just got. But we're only advisers. We can tell them how we think they should do it, but they can just tell us to shove off if they want to. I'm only an adviser, and I've made suggestions until I'm *blue in the face!* Actually, though, we've seen some improvement over the last year. This is a lot better than what we used to have."

I asked if the day's interrogations had so far turned up any important information.

"Not much today," he answered. "They're not telling us much. Sometimes they'll just tell you, 'Hey, I'm a V.C., I'm a V.C.' You know—proud. Today, we had one old man who told us his son was in the V.C. *He* was proud of it." Then, shaking his head again, he said with emphasis, as though he were finally putting his finger on the real cause of the difficulty, "You know, they're not *friendly* to us at this place, that's the problem. If you build up some kind of trust, then, once some of them come over to your side, they'll tell you anything. Their brother will be standing near them and they'll tell you, 'Him? He's my brother. He's a V.C.' It's hard for us to understand their mentality. They'll tell you the names of their whole family, and their best friends thrown in." Of the Front soldiers he said, "They don't know what they're doing half the time. Outside of the hard-core leaders, it's just like those juvenile delinquents back home, or those draft-card burners. They're just kids, and they want excitement. You give those kids a gun and they get excited. Half of the V.C.s are just deluded kids. They don't know what they're doing or why. But the V.C. operates through terror. Take this village. Maybe everybody doesn't want to be a V.C., but they get forced into it with terror. The V.C. organizes an association for everyone—the Farmers' Association, the Fishers' Association, the Old *Grandmothers'* Association. They've got one for everybody. It's so mixed up with the population you can't tell who's a V.C. Our job is to separate the V.C. from the people."

At that moment, a helicopter came in sight five hundred yards away, cruising low over the woods and emitting a steady chattering sound that was too loud to be the engine alone. Breaking off his explanation to look up, Captain Shipman said, "Now, there's a new technique they've developed. That sound you hear is the 7.62-calibre automatic weapon on the side. They have a hell of a time finding the V.C. from the air, so now when they hear that there's a V.C. in the area they'll come in and spray a whole field with fire. Then, you see, any V.C.s hiding below will get up and run, and you can go after them."

Captain Shipman went off to attend to other business, and I walked back to the interrogation hut. The fat American in the tiny chair was still looking at his hands, and the prisoner was still sitting stiff-spined on the floor, his lips tightly compressed and his gaze fixed in front of him. The young lieutenant with the map cover held it above the suspect's face and stared intently down at him. All three lieutenants were wholly engrossed in their work, excited by their power over the prisoner and challenged by the task of drawing information out of him. After twenty seconds or so, the American looked up and said to me, "They been usin' a little water torture." In the water torture, a sopping rag is held over the prisoner's nose and mouth to suffocate him, or his head is pushed back and water is poured directly down his nostrils to choke him. Again the lieutenants had not noticed me when I entered, and when the American spoke one of them looked up with a start. The tension and excitement in his expression were immediately replaced by a mischievous, slightly sheepish grin. Then all three lieutenants smiled at me with their self-deprecating grins, inviting me to smile along with them.

Captain Shipman came in, looking even more harried than before. One of the lieutenants spoke to him in a sugary, pleading tone, and Captain Shipman turned to me with a fatalistic shrug and said, "Look, I'm really sorry, but I get it in the neck if I don't take you away." Glancing over my shoulder as I left, I saw that the lieutenants were already crouching around their prisoner again and were all watching my exit closely.

Outside again, Captain Shipman explained that this was only a preliminary interrogation—that a more extensive session, by the Province Police, would be held later. He pointed out that American advisers, like him, would be present at the police interrogation.

At the end of an interrogation, the questioner, whether American or Vietnamese, tied an eight-inch cardboard tag around the neck of the bound prisoner. At the top were the words "Captive Card," in both Vietnamese and English, and below were listed the prisoner's name, address, age, occupation, and the kind of weapon, if any, he was carrying when caught. None of the captive cards on the first day listed any weapons.

At one o'clock, the official count of "V.C.s killed" stood at twenty-four, with no friendly casualties reported. Soldiers on the spot told me of six shootings. I learned that three men had crawled out of a tunnel when they were told that the tunnel was about to be blown up. "One of them made a break for it, and they got him on the run," the soldier said. An officer told me that a man and a woman were machine-gunned from a helicopter while they were "having a picnic." I asked him what he meant by a picnic, and he answered, "You know, a *picnic*. They had a cloth on the ground, and food—rice and stuff—set out on it. When they saw the chopper, they ran for it. They were both V.C.s. She was a nurse—she was carrying medical supplies with her, and had on a kind of V.C. uniform—and he was, you know, sitting right there with her, and he ran for it, too, when the chopper came overhead." A soldier told me that down near the river three men with packs had been shot from a distance. Inspection of their packs revealed a large quantity of medical supplies, including a surgical kit, anti-malaria pills, a wide assortment of drugs, and a medical diary, with entries in a small, firm hand, that showed the men to have been doctors. (The *Stars and Stripes* of January 12th gave an account of seven additional shootings: "UPI reported that Brigadier General John R. Hollingsworth's helicopter accounted for seven of the Vietcong dead as the operation began. The door gunner, personally directed by the colorful assistant commander of the 1st. Inf. Div., shot three V.C. on a raft crossing the Saigon River, another as he tried to sneak across camouflaged by lily-pads, and three more hiding in a creek nearby.")

I asked the officer tabulating the day's achievements how the Army disposed of enemy corpses. He said, "We leave the bodies where they are and let the people themselves take care of them." It occurred to me that this was going to be difficult, with only women and children left in the area. Later in the afternoon, I heard the following exchange on the field radio:

"Tell me, how should we dispose of the bodies, sir? Over."

"Why don't you throw them in the river? Over."

"We can't do that, sir. We have to drink out of that river, sir."

The captured-weapons count stood at forty-nine—

forty booby traps, six rifle grenades, two Russian-made rifles, and one American submachine gun. All were captured in caches in tunnels.

In the early afternoon, I went over to the field where the Americans were resting to ask them about the attack in the morning and what their feelings were concerning it. When I told one soldier that I was interested in finding out what weapons, if any, the Vietnamese dead had been carrying, he stiffened with pride, stared me straight in the eye, and announced, "What do you mean, 'Were they carrying weapons?' Of course they were carrying weapons! Look. I want to tell you one thing. *Anyone killed by this outfit was carrying a weapon.* In this outfit, no one shoots unless the guy is carrying a weapon. You've got to honor the civilian, that's all." With that, he terminated our conversation. Later, he and I walked over to a small tent where several men sat on the ground eating Spam and turkey from canned rations. They ate in silence, and, in fact, most of the men preferred to be alone rather than talk over the morning's attack. The men who did say anything about it laconically restricted themselves to short statements—such as "C Company had some light contact in the woods over there. Snipers mainly"—usually brought out in an almost weary tone, as though it were overdramatic or boastful to appear ruffled by the day's events. Nor did they kid around and enjoy themselves, like the ARVN soldiers. One young soldier, who looked to be not out of his teens, did come riding by on a small bicycle he had found near one of the houses in the village and cried out, with a big, goofy smile, "Hey! Look at this!," but the other men ignored him coldly, almost contemptuously.

I entered into conversation with Major Charles A. Malloy. "We're not a bunch of movie heroes out here," he said. "I think you'll find very few guys here who really hate the V.C. There's none of that stuff. I'll tell you what every soldier was thinking about when he stepped out of the helicopter this morning: Survival. Am I going to make it through? Am I going to see my wife and kids again? O.K., so some people without weapons get killed. What're you going to do when you spot a guy with black pajamas? Wait for him to get out his automatic weapon and start shooting? I'll tell you I'm not. Anyway, sometimes they throw away their weapon. They'll throw it into the bushes. You go and look at the body, and fifty yards away there's the weapon in the bushes. You can't always tell if they were carrying a weapon. Now, this man here has just heard that his wife had his first kid, a baby girl." He indicated a short, young-looking soldier with bright-red hair. "Now, if I told any one of these men they could go home tomorrow, they'd be off like a shot." The men listened with quiet faces, looking at the ground. "No, there's very little fanatic stuff here," he went on. At that moment, a middle-aged Vietnamese wearing the customary black floppy clothing was led by, his arms bound behind his back. Major Malloy looked over his shoulder at the prisoner and remarked, "There's a V.C. Look at those black clothes. They're no good for working in the fields. Black absorbs heat. This is a hot country. It doesn't make any sense. And look at his feet." The prisoner had bare feet, like many of the villagers. "They're all muddy from being down in those holes." In a burst of candor, he added, "What're you going to do? We've got people in the kitchen at the base wearing those black pajamas."

At three-forty-five, the male captives between the ages of fifteen and forty-five were marched to the edge of the helicopter pad, where they squatted in two rows, with a guard at each end. They hid their faces in their arms as a Chinook double-rotor helicopter set down, blasting them with dust. The back end of the helicopter was lowered to form a gangplank, leading to a dark, square opening. Their captive cards flapping around their necks, the prisoners ran, crouching low under the whirling blades, into the dim interior. Immediately, the gangplank drew up and the fat bent-banana shape of the Chinook rose slowly from the field. The women and children braved the gale to watch its rise, but appeared to lose interest in its flight long before it disappeared over the trees. It was as though their fathers, brothers, and sons had ceased to exist when they ran into the roaring helicopter.

Inside the Chinook, the prisoners were sitting on two long benches in a dim tubular compartment, unable to hear anything over the barely tolerable roaring of the engines, which, paradoxically, created a sensation of silence, for people moved and occasionally talked but made no sound. Many of the prisoners held their ears. Up front, on each side, a gunner wearing large earphones under a helmet scanned the countryside. The gunners' weapons pointed out, and there was no guard inside the helicopter. A few of the prisoners—some bold and some just young—stood up and looked out of small portholes in back of their seats. For the first time in their lives, they saw their land spread below them like a map, as the American pilots always see it: the tiny houses in the villages, the green fields along the river pockmarked with blue water-filled bomb craters (some blackened by napalm), and the dark-green jungles splotched with long lines of yellow craters from B-52 raids, the trees around each crater splayed out in a star, like the orb of cracks around a bullet hole in glass.

That night, the women, children, and old people were allowed to return to their houses under a guard of ARVN soldiers. Being of peasant stock themselves for the most part, the ARVN soldiers knew just how to catch, behead, and pluck a chicken. Most of the battalion helped itself to fried chicken—a rare luxury for them. In the hot sun the next day, they went inside the houses to keep cool. Except for the guards on the perimeter of the village, the Americans stayed apart in the field next to the landing pad; even so, a few of them managed to get some chicken to fry.

The next morning, trucks arrived in Ben Suc to begin the evacuation. The Americans on the scene were not sure just how many possessions the villagers were supposed to take with them. The original orders were to "bring everything." In practice, the villagers were allowed to take anything that they themselves could carry to the trucks. Families near the spot where a truck was drawn up took furniture, bedclothes, bags of rice, pigs, cooking utensils, agricultural tools, and just about anything else they wanted to, but, without their men to help them, families living at any distance from a truck could carry only clothing, a few cooking utensils, and one or two bags of rice. By government decree, any rice beyond fifteen bushels per family was to be confiscated as "surplus," potentially intended for the enemy, but although many families had as much as four times this amount at their houses, they could never carry more than fifteen bags with them to the trucks, so no scenes of confiscation took place at the loading. (During the next few days, all the cattle still in or near the village were rounded up and brought to join the villagers.) Several of the ARVN soldiers helped the women and children load the heavy pigs and bags of rice on the trucks. Later, an American officer who saw this exclaimed in amazement, "You saw it! The Arvins loaded those trucks. We've never seen anything like it."

ARVN's willingness to load and unload trucks during this whole operation became quite famous, evoking a few compliments for the ARVN troops amid the usual barrage of American criticism. Hearing about the truck-loading, another officer remarked, "You pat the little Arvin on the ass and he just might do a good job." Because the Americans were very eager to find the Front's storage places for the rice collected as taxes, they had a Vietnamese officer announce to the assembled women that by divulging where this rice was they would gain permission to take it with them to the resettlement area, but no one responded. Several Americans speculated about whether this showed loyalty to the Vietcong.

Jammed with people, animals, and bundles of possessions, the trucks left Ben Suc in convoys of ten. The first few miles of the journey took them along a bumpy dirt road in a choking cloud of dust, which quickly coated everything. After an hour, they turned onto another road, near Phu Cuong, and headed for Phu Loi, their destination. Finally, the trucks swung right into a vast field of at least ten acres, empty except for a row of a dozen or more huts standing in the shade of a line of low palm trees along a narrow dirt road. Since there was nothing resembling a camp for the villagers, the American drivers brought their charges to these huts— the only shelter in sight. They were the houses of families who farmed fields nearby and who were totally surprised to discover themselves playing host to several thousand strangers—strangers not only from Ben Suc but from several other villages. Earlier that day, truck-loads of people from other villages in the Iron Triangle had been arriving in a steady stream. ARVN soldiers again won praise by helping to unload the trucks, and American soldiers also gave a hand with the unloading. Dusty, squealing, desperately kicking pigs were slid to the ground down ramps improvised from boards. One American soldier put his hands under the arms of a tiny, very old deaf woman and whisked her to the ground, setting her gently down as though she were as light as a bunch of straw. Several children smiled at seeing the old lady lifted down. As for the lady herself, she simply stood motionless among the pigs and rice bags, staring in front of her with blank unconcern; ap-parently she was too old to realize that she had just flown through the air from truck to ground. The Ameri-cans also lifted down several small, amazed, pantless children. After the unloading was finished, some of the Ben Suc people jammed themselves into the already jammed houses of the Phu Loi peasants, and others simply tried to find some shade. Soon they began to talk with the people from the other villages, who had their own tales of misfortune to tell.

Late in the morning of that day, I made my way to the northern edge of the Iron Triangle to see what was happening in these other villages. Arriving at a point near the northeastern tip of the Triangle at noon, I was offered a ride in a jeep with two Psychological Warfare officers and an Army photographer who were heading west across the top of the Triangle on a tour of inspection. Driving in the wake of heavy military traffic, we soon found ourselves in the midst of an immense demolition job being performed on a large rubber plantation, four villages, and large areas of the jungle itself. On both sides of the road, bulldozers had already pushed back the jungle for fifty yards, forming six miles of rough, hilly field that contained torn-up tree trunks, broken branches, and upturned stumps with their roots sticking out in every direction. In places, the stretch of road was alive with bulldozers, flashing yellow and silver in the forest and bobbing up and down in a hilly sea of mangled trees. Soldiers with machetes were walking down rows of tall, slender rubber trees and felling them at waist height, while engineers placed explosives around the brick buildings of the plantation managers. In the villages of Rach Kien, Bung Cong, and Rach Bap, the sequence of attack, evacuation, and demolition had been compressed into a single day. Across from the rubber plantation, the villagers crouched along the road with their bundles of belongings while American infantrymen ducked in and out of the palm groves behind them, some pouring gasoline on the grass roofs of the houses and others going from house to house setting them afire. When we came upon this, a major in my jeep exclaimed, "Oh, God, this is bad! This is like the Marines." Then, to the Army photographer, who had got out to take pictures, he called out, "Be careful not to get any of our men in those shots!" At the village of Rach Bap, many of the houses were already burned to the ground and bulldozers were crushing whatever was left standing. To find the houses, the bulldozers would plow into the groves of palm trees, snapping the trunks as they went, and then, discovering a house, crush it. Columns of heavy black smoke rose from the burning village. The villagers had been assembled next to a masonry building in the center of this activity, and the air around them was filled with the snapping of palm trunks and the high-pitched roar of the bulldozers cutting into the walls of a few masonry houses near the road. Standing or crouching without speaking, their faces drawn tight in dead masks, the people seemed not to see or hear what was happening around them.

At Rach Bap, I asked a captain in charge of one phase of the evacuation why it was necessary to destroy the villages and the jungle. "We're going to deprive the V.C. of lodging and food in this area!" he shouted over the noise of the bulldozers and of the explosions in the jungle. "We want to prevent them from moving freely in this area. By making these paths in the jungle, we're going to be able to see them a lot more easily than before. From now on, anything that moves around here is going to be automatically considered V.C. and bombed or fired on. The whole Triangle is going to become a Free Zone. These villages here are all considered hostile villages."

I asked what would happen to the men of Rach Bap.

"We're considering all the males in this district V.C., and the people as hostile civilians," he replied.

The term "hostile civilians" was a new one, invented during Operation Cedar Falls for the people in the villages that had been marked for destruction. The question of what to call these villagers was one of many semantic problems that the Army had to solve. At the scene of an evacuation, they usually used the phrase "hostile civilians," which hinted that all the villagers at least supported the enemy and thus all deserved to be "relocated." But later, at Phu Loi, the officials in charge reverted to the more familiar term "refugees," which suggested that the villagers were not themselves the enemy but were "the people," fleeing the enemy.

When I asked the captain at Rach Bap how the Army sorted out the enemy from the friendly civilians, he answered, "In a V.C. area like this one, there are three categories of classification. First, there are the straight V.C. They're the activists, the real hard core. Then, there are the V.C. sympathizers, who support the V.C. with taxes. Then, there's the . . . there's a third category. There are three categories. I can't think of the third just now, but I can say that there's no middle road in this war. Either you're with us or you're against us. We've captured eleven straight V.C.s and sixty-three suspects, and had thirty-two *hoi chanh*. The body count isn't in yet."

As we were driving in the vicinity of Rach Bap, our jeep pulled up next to a Vietnamese officer at the side of the road who was carrying an electric bullhorn on one shoulder and a submachine gun on the other. Hearing that I was a reporter, he introduced himself proudly in broken English. "I am Captain Nguyen Hué. I am district chief of Ben Cat area. I control forty-four thousand people. Now we chase away the V.C.—they never come back. If they come back today, O.K., but if don't come back—all killed!" District Chief Nguyen Hué had not been able to exercise real control over these villages until that day, and he could not look forward to controlling them in the future, because they would soon cease to exist. From what I saw later, I gathered that he was bent on squeezing a maximum of exercise of control out of his day and a half of authority. He drove around in a station wagon and frequently jumped out to give a short, excited lecture to groups of villagers crouching along the road waiting for the evacuation trucks. "I am Captain Nguyen Hué, district chief of the Ben Cat District," he told them, adding that he and the Americans had come to save them from the Vietcong and urging them to persuade their friends who were still hiding to give themselves up, because those who didn't would be killed.

Farther along, in an area that, according to the original plan, should already have been fully evacuated, one of two majors in our jeep noticed the figures of two little girls by the edge of the forest. Going into four-wheel drive, we lurched over the plowed stretch to where they were standing. Just beyond the border of the fifty-yard demolition, a number of tiny huts still stood in a grove of tall trees sloping down to rice fields along the river. The little girls appeared to be sisters, about nine and twelve years old. They were barefoot, wore simple, short beltless dresses, and had their black hair in long braids. A few yards away from them, a very old man and woman watched us approach. When we arrived, no one seemed quite sure how to deal with the situation. Then the two little girls took charge. Speaking slowly and clearly, and repeating everything several times, they informed a major who had attended six weeks of language school that their parents had been taken away in a truck and that they now wished to load their rice and furniture into a truck and go themselves. They laughed freely when the major failed at first to understand them. Without waiting for a response, they beckoned to us to follow them. One of the officers muttered, "Better watch it—it could be a trap," but the others followed the little girls. Upon reaching one of the huts, the girls hoisted onto their shoulders sacks of rice that I thought would surely crush them, and pointed to things for us to carry. One almost full bag of rice was open at the top. The younger sister gave me a handful of straw, indicating that I was to tie it closed. She watched me fumble for a minute, and then took the straw from my hands and expertly twisted it around the top of the bag in a way that made it secure. They insisted on bringing a large jar full of rice that could be carried only when it was suspended by its wire handles from a pole and there was a person at each end to man the pole. I took one end and the sisters took the other, and we had just started toward the jeep when the pole snapped and the jar fell—without overturning—on the ground. The little girls burst out laughing, and it was a full fifteen seconds before the elder sister ran back for another pole. Meanwhile, an empty truck had been hailed and brought over to the edge of the forest. A minute later, I noticed that the little girls had disappeared. After a brief search, they were discovered out in the rice fields stuffing unwinnowed rice into burlap bags. They came immediately when the Vietnamese-speaking major called to them. One of the officers said that he had found a rowboat and wanted to blow it up with a hand grenade. While he was performing this mission, the other Americans loaded the rice on the truck and hoisted up the girls and the aged couple, who had fetched a few bundles themselves by this time. Holding their sleeves over their mouths against the dust, they set out down the road for Phu Loi. The officer who had gone to attend to the rowboat returned after an explosion had sounded from the woods, and reported that, to his surprise, the hand grenade had blown only a six-inch hole in the bottom of the skiff.

We pushed on in our jeep to the end of the plowed boulevard in the jungle, and here we came on five armored personnel-carriers sitting parked, facing the jungle in fan formation. Perched in the turrets of their massive vehicles, the men ate canned rations and kept an impassive eye on the edge of the jungle fifty yards away. On the high metal deck of one of the personnel-carriers, two monkeys no bigger than cats were tied with five-foot pieces of cord to the base of a machine gun. A soldier sitting in a turret above them alternately threw scraps of food to them and grabbed at them, so that they rushed screeching to the far ends of their cords. Sometimes, when the monkeys bared their teeth and chattered, the soldier would lean down, bare his own teeth, and cry "Nyahhh," terrifying the monkeys. Watching this from a distance, a young soldier who had just spent most of the morning in the area of the burning villages suddenly shouted, "I can't stand it! I just can't stand it! Whenever I see people with monkeys, they're always teasing them, or something. Always poking at them or annoying them. Why do they have to torture the monkeys? Why can't they just leave the monkeys alone?"

We returned across the top of the Triangle to Ben Cat, a village that was to be spared destruction. The people living in the vicinity of Ben Cat had already been "relocated" several times in the last five years, in an unsuccessful attempt to break the influence of the National Liberation Front in the area. Now, as trucks full of villagers poured out of the Triangle, the Army was using one of the smaller former resettlement areas as a headquarters and relay point for the villagers. The huts there were the architectural equivalent of a crazy quilt. Straw, bits of cardboard, corrugated iron, planks, flattened beer cans, mats of woven branches, burlap, and anything else thin and flat that might keep out rain were tied, nailed, pegged, and wired to crude frames made of tree trunks lashed together at the joints with vines or wire. A coil of barbed wire had been thrown around a half acre of these huts, and inside this enclosure the new homeless moved in with the old homeless and both groups mingled freely with the soldiers of the two armies. A heavy traffic of trucks, jeeps, tanks, carts, bulldozers, and armored personnel-carriers moved slowly through the enclosure, heading into the Iron Triangle. The children had quickly invented games involving the parked or slow-moving tanks and personnel-carriers. They climbed up on them and hung on the back for rides, to the annoyance of the American soldiers, who could not see all sides of their vehicles from their high turrets and were afraid that a child would slip under the treads. Several women and children from the village of Ben Cat had already set themselves up in business, selling bottled orange drinks and beer at more than sixty piastres a bottle (about fifty cents) to the parched and affluent Americans. Beyond this, however, there was little intercourse between the different groups in the enclosure. Carts drawn by water

buffalo moved in the tracks left by tanks, and soldiers
carrying submachine guns milled about among villagers lugging possessions, but each of them was on
his own urgent errand, and they rarely communicated,
or even looked at each other. Only the children, always curious, stared in wonder at all the new things.
For a minority of the villagers, Ben Cat would be the
permanent resettlement area. The majority were to be
taken on to Phu Loi. Captain Nguyen Hué was to
decide which families went and which stayed.

At Phu Loi, truckloads of villagers from the north
end of the Triangle and from Ben Suc continued to
arrive in front of the little row of huts in the huge field.
On the first day, over a thousand people were brought
in. When they climbed slowly down from the backs of
the trucks, they had lost their appearance of healthy
villagers and taken on the passive, dull-eyed, waiting
expression of the uprooted. It was impossible to tell
whether deadness and discouragement had actually replaced a spark of sullen pride in their expression and
bearing or whether it was just that any crowd of people
removed from the dignifying context of their homes
and places of labor, learning, and worship, and dropped,
tired and coated with dust, in a bare field would appear broken-spirited to an outsider.

The reason for the total lack of shelter and facilities
for the villagers at Phu Loi when they arrived was
simply that the Vietnamese who were to provide these

knew nothing about their assignment until twenty
hours before the influx began. On the morning of the
attack on Ben Suc, Lieutenant Colonel Ly Tong Ba,
the chief of Binh Duong Province, learned, to his surprise, that American troops had already set in motion a
plan to destroy four villages in his province and evacuate the villagers to Phu Loi, where he was expected to
provide them with what the Americans called a "refugee camp," and also with food, and with a form of security around the camp that would keep the villagers in
as well as enemy organizers out. One AID official observed to me that day, "Refugees are a real headache.
Nobody likes to have to take care of refugees." Colonel
Ba was annoyed at being suddenly saddled with the
tedious and thankless task of caring for anywhere
from six thousand to ten thousand homeless, hostile villagers, but at the same time he was a little flattered
when the Americans told him that they were thrusting
on him a position of "command" in the largest operation of the Vietnam war. As the highest official of the
South Vietnamese government in the province, he was
to assume responsibility for villagers recently freed
from Communist domination. The Americans had
taken care of the "military half," and now it was up to
him to lead "the other war—for the hearts and minds of
the people," which could be really won only by "the
Vietnamese themselves." His first task, they said, was to
come out to the battlefield in a helicopter and talk to
the people. They explained that they had been unable

to inform him of the operation earlier because the security risk forbade their telling any local Vietnamese about it, and that they had been unable to do anything more than stockpile rice at an AID warehouse in preparation for the camp because any major construction would have given the operation away to the enemy. However, because Province Chief Ba was acquainted so late with the nature of his task, several officials from AID who knew the details of the operation thoroughly and had already decided on the site for the construction of the camp were assigned to him to suggest plans of action. These officials were very clear on the point that all credit for building the camp was to go to the Vietnamese—that, from that point on, "Vietnamese had to deal with Vietnamese." Explaining the policy later, Philip L. Carolin, Jr., and chief AID official for Phu Cuong, said, "We can't do it for them. They have to learn to do it themselves someday. One of our most important jobs here is to teach these people to stand on their own feet. Otherwise, what's going to happen when we leave?" Colonel Ba, therefore, soon overcame his initial pique and became an enthusiastic promoter of the operation as well as its commander. At times, perhaps thrilled by his sudden direct connection with the Americans' awesome military power and by his own vital role in its operations, he exaggerated the aims of the current project, indulging in bursts of enthusiasm as he talked to reporters. On the second day, after the villagers began to arrive, he triumphantly announced to four assembled American correspondents, "We are going to destroy everything in the Iron Triangle. Make it into a flat field. The V.C. can no longer hide there." Actually, instead of flattening the entire area of forty square miles, the Americans restricted themselves to bulldozing several wide avenues across the jungle.

Although two AID officials were brought in from other provinces expressly to help with the construction of the camp, the principal full-time AID official was Carolin, a big man of twenty-eight, with curly blond hair and a young, almost collegiate sunburned face with a small turned-up nose. He had worked in Vietnam for six months after teaching history and doing social work in the United States. Temporarily superseding him in the hierarchy of American officials, however, was a man introduced to me as "Lieutenant Colonel Kenneth J. White, province representative for the Office of Civilian Operations, and top civilian in the area." When I asked him how it came about that the top civilian was a colonel, he explained that he was "on loan from the Army" for the period of the camp's establishment. Because the United States Army 1st Division would supply most of the building supplies and the ARVN 5th Division would do most of the construction, the Americans felt that a man of high military rank would get faster results as top civilian than a full-time civilian would. I asked him how he liked being a civilian. "This is my first stretch as a civilian," he answered. "You find that certain things just don't get done the way you're used to." A cheerful man of trim, athletic build, Colonel White is thirty-seven, and in talking business he speaks so rapidly that you wonder if he's going to be able to get all the words out. He maintained a buoyant enthusiasm throughout the construction of the camp. Whether he was offering advice to Colonel Ba, in a self-consciously humble, soft-spoken manner, or moving from task to task with his characteristic rapid, almost bounding gait, he displayed unflagging energy and almost unclouded high spirits, not unlike an eager camp councillor managing a large and difficult but highly successful jamboree.

Since there was no central advance plan for the camp, it grew through hundreds of separate improvised decisions taken by a great number of organizations, with the Vietnamese organizations reporting to Colonel Ba and the American organizations reporting to Colonel White. On the Vietnamese side, there were the province administration, the ARVN 5th Division, the Revolutionary Development teams, and, arriving later in the week, several Vietnamese groups formed for "nation building." On the American side, there were the Army's 1st Division, AID, the sizable American advisory group to the ARVN 5th Division, and the American advisers to other Vietnamese organizations, like the Province Police. There was also a team of Philippine doctors. In speaking of the planning of the camp, Colonel White remarked, "We're winging it all the way!"

As a site for the camp, AID had chosen the empty

field at Phu Loi. Fronting on the road, it was bordered on one side and at the back by forest, and on the other side by barracks for the ARVN 5th Division's thousands of dependents. This housing consisted of long, straight rows of unpainted wooden sheds divided into compartments, each with a doorway but rarely a door. In between the rows, the earth was bare except for an occasional vegetable patch. Like so much of wartime Vietnam, particularly in and around the cities, the dependents' area had a rough, half-finished look, as though it were just being built, or were being torn down. It had been made by simply flattening the previous landscape and laying out the structures according to a strictly symmetrical crosshatch plan. There had been no attempts at beautification by either the builders or the inhabitants. The ARVN dependents were displeased at having to live in the neighborhood of the dirty, impoverished new arrivals, and they tried without much success to keep their children from going over to watch the soldiers at work. Later, when they spotted a movie screen inside the camp during the showing of a propaganda film, a few of the women indignantly demanded to know why the enemy people were shown movies and the loyal supporters had none.

At the moment that the Ben Suc villagers got off the trucks at Phu Loi, the military plan that had started with the attack on Ben Suc and had proceeded precisely on schedule came to an end. This was the point in the plan at which the villagers came under the

control of the provincial authorities. But Colonel Ba
and his advisers were not yet ready to assume control,
and the result was a planless interlude of about a day.
Colonel Ba and Colonel White managed to borrow men
from the United States 1st Division and the ARVN 5th
while they waited for the Revolutionary Development
workers to arrive, but these men were unprepared for
their brief assignment, and the tight guard that had
been mounted over the "hostile civilians" until that day
all but faded away. Any of the villagers who wished to
escape could easily have done so at this point, and any
outsider could easily have come to join them. At about
three o'clock, the 1st Division parked a water truck
with spigots in the yard of one of the absurdly jammed
houses under the row of palms. Mothers and children
crowded around it with pots and pitchers, and soon six
inches of mud had formed under their feet. Several
mothers thrust bawling babies directly under a spigot
to wash them, or made their children stand under the
streams of water. A medical tent was set up as at Ben
Suc, and next to it blossomed a yellow nylon pavilion,
shaped like a circus tent, with chairs and a table in its
shade. This was referred to as the "command tent," but
most of the commanders were too busy arranging for the
construction of the camp to sit down. At one point in
the late afternoon, three weary locally recruited Revolutionary Development workers, wearing cowboy hats,
availed themselves of the chairs and the shade to take a
rest. Shortly after they had sat down, an old woman in

black, with bare feet and straggling hair, came shuffling toward them, talking angrily to herself. Upon reaching the threesome, she focussed her annoyance on them. She said that she wanted to go back to Rach Bap to get a baby that she had left there. The three R.D. men looked uncomfortable, and one answered with resigned politeness that they could do nothing just then, and that she should ask some soldiers standing by a truck. The old woman walked away muttering, and did not speak to the soldiers.

In the evening, as Colonel Ba began to mobilize his forces, coils of barbed wire were unrolled around the villagers wherever they had squatted down, and guards were posted, signalling the end of the planless interlude. The attempt to provide security was still only halfhearted, though. (I accompanied an American major on a tour of the grounds that evening, and in the darkness we passed through two barbed-wire barriers without being challenged. The guards we did encounter did not seem to know whether they were keeping the villagers in or the enemy out. The major thought they should face outward, and reprimanded one, a Vietnamese, for failing to do so.) As the sun set, the warmth left the dry air, and the light dimmed quickly in the unclouded sky. A few small cooking fires sprouted up among the villagers as some of them prepared a supper of the rice they had brought with them, and a low sound of talking rose from the dark field.

A hundred yards away, soldiers of the ARVN 5th

Division set up floodlights and began construction of the camp. That afternoon, bulldozers had flattened several hundred cone-shaped anthills, six feet high, which had covered the site for the camp, leaving an expanse of several acres of level earth. On this the Vietnamese soldiers first erected a long, peak-roofed frame of bamboo poles, fastened together with pieces of wire. The frame was of the most basic simplicity, having no supports or poles that would not appear in a child's line drawing of a three-dimensional transparent rectangular house. Over this the soldiers pitched a single hundred-foot piece of nylon cloth and pegged it down on each side with ropes and stakes, thus forming a roof over the frame and completing the structure. The final product was a long nylon canopy over the bare earth, without floors or walls. Around ten o'clock, having constructed five or six of these canopies, the ARVN soldiers roused several hundred villagers from their resting places in the dark and led them through a gap in a long barbed-wire fence circling the canopies and into the harshly lighted construction area. Each family was assigned a space about ten feet square between the vertical poles that held up the nylon. At eleven o'clock, the soldiers turned out the lights. That night, the temperature dropped into the low fifties, making sleep difficult for the villagers, most of whom lay, without blankets, on mats or in the dust itself. About five hundred people remained in the field outside the camp.

With no walls to keep out the light, the people under the canopies were awakened at six-thirty by the sun, to find themselves in one corner of a vast earthen expanse enclosed by barbed wire and guarded by a few tired soldiers standing, singly, around them in the early-morning light. They noticed that the canopy over them was gaily colored red and white, the two colors alternating every twenty feet. Now helpless to do anything for themselves, they began a life of sitting and waiting. Not long after they awoke, a little gray truck on which were mounted two speakers facing in opposite directions began to pass up and down inside the barbed wire, blaring loud, cheerful Vietnamese music into the camp. After several runs back and forth, the driver stopped the truck and slumped exhausted in the front seat, fighting off drowsiness as the day grew hot and the music played on. The music consisted of a number of songs performed in the rapid, high, inflected nasal style of Vietnamese popular singers. The lyrics praised the government in Saigon and urged the people to pitch in and help with the reconstruction of their country. The songs, interspersed with propaganda tapes on which a warm, vigorous, manly voice boomed questions and a chorus of young voices shouted answers in unison, were played again and again.

Under the canopies, the people had embarked on a common existence with their animals. Because the vertical poles supporting the canopies were the only places where the big, gray, muddy, bristle-backed pigs could be tied, it was impossible to keep them from entering the compartments to escape the burning sun. The animals were everywhere and in everything. If the people grew tired and quiet as they got hungry, the animals became more and more aggressive and active. A ravenous, snorting pig would occasionally break its tether and range wide in search of food, sometimes finding it in a villager's unprotected store. And the chickens, now released from their baskets, ran everywhere, pecking at anything that looked like food. The pure, high peeping of baby chicks rose on all sides as flocks of the little creatures raced at breakneck speed down the fresh bulldozer tracks, their fuzz blending into the yellow earth so that they were difficult to see. Later in the day, as the heat grew more intense, the animals calmed down a bit—especially the pigs, which keeled over on their sides and lay panting in the dust.

By official calculation, there were almost three times as many women as men in the camp, and almost twice as many children as adults. On the morning after the construction began, the camp held about a thousand people, approximately seven hundred of them children. Growing restless with nothing to do, the children old enough to walk but too young to know where they were going tended to drift away from their compartments, sometimes following a chicken or a dog, sometimes with no purpose at all. Soon, wandering among the identical canopies, they would stop, look about them, and start crying for their mothers. (On the first day, the mothers could often find their lost children themselves, but in succeeding days, as the population rose to nearly six thousand, this became impossible. When Vietnamese Revolutionary Development teams arrived on the scene, two days later, returning these lost children constituted one of their major jobs.)

The ARVN soldiers resumed the construction of canopies at about nine-thirty in the morning. They also constructed a temporary latrine, consisting of two fifteen-yard parallel ditches, one for men and one for women, divided from each other and also surrounded by a waist-high fence of gleaming silver corrugated iron. The entire arrangement, including the interior, was visible from the busy main entrance to the camp, which was not more than fifty yards away. The designers of this mass toilet apparently intended its users to balance themselves on the brink of the ditch in order to relieve themselves into it. This latrine got very little use. Instead, most of the villagers restrained themselves until dark and then slipped out beyond the lighted part of the camp to a place where the bulldozed earth had been left in rough hills and mounds. But there was no grass or brush cover within the bounds of the barbed wire, and on the first day under the canopies a few of the old people, who could not stand to relieve themselves semi-publicly, sneaked through the barbed wire in search of brushy, protected areas outside the coils. This became considerably more difficult on the second day, when two coils of barbed wire were added to the first to form a barbed-wire pyramid—two coils on the bottom and one on top. The children slipped in and out with no trouble, but the old people required help. The helper would part the wires while the escaper entered the inner coil and attempted to negotiate the inner wall between the two coils himself, with the helper unhitching him from the wire if he got stuck. One afternoon, I came upon an old woman caught on the barbs on the inside of the inner coil and a boy about eight years old attempting to free her by reaching into the coil. When I approached, the little boy jumped back and the old woman's eyes filled with panic, but she produced a thin smile, and then, stuck inside the coil, attempted to bow to me. Speaking to my interpreter, she explained that she had been relieving herself in the brush outside the camp. The ARVN guards, although they could not condone these temporary escapes outright, apparently adopted a lenient policy toward them.

Arriving at the camp early in the morning of the first day dressed in a freshly ironed plaid sports shirt and a cowboy hat, against the sun, Colonel White met informally with two AID officials and, looking out at the newly constructed red-and-white canopies fluttering in a fresh breeze under a flawless blue sky, exclaimed, "This is wonderful! I've never seen anything like it. It's the best civilian project I've ever seen." Throughout, the camp was referred to as a "civilian project" or as "the civilian half of what we're doing here." "We've got shelter up for almost a thousand people here in one day," the Colonel went on. "The ARVN boys have been working just like coolies loading and unloading those trucks. It's been highly gratifying." Then, suddenly remembering something, he waved an arm between the tall shoulders of the AID officials in the direction of an officer of the South Vietnamese Army who was standing half outside the ring of Americans and focussing his whole attention on an attempt to grasp Colonel White's rapid English. The shoulders parted, and the officer, whose beret hardly reached the chins of the Americans, was startled out of his single-minded concentration. "This is Lieutenant An," Colonel White announced, extending his hand to one side and smiling warmly down at the Lieutenant as though he were introducing someone to a television audience. All eyes moved to Lieutenant An, and Colonel White continued dramatically, "Here's the man who did it. Here's the man who deserves the credit." Lieutenant An nodded, his eyes following Colonel White's lips in a desperate but futile attempt to understand. "He did a wonderful job with his men. He deserves all the credit." Noticing the Lieutenant's confusion, Colonel White ran through the words of praise again, trying to warm up a smile that he had been wearing too long already. "He did a wonderful job. His men stayed up until eleven o'clock doing this last night. We didn't do anything. He deserves the credit." Recognizing that attention was centered on him, Lieutenant An stepped forward with a smile. There was a silence. Colonel White turned to the

Americans again and said, "About the water trucks
. . ." Lieutenant An stepped back, and the shoulders
closed. After the two AID officials had left, Colonel
White paused, again looked out over the coils of barbed
wire toward the bright canopies, and, turning to Philip
Carolin, said with warm satisfaction, "You know, Phil,
sometimes it just feels *right.*"

Colonel Ba, when he arrived, was no less exuberant
than Colonel White. He stationed himself in the round
yellow command tent, which had been moved to a
point near the main entrance to the camp. His men
brought several more chairs, another table, a large map
of the Iron Triangle, and a small cooler containing beer
and soft drinks on ice. Colonel Ba, a short, powerful
man who gestured strongly with his arms and usually
faced the world through a pair of sunglasses, was
clearly in a state of eager excitement. He issued a
stream of orders and talked with gusto to American
reporters in broken English, frequently laughing
abruptly at his own remarks, although there did not
always seem to be any joke. His American advisers
politely murmured suggestions to him, almost as
though their presence were a secret. American reporters repeatedly turned to Colonel White to ask questions, but usually the Colonel tactfully redirected them
to Colonel Ba. As soon as a public-address system had
been set up to supplement the sound truck, Colonel Ba
had a microphone installed in his command tent. This
put him in direct contact with the villagers, none of

whom had heard the voice of any official representing the government in Saigon for two years. In addition to official announcements, Colonel Ba took care of many small problems and interrupted the taped propaganda to make extemporaneous announcements of his own. He took particular pleasure in announcing the names and descriptions of lost children in an attempt to find their parents. On the second day of the camp's existence, a Vietnamese soldier moved down the aisles between the canopies, blasting insecticide on the villagers and their belongings from a machine that resembled a large rotary lawnmower. There was a mild panic among the villagers, who had been told by the Front that American defoliant sprays were poisonous to people. To reassure them, Colonel Ba went to his microphone and announced, "Don't worry! The poison will not harm you. It kills only insects. The Vietcong say the government and the Americans will poison you, but instead we improve your welfare by killing the insects." Then, turning to two reporters seated in his tent, he said, "You see? The Vietcong say we will kill the people, but instead the poison kills only the insects!" At every opportunity, Colonel Ba drummed away at the point that conditions at the camp were much better than enemy propaganda had predicted: he did not poison them; he did not beat up pregnant women; soon he would give everyone food.

A reporter asked him how the present program of "resettlement" differed from the earlier "strategic-hamlet" program, which both Americans and Vietnamese regard as a failure.

"In the strategic hamlet, we could not stay with the people," he answered. "We would leave and the Vietcong would come again. Now we have the Revolutionary Development workers to win their hearts and minds, and teach them about the government. This time we will stay with the people. We can educate them."

In the camp itself, the educational program was represented by the sound truck and the public-address system, the two of which often broadcast propaganda simultaneously. Along with patriotic songs and speeches, announcements were repeatedly played on tape. The following announcement played for about an hour one afternoon: "The 32nd Tactical Area Division and Binh Duong Province welcome you and promise to help you in every way. We know that in the areas under Vietcong control you are terrorized and forced to pay enormous taxes. They promise you everything but never actually do anything good for you. So now the government operation has brought you all here so you can escape from the Vietcong. We are doing our best, but know that food and space are a little short at the moment. In a few days, conditions will improve. The government will soon find a new job for everyone. The Army would like to warn you against the presence of scheming Vietcong cadres in your midst who disguise themselves as refugees. When you see such cadres, come immediately to tell the government troops. We hope that you will be able to go home soon. We also want to request Vietcong cadres to turn themselves in. They will be made welcome in the Open Arms program of the government. This is the only refugee camp in Binh Duong, and we advise all families with relatives still hiding in Ben Suc or in the other towns to come with the Army and try to persuade their relatives over the loudspeakers to come back. The government will always stay with its people!" Propaganda signs were also posted at various points around the camp. One sign, painted on cloth that was draped over the barbed-wire coils at the entrance to the camp, announced in large letters, "WELCOME TO FREEDOM AND DEMOCRACY." A sign farther in, also hanging on the barbed wire, read, "WELCOME TO THE RECEPTION CENTER FOR REFUGEES FLEEING COMMUNISM."

Presently, an N.B.C. reporter asked Colonel Ba where the villagers would be moved for permanent resettlement, and when they would leave the Phu Loi camp.

"We are not sure where they will go yet. They will go to another province in about two months, I think," he answered.

The reporter asked what military operations had been launched in Binh Duong before Operation Cedar Falls.

"Before?" asked Colonel Ba.

"Yes—last year, or the year before."

"Last year?" Colonel Ba slapped his knee and laughed his abrupt laugh. "*I* don't know about last year. I wasn't here." He pointed to himself with both hands in a gesture that cleared him of all responsibility for what had happened last year. "Ask someone else about last year!" he said, dissolving in merriment.

The reporter pursued the matter of a permanent-resettlement area with Colonel White. "Tell me, Colonel, in the new area, will these people be working at the same occupations as they did before?"

"Yes, they will. They will be able to farm just as before. We are giving each family a compensation of five thousand piastres [about thirty-eight dollars]."

"Most of these people are rice farmers. Could you tell me about some of the problems of getting a paddy going? I understand that there are a lot of difficulties at the beginning."

"Yes, we are aware of this, and plan to do everything that's necessary for that," Colonel White answered. As an afterthought, he added, "Maybe they'll grow vegetables."

When the reporter had left the tent, a shadow of perplexity passed over Colonel White's usually cheerful face, and he turned to me and said, "That fellow from N.B.C. didn't look as if he was going to be very nice about what we're doing out here, did he?"

I agreed that he didn't.

Colonel White had a theory about how a reporter might receive an unfavorable impression of the camp.

"I bet that when they talk to the refugees, if they talk to the families *without* men along everyone seems unhappy, but if they happen to talk to families *with* men along everyone seems relatively happy," he said.

A number of American officers assisted Colonel White with matters concerning the camp, but they did not work there full time. Several high-ranking officers, including two generals, made personal tours of inspection in Ben Suc and in the camp. At Phu Loi, the sight of a colonel or a general striding down the aisles between the canopies, followed by staff officers with notebooks, was a common one. I accompanied Colonel John K. Walker, Jr., Senior Adviser to the ARVN 5th Division, on a tour of Ben Suc, and also stayed several days at Gosney Compound, the living quarters of the American Advisory, where I had an opportunity to see what life was like for the Americans after they had finished their day's work at the camp.

Colonel Walker, a tall, forty-eight-year-old man, has a serious, slightly formal air that contrasts with the generally easygoing manner of most of his staff officers, who respectfully refer to him as the Old Man. Living in a room of his own above a dormitory for six staff officers, he often listened to classical music on a tape recorder and, in general, seemed to seek out the company of his fellows less than the other officers did. Sitting in the staff quarters of the compound on the evening before his inspection tour of Ben Suc, I had a chance to talk with him about the war. On the subject of Cedar Falls and the attack on Ben Suc, Colonel Walker said, "What I want to know is: Did you get a feeling of the tremendous firepower we were able to bring to bear, and the precise coördination? The infantryman today has six times the firepower of his Korean counterpart. The troops of the 2nd Brigade were able to land and move to their positions within five minutes. That kind of precision saves American lives. And I'd like to mention that the 2nd Brigade is the finest in the United States Army. You can ask anyone about that. Ask General DePuy about it. And it hurts me to say so, because it's not one of my own. That's what a brigade is—a unit of power. But in this war it's got to be a lot more than that, too. The soldier in Vietnam has to have diverse talents, for dealing with any situation. The military side is only one part. Our men have to fight a war and carry on reconstruction at the same time. This isn't a war for territory, it's a war for the hearts and the minds of the people."

When I asked about the war in general, Colonel Walker said, "This war has many different facets, with the light reflecting in a different way off each of them as it changes. For instance, when we first came here we were losing a lot of men to the V.C.'s night ambushes. Now we're employing his own techniques against him, and a number of V.C. groups have been surprised to find some of our men out there waiting for them when they try to come into a village or move some supplies at night. This is a war with a difference—a weird and beautiful difference. Personally, I feel challenged by it. I'll tell you one thing—it's a heck of a lot more challenging than running a string of gas stations or supermarkets back in the States. But we don't have all the answers yet. The Vietcong is a tough soldier and highly dedicated. When you see people that dedicated, sometimes you wonder: Am I right? Should we be killing them? It gives you pause. But, even with all these problems, the soldier we've got over here today is the best soldier I've seen in three wars. Morale is tops. What I mean by that is that there is less of the kind of complaining from the troops that we used to have in the Second World War and the Korean war. You saw those soldiers helping to unload those trucks for the refugees. They just pitched right in without a word."

The next morning, Colonel Walker flew by helicopter to Ben Suc. The center of the town was empty of villagers now, but some women and children remained in their houses, waiting for boats that would take them down the river to Phu Cuong. A crew of ten-year-old Vietnamese buffalo boys had been helicoptered into the village to round up a herd of buffaloes and take them to boats on the Saigon River. But, aside from these few people and the animals, Ben Suc was now populated by ARVN soldiers. After talking with an American captain about the ARVN search operations in the village, Colonel Walker ordered a jeep in which to drive out from the center of the village along a narrow road. Six

Americans piled onto the jeep, each of them holding a submachine gun. After about five minutes, Colonel Walker stopped the jeep at a clearing on the edge of the woods, jumped out, and strode over to a place where a patch disappeared into a gully. He peered into the undergrowth and suggested that the path was probably used by the enemy. Then, leaving the jeep in the clearing, he struck out across country into the vegetable fields and back yards at the head of a small column of Americans, apparently unconcerned about the danger of land mines, which the Front often plants in such areas. Earlier, one of his staff officers had told me, "An inspection tour with Colonel Walker is quite an experience. He always wants to go right into the brush himself." Coming to a village house, he found that half a dozen ARVN soldiers had moved right in and were enjoying a dinner of the original resident's rice, cooked in his kitchenware and on his hearth. Chicken bones were strewn on the floor and heaped in bowls on a table. Colonel Walker registered a complaint with the soldiers' headquarters over a field radio. Walking back to his helicopter through sunny back yards and copses of palm trees, he told the pilot that he wanted to have a look at the camp at Phu Loi. The pilot flew over the Saigon River at twenty-five hundred feet, and when we neared the camp he circled it twice, coming down to an altitude of five hundred feet. At first, as we wheeled down over the camp, only the red-and-white canopies were visible, but at five hundred feet individual people could be dimly distinguished. The helicopter continued to the ARVN 5th Division landing pad. Helicopters, with their ability to move slow or fast, to circle, and to hover, enabling a viewer to scrutinize a landscape from the top or from any angle, give him a feeling of mastery over a scene, for it seems to him that he has examined it thoroughly, almost scientifically.

At Gosney Compound, I met Major Wade Hampton, who was a member of Colonel Walker's staff and worked full time at the camp. A slender, mild-mannered, courteous man in his mid-thirties, with a strong Southern accent, he told me he usually got up at about six-thirty, to give himself time to eat a leisurely breakfast and finish up his business around the base before leaving for the camp, at about eight-thirty. On his own initiative, I gathered, he had moved his post of operations from an office on the base to a tent at the camp. He came back to Gosney at lunchtime, to eat in the dining hall, and again early in the evening, in time for a hot shower and dinner. Perhaps the most important of his several duties at the camp was to organize and coördinate the dropping of leaflets over the area covered by the Cedar Falls operation. The leaflets, dropped by the tens of thousands, were mainly of two kinds, the Major explained, and he handed me a sample of each. One shows a happy family eating a meal in a cozy grass-roofed house, with their dog sitting outside, near a pretty young girl who stands leaning against a shady tree with her arms folded behind her back, looking sad. The message on the other side reads:

To Our Friends the Cadremen Who Are Still in the War of Liberation for the South

At present, your parents, your wives, your children, and your brothers and sisters who were living in Ben Suc have taken refuge in the township of Binh Duong in order to avoid the exploitation and the suppression of the Vietcong.

Your families have been supplied by the Army and the government of the Republic of Vietnam with money, rice, and decent places for living. Besides all of this, their health is being taken care of by doctors, who give them all kinds of medicine every day. Thus, friends, do not hide in the desolated villages and hamlets anymore and die unreasonably by bullets and bombs.

Come back to the republican regime and live happily and peacefully with your families in this coming spring. How can you forsake your families and let them live in loneliness? The government and the Army are always ready to welcome you back, so that we can build a strong and rich nation together.

With friendly greetings to you all,

The Commanding Headquarters of the 32nd Strategic Area

The second leaflet shows an ARVN soldier, carrying the government flag, mounted on a rearing white horse that has just trampled a tattered flag of the Front on the ground. A tall white cloud rises up behind him. The text reads:

Dear Inhabitants
of the Nhon Trach Area

For a long time the Vietcong have threatened your lives, forced you to pay taxes and supply them with rice so that they can lengthen this painful war. They destroy roads and bridges and hinder you in your work.

The Army of the Republic of Vietnam has come here to help you destroy them. So come to your senses and listen to the notices and give the Army and the regime a hand in destroying the Cong and pacifying the people.

You must boldly expose the Vietcong elements who are sneaking into your villages and hamlets to threaten and capture you.

The Army is decisively destroying the barbaric Vietcong with your coöperation, looking forward to the day when peace comes back to your villages.

THE ARMY PROTECTS ITS PEOPLE SO THAT THEY CAN REAP THEIR RICE AND TAKE IT BACK TO THEIR VILLAGES

The People's Hearts Offensive 81

Major Hampton explained that Operation Cedar Falls was expected to be particularly effective because "this time we've got their families, and if you've ever been separated from your family like that, you know that it's pure hell—and family ties are particularly strong here in Vietnam, which explains why we've had so many *hoi chanh.*" Oh his bureau Major Hampton had a picture of his wife and children.

I asked why he thought it had been necessary to destroy the villages and evacuate the villagers.

He, in turn, asked if I recalled the villages along the northern edge of the Triangle, and went on, "Tell me, what was the most striking feature of those villages? To me, it was that those people were virtually living underground. It was like a military fortification up there, with bunkers and pillboxes. It looked like the Maginot Line. There was nothing aboveground but a few sticks holding up grass mats."

I suggested that most of the underground rooms might have been used principally for protection against bombs, and not as fortifications.

"I don't think so," he said. "But, at any rate, that was a life of fear they lived. Fear of the Vietcong, fear of the bombs. That wasn't a natural life at all."

Major Hampton had an unusually relaxed and friendly relationship with the men and women who worked for him in his office. He had high praise for one young Vietnamese who prepared translations for him, but sometimes he criticized the Vietnamese, too. Once, when a young woman in the ARVN women's corps told him that she intended to take the customary two-hour midday siesta, he said, in a kidding tone, "That's why you lose the war, Co Ninh, that's why you lose the war."

I mentioned to him that since I had been in Vietnam I had heard almost nothing but criticism and complaints against ARVN troops from the Americans who worked with them. (For instance, one captain who advised ARVN troops told me, "I just can't take it any longer. You can't get anything done with these Arvins, and I'm going out of my mind. I've applied for reassignment to work with our own men again." And when I asked a sergeant who worked under Major Hampton what he thought of the Vietnamese, his reply was "I've worked, eaten, and slept with those villagers for six months, and I want to tell you I have no sympathy for those people. I really don't." One sergeant in the Gosney mess hall, when I asked him whether civilians weren't occasionally killed in the bombings, answered, with a laugh, "What does it matter? They're all Vietnamese.")

Replying to my comment, Major Hampton said, "Speaking for myself, I have great admiration for many Vietnamese. Some of the people I work with are just tops. To me, many of the villagers have a quiet dignity that's extremely impressive. I remember visiting the house of a village elder once. He immediately offered me the greatest hospitality, bringing me a cool drink and inviting me to sit down with his family in their house. We're not supposed to drink unpurified water around here, but I couldn't refuse that drink, although I didn't know what I might get from it."

I told Major Hampton about the cyclist I had seen shot during the attack on Ben Suc, and he said, "When I was out in the field once, a suspect made a break from a group I was guarding. I could have dropped him like that. But I just couldn't do it. I couldn't shoot him like that. So I ran around in front of him and headed him off, and he was recaptured."

Gosney Compound is about five hundred yards up the road from the Phu Loi camp, on one edge of the ARVN 5th Division's base, from which it is separated by a barbed-wire barrier. To enter the compound, one has to pass through a guarded gate. No Vietnamese are permitted to enter on anything but emergency business after 10 P.M. Gosney has much the appearance of an extremely simple but well-kept motel on an American highway. Rows of small white clapboard dormitories for the enlisted men, with neat strips of lawn in front, are grouped across from two larger clapboard buildings, which contain the dining hall and the officers' quarters. The American flag flies from a pole in front of the officers' quarters. Gosney has three clubs, equipped with bars, pinball machines, slot machines for nickels, dimes, and quarters, and a pool table. The smallest club is for the enlisted men, the middle-sized one is for the noncommissioned officers, and the largest—the one with the pool table—is for the commissioned officers. ARVN soldiers serve as bartenders in the enlisted men's and the noncommissioned officers' clubs, but an attractive Vietnamese girl in a gauzy light-purple dress serves the drinks in the club for the commissioned officers. After a hot, dusty day, the men return for a fully American meal, cooked and served by Vietnamese, and perhaps a beer or two, at fifteen cents a can, in one of the clubs. Because it is highly dangerous to go out after dark, and there is nowhere to go anyway, a different movie is shown in the compound almost every night. One night when I was there, they showed "Beau Geste."

On some evenings when war films are shown and the ARVN 5th Division's big guns begin to fire their nightly rounds into the Free Strike Zones, there is momentary confusion in the audience over whether the booming is the Vietnam war outside or, say, "Beau Geste's" Arab-French war in the Sahara. Sometimes the men in Gosney Compound become spectators of the real war, too. Although the compound has never been hit, mortar barrages once landed only a few hundred yards away, and night skirmishes often erupt nearby. On one evening during my visit, as the officers sat out on the porch in front of their quarters sipping soft drinks and criticizing a science-fiction film they had just seen, the slowly moving red lights that indicate helicopters rose into view not more than half a mile away. After drifting back and forth over the treetops for a few minutes, one of the helicopters, apparently finding a target, opened fire with both of its machine guns, directing their aim by red tracer bullets. At first, the fire was wildly diffused, but then the flecks of red from the left side straightened out into a single wavering line of light as the helicopter bore down on the target. The gun on the right continued to send its fire wildly into the landscape immediately below it. Colonel Walker remarked, "The gunner on the left has got his aim all right, but the guy on the right is just spraying those villages over there." The men on the porch could hear the machine-gun fire only as a faint chattering, but after a minute or so there was a series of loud swishes and thumps as the helicopters fired some fifteen rockets at their target. One man on the porch remarked, "If we kill seven of those slant-eyed little bastards tonight, it'll cost the American taxpayer five grand apiece."

For the Americans living in Gosney Compound and working at the Phu Loi camp, the camp created an unpleasant strain, requiring them to work longer hours than usual, but it did not disrupt the basic framework of three solid American meals a day and a movie at night. Although life at the compound was extremely limited and rapidly grew tedious, the wholly American atmosphere, the familiar food, the strong hot showers, and the movies blotted out—for a few hours, at least—the war, the camp, the tension, and the perpetual sense of danger. Once the men had returned to the compound, showered, and put on fresh clothes, they liked nothing less than to have to go out again. On the evening of the villagers' arrival in Phu Loi—when the camp had yet to be constructed and the people were still sitting out in the field—Major Hampton decided that he should go down to the area to see how things were progressing. Stepping out on the porch where his fellow-officers were sitting, he said, "I'm going down to the refugee camp. Does anyone want to come along?"

The men on the porch laughed, and one said, "Are you kidding us, Wade?"

"No. I think we should go down and have a look."

"You're pulling my leg, Wade. Go out? Now? At night?"

Major Hampton went alone.

There is one diversion available outside the compound. Right next to the ARVN dependents' barracks, and about two hundred yards from the Phu Loi camp, the road is suddenly crowded on both sides for about a hundred yards with unpainted, and often freshly constructed, two-story buildings bearing signs, all in English, that read, "Hollywood," "Tokyo," "The Fanny Bar," "Hong Kong," "Happiness Bar," "Snack Bar Sexy," "Scientific Health Massage," and the like. These are bar-brothels, about thirty of which sprang up in immediate response to the buildup of American troops in the area, particularly after the arrival of the 1st Division nearby. A drink for oneself costs about fifty cents, and a drink for one of the "hostesses" costs twice as much. The hostess herself, if she is a prostitute, as about half of the girls are, costs from three hundred to seven hundred piastres (from about two dollars and a quarter to six dollars and a quarter). One of the 1st Division's Military Police told me that his superiors were preventing radical inflation of the prostitutes' fees by the simple expedient of placing establishments off limits—or threatening to—if they got too expensive. If the threat were carried out, it would cut off business completely, for the clientele is entirely American. If the ARVN soldiers should be inclined to go, their base salary of the equivalent of sixteen dollars a month would prohibit it. The strip at Phu Loi is modelled precisely on the original bar district for American servicemen in Saigon, except that what goes on in Saigon at night takes place in sweltering broad daylight—from noon until 5 P.M.—in the rural setting of Phu Loi. The strip is obliged to operate during these peculiar hours because in Phu Loi it is unsafe for an American soldier to venture out after dark. The night still belongs to the enemy. Phu Loi is a small village, and there are as many bars in it as there are all other shops put together. The hot, dusty afternoons at Phu Loi are dominated by the nightlike scenes of the bars. Vietnamese girls from their early teens on up, garbed in low-cut high-hemmed, tight-fitting imitations of evening gowns, wearing Western hair styles, neon-bright lipstick, and heavy eye shadow, stand in the doorways of the bars, in the thick dust from the constant flow of military traffic. Girls just beginning the trade are often shy and wear no makeup, but the ones who are more accustomed to the ways of business on the strip grab at the American soldiers as they pass by in small groups, often carrying opened cans of beer. If the soldiers don't come in, some of the girls taunt them with their few English phrases: "Hey, you cheap Charlie," or "You Number Ten" (the opposite of the phrase for approval, "You Number One"). Among these hostesses, there are occasionally faces of piercing beauty. Mingling with the soldiers out for amusement are soldiers on errands of business, who are distinguishable by the rifles they carry. Most American soldiers carry rifles or submachine guns everywhere they are allowed to, and few Americans appeared at the Phu Loi camp without guns on their shoulders. Carrying a gun becomes second nature, like wearing a watch. A soldier who was about to leave the Gosney Compound for his "r. and r."—rest and relaxation—told me that he felt naked without his gun. Also attracted by the unprecedented flow of money from American hands are beggars of all kinds. They have collected in large numbers at Phu Loi, and, like the bars, they display signs in English. One boy about twelve years old leads his blind mother back and forth in front of the bars on a string, with an English-language sign around his neck asking for money. He is an aggressive beggar and directly confronts soldiers as they step out of the bars onto the dirt road. His mother murmurs something in Vietnamese and bows when her son receives money. At the five-o'clock closing hour, the soldiers all emerge from the bars, often arm in arm with girls and occasionally embracing them on the street. Five o'clock, however, is not the end of the working day for the girls. With imitation-fur stoles over their shoulders and bandannas over their hairdos, they crowd onto a small, dirty blue-and-white bus with a number of other local people and make the bumpy hour-long journey to Saigon, where they go to work again, in the city bars. Most of the Ben Suc villagers in the camp at Phu Loi were not allowed to leave the camp, but on several afternoons groups of women were escorted by ARVN guards to the Phu Loi strip to buy or sell things at the stores that were tucked in between the bars.

On the second and third days of the camp's existence, Lieutenant An's men continued to erect canopies at a feverish rate, and they completed sixty-eight of them before the nylon roofing ran out. Six or seven hundred villagers were still without shelter, and to accommodate them the U.S. 1st Division set up a hundred and fifty hexagonal Army tents about ten feet in diameter and assigned one family to each. The villagers living in these tents stayed outside them in the daytime, because it was impossible to stand up inside except at the very center and the heat under the canvas was suffocating. During the first two days, ARVN soldiers distributed a ration of rice in the camp. The Americans actually supplied the ration, in AID bags printed with a design of two hands clasped in front of a red-white-and-blue shield, but they insisted that the ARVN soldiers distribute the rice to the people. Colonel White said, "We've got to teach them to do this themselves. We could go ahead and hand it out, but we're not here to sell ourselves." When the ARVN soldiers brought the first bags of rice into the camp, at lunchtime on the day after the first canopies went up, women, children, and old people crowded four-deep around them, stretching

out containers of all sizes to be filled. A certain allotment had been planned for each family, but the ARVN
soldiers were unable to tell who belonged to what
family, so were apt to give each person a whole family
allotment, and the rice was exhausted in ten minutes,
leaving a crowd of disappointed women still thrusting
out their pots. Some complained that their families had
not eaten in two days. This scene was repeated in the
evening.

On the third day, a group of fifty Revolutionary
Development workers arrived from Saigon. On the example of the cadres of the National Liberation Front,
most of them were between the ages of eighteen and
twenty-five and wore the simple black peasant garment
first adopted by the Front cadres. At the camp, they
went about their work silently, speaking little to anyone, and leaving the propaganda entirely up to the
loudspeakers, which broadcast ceaselessly thirteen or
fourteen hours a day. (The Psychological Warfare
Office measures its achievements in part by the number
of hours of propaganda played. Thus, in a report on a
so-called New Life Hamlet program carried out at the
southern tip of the Triangle in the last months of 1966,
among such items as "5,269 Medcap patients," "2,200
liters of chemical used for defoliation," "250 acres
cleared by bulldozer for security," and "20,860 sheets of
roofing issued to 1,156 families" are the achievements
"524 hours of Psywar by loudspeaker" and "4 music
concerts conducted.") In sharp contrast to the noisy,

playful ARVN soldiers and their flamboyant officers, the Revolutionary Development workers usually gave no indication of their mood. Like the villagers' withdrawal from contact with anyone around them during the period of the attack and evacuation, the R.D. workers' posture of attending exclusively to their own business and generally drawing as little attention to themselves as possible was very noticeable among a frequently demonstrative, theatrical, hot-blooded people such as the Vietnamese. On those occasions when the R.D. workers did speak to the villagers, the exchanges were extremely short, both sides appearing relieved at being able to terminate the contact quickly. The R.D. workers' first job at the camp was to coöperate with the Province Police in registering, fingerprinting, and photographing the villagers. To solve the problem of food distribution, they issued each registered family a green tag as a ration ticket, which would be marked each time the family received rice.

When I asked to speak to the leader of the R.D. workers, I was introduced to Tran Ngoc Chang, a slight young man who stared off to one side of me as he delivered brief, factual answers to my questions in a soft, deliberate voice, as though he were reciting. He said that his workers slept inside the camp and received a salary of three thousand two hundred and fifty piastres a month (about twenty-four dollars). As leader, he received fifty-two hundred piastres a month (about thirty-nine dollars). When I inquired whether he had any problems with his job at the camp, he answered that he was afraid his crew of only fifty would not be able to handle effectively the needs of the six thousand people who were totally dependent on them. When I inquired about the satisfactions and drawbacks of his job, he answered quickly, "I like to work, and I want to enable the people to realize their aspirations and fulfill their hopes for a new life." I asked for an example of what he meant, and, after a pause for thought, he replied, "For instance, if the people want water, I can get it." Concerning the people's needs at the camp, he said that the most frequent demands were for more food, for permission to leave the camp to relieve them-selves, and for permission to return to their villages for more of their possessions. One day, he said, a truckload of women had been taken back to a village that had not yet been destroyed, to fetch their belongings. However, permission to leave the camp for any reason could be granted only by the military, who were very reluctant to let anyone out, so the R.D. workers could not be of much help to the people in this respect.

That day, the ARVN troops began the construction of another latrine, of a more. permanent type, which would hide the users from public view. A short time later, a team of Americans with a derrick entered the camp to dig a well. To the desperately bored children, the derrick was a focus of attention. So were sections of piping four feet in diameter strewn around on the ground near it; the children made use of them as a playground, crawling through the sections that were lying on the ground and climbing into the sections standing on end. Also on the third day, water buffaloes and cows began to arrive, in trucks, and were placed in a fenced-off section of the field. On the fourth day, a hundred of the men from Ben Suc were released by the Province Police to join their families in the camp. Just outside the barbed wire near the command tent, the 1st Division set up a mess tent that served hot dogs, chicken, potatoes, Spam, and Keen to the American and Vietnamese soldiers. The wind nearly always blew from the tent toward the camp, and the smell of the cooking wafted down among the villagers, bringing out small crowds of children to stand at the edge of the barbed wire and watch the soldiers receive their dinner on paper plates.

Throughout the first week, work teams from South Vietnam's profusion of patriotic groups for "nation building" arrived at the camp, wearing a wide variety of uniforms. The first to come were five locally recruited girls in their late teens and early twenties, at least three of them strikingly beautiful, who wore conical straw hats and long, flowing, spotlessly white *ao dai*— the traditional women's dress in Vietnam, which consists of wide, ballooning trousers under a long dresslike garment split up the sides to the waist. The girls' job was to help the medical teams by searching through the camp for those in need of medical attention. They were doing this kind of work for the first time and were afraid to approach the villagers directly. For the most part, these young girls—shy, beautiful, and useless—simply clung tightly to their clipboards and kept their eyes trained properly on the air in front of them as they bravely sailed down the dusty aisles between the rows of squatting villagers, like lovely angels in white robes who had been dropped into the camp by mistake. Next to arrive was a wholly different type of girl—a troop of ARVN women, who were clad in tight-fitting Army-green trousers, jackets covered with pockets, and small, high-heeled black leather boots. Many wore sunglasses and sported broad-brimmed green hats of a sort that have lately become very popular among the Vietnamese military. Wholly preoccupied with chattering to each other in low, nervous voices as they made their first appearance, they seemed ready, as a group, to giggle at the entire universe. When I asked a little knot of four of them, through an interpreter, what their job at the camp would be, they all broke into giggles and looked desperately at each other for someone to answer me. Finally, one girl replied, "We don't know yet. We're here to help the refugees." The giggling that followed precluded any further conversation. It seemed to me that every time I walked by the mess tent there was a line of them waiting, paper plates in hand, for hot dogs and Keen. Later, reading a report put out by the American Advisers in the 32nd Division Tactical Area, which described "the relocation of civilians" as "an outstanding success," I read that the ARVN women, who were referred to as "social workers," were "assisting in the necessary administration required in processing the refugees and giving adult hygiene and sanitation classes," and also "taking care of children and looking after anyone requiring medical care."

The villagers themselves began to improvise improvements for their quarters. ARVN soldiers having laid out bamboo poles for them, they split these into long strips, which they lashed together to construct flat panels that could become raised platforms when they were rested on rows of notched bamboo poles driven into the ground. Rudimentary partitions, made of mats, rice bags, and bedclothes, also appeared. After a week in the camp, the children began to show signs of a universally lamented transformation that seems to occur inevitably whenever Vietnamese children are brought into frequent contact with Americans. At first, the G.I.s, charmed by the shyness and reserve of the Vietnamese children and wanting to be friendly, offer pieces of candy or gum. Perhaps the children accept and politely offer thanks, but the next time there is less hesitation, and after several times the children, far from hesitating, demand the handouts. Walking along the road to the camp, for instance, a soldier would often be virtually attacked by groups of children from the ARVN dependents' area. They ran at him screaming, "O.K.! O.K.! O.K.! O.K.!" and turning smiles full of excitement and anticipation up to him as they grabbed both his hands and rifled his pockets. When turned down, they called out, "Cheap Charlie!" with terrible disappointment. The Americans, finding themselves in the unpleasant position of having constantly to refuse candy to smiling children, soon tired of this game. Inside the camp, the children were not yet attacking the Americans, but they had already learned to hold out their hands and shout, "O.K.!" Another more or less inevitable development was the hasty construction just outside the camp, by local Vietnamese, of a whole row of little stands selling beer and soft drinks to Vietnamese at high prices and to Americans at exorbitant prices. When an American objected to paying seventy-five piastres (about fifty-five cents) for a soft drink, the venders, like the prostitutes, the beggars, and the children when they met resistance, would call out, "Cheap Charlie!" and "You Number Ten!"

After most of the villagers had been evacuated from the Triangle, I drove a mile down the road from the camp to the Open Arms center. An armed Vietnamese guard let me pass without identification through a gate. Surrounded by high barbed-wire fences, heavy sandbagging, bunkers, and sentry posts, the Open Arms center consisted of a dirt yard in which several tents had been pitched opposite a long building containing a small café, a room with administrative desks, two interrogation rooms, and a dormitory filled with doubledecker beds for the returnees. The interrogators kept one or two returnees busy, propaganda sessions occupied a group in the morning and the early afternoon, and construction work on a small wooden house that was to be a recreation center occasionally occupied another group, but the majority of the returnees spent most of their time asleep, or simply lying on their bunks in the heat. One group of twenty or thirty stood or crouched in a circle, absorbed in a game of cards. Five or six lay stretched out asleep on the board floor of an open-sided Army tent. Some sat around in small groups smoking and talking. (Upon arriving, each man had been issued a package of Cambodian cigarettes and a toothbrush.) All these men were listed in official reports as "Vietcong defectors," but the majority of the returnees from Ben Suc, evidently not yet realizing they were defectors, rather than just prisoners given a special amnesty, claimed that they had never participated as soldiers in the National Liberation Front or coöperated with the enemy in any way, though most said they had paid taxes. They seemed to have been unaware at the moment of their capture that they were "defecting." One returnee, after telling me that he was married and the father of two, went on, in a soft voice, "When the bombs started falling and the helicopters came, I ran into a bomb shelter under my house with my wife and children. Later, the government troops came to the mouth of the tunnel with a loudspeaker and told us to turn ourselves in or be shot. We were scared of being shot! We turned ourselves in and handed the Americans leaflets. Then I was brought here by helicopter. They tell me my wife and children are in a camp nearby."

One American officer concerned with classification problems said, "We aren't going to accept them as *hoi chanh* if they don't turn themselves in until we come along and tell them we're going to blow up their hole and *then* they come running out waving their leaflet."

A seventeen-year-old returnee with his toothbrush sticking up out of his shirt pocket said simply, "When the troops came and the artillery started firing, I hid in the fields. Later, I heard the helicopter announcement. Then I turned in a leaflet I had found a month ago."

Another man, who admitted he had led a squad of five soldiers, said, "When the helicopter came, I ran around from place to place trying to escape, but I couldn't, so I turned myself in to a unit of government troops with a leaflet I had picked up."

In a situation where everyone, whether a defector or not, had to give himself up or be shot, possession of one of the safe-conduct passes dropped at the beginning of the attack had apparently been the key factor in determining who was to be placed in the category of "defector." Generally, the returnees' conversion to the government cause seemed to have involved a minimum of initiative on their part. According to a United States Army report, there were five hundred and twenty-nine returnees in Binh Duong Province in the month of January. In the two neighboring provinces of Phuoc

Long and Binh Long, where no large operations took place, there were only four returnees all told in the same period.

Before leaving the Open Arms center, I sat down for a minute in an open Army tent, whereupon ten or fifteen returnees came over to look at me with sleepy curiosity. Through my interpreter, I asked again about life in Ben Suc, and a young man began to tell me about the bombing of the center of the village and about the government flag they had posted on the rice-storage building to protect the village. I noticed that he was glancing at the other returnees as often as at me, and that he was warming to his story with the relish of a man telling a favorite anecdote to an appreciative audience. Like any good storyteller, he allowed only a twinkle of amusement to appear on his own face, but the other returnees were plainly having a hard time controlling their laughter. Their deadpans were cracking, and I felt that the whole group was suddenly coming to life. "The government told us that if we flew the government flag on any building it would not be bombed," he said, as though he had innocently placed his whole trust in the government. "So we bought a government flag in Phu Cuong and put it on top of the rice-storage building—a big flag it was." He stretched his arms to show his audience just how big. "But then the planes came and they bombed it anyway, and the government flag went down in the bombed building." By this time, several young men in the group had burst out laughing, although most of them were not from Ben Suc. It was a full minute before they resumed their dull, sleepy stares.

During the Phu Loi camp's first week, I spent several afternoons there interviewing villagers from Ben Suc through an interpreter. Before I asked them any questions, I would say that I was a reporter, not connected with the Army. They clearly disbelieved me. At first, they would nod understandingly, but later they would ask me for salt, cooking oil, or rice, or for permission to leave the camp, and I would have to explain again that I had no authority in these matters. They would nevertheless ask several more times for food or privileges, as though my claim to be a journalist were part of a game they had played with many interrogators before me. They refused to believe that this young man—the latest in a long procession of young men, of many political colorations, in their lives—did not want to persuade them of something or use them for his own ends. As we spoke, it was difficult to hear each other above the din of loud, enthusiastic taped voices coming over the public-address system.

When I ducked, with an interpreter, into a section of one canopy and asked a young man who was holding the hand of his three-year-old son if we could talk with him for a minute, he leaned down, smiled at the boy, and told him to go to his mother, a young woman with a broad, open face and large, dark eyes, who was standing nearby. The young man came forward to meet us with an unruffled composure that I encountered again and again in the Ben Suc villagers, as though nothing in the world could be more natural for them than to have a talk with an American. He stood before us with a faint smile of amusement. After introducing myself in my usual way, I asked what he thought about coming to the camp. Through the interpreter he said, "I realize now that there is a war going on and that I have to leave to be defended by the government troops and the Americans. Here it is safe—there will be no bombs and artillery. The crops in my field have all been destroyed by chemicals, and my elder brother was killed by a bomb. Many people were killed when the center of the village was bombed last year. Here we are protected by the American troops."

I asked him what he had enjoyed most in his life at Ben Suc.

With a laugh at being asked such a question, he answered, "I play the guitar, and I liked to sing at night and drink with friends—to eat fish and drink until the sun came up. I am thirty-one now, and was married when I was twenty-three. I have three children. I believe in Confucius and pray to Confucius to keep me from misfortune, to send me good luck, and for peace. On most days, I would get up at six o'clock, eat, have a bath, and then go out to the fields. At midday, I would come back, have another bath, and eat, and I would have a bath again when I stopped working at night. I haven't had a bath in four days now. Do you think we'll be able to have one soon?"

I expressed surprise at his taking so many baths, and told him that most Americans take only one bath a day.

"I don't believe it!" he answered. "We always take three baths a day—four when we are sick. After a bath, you feel healthy and feel like eating a lot. We have become very tired here waiting for food, and for water for a bath."

Outside another canopy, I approached a middle-aged man with long, mussed-up hair who sat cross-legged on a straw mat in front of his compartment, scowling frankly while his wife, squatting next to him, tried to blow life into a small twig fire. It was late afternoon, and a chilly breeze had picked up as the sun moved lower in the sky. The thin, scowling man, who wore only a black shirt and green short pants, was shivering slightly. "I have a stomach ache," he told me, pressing his hands over his belly. "I got here yesterday morning on a boat, but we couldn't bring anything with us. All our things are still in Ben Suc—our oxen, our rice, our oxcarts, our farming tools, and our furniture." He related this without looking at me, in a restrained but disgruntled tone. "Now we have only plain rice to eat—nothing to flavor it, not even salt. They don't bring any food. And there's not enough water to take a bath."

I asked him how he felt about leaving his village.

"Anybody would be sad to leave his village," he said. Then, quoting the loudspeakers, he added, "But we have to be protected by the government and American troops."

At this, his wife turned and said furiously, "We have nothing! I have no cooking oil, no rice! We have to beg from the people next to us!"

I asked her if she knew about the rice distribution by the Revolutionary Development workers.

Now losing all control of her temper, she snatched a green meal ticket out of her pocket and waved it at me. "They gave me a ticket a day ago, but they never have enough rice. We couldn't even bring blankets or clothes. My son is naked. Look!" She pointed to a little naked boy of about four, who stood watching his angry mother. "It's no good for children here. Not good for their health. They get cold at night, and there is nowhere for them to go to play." Abruptly, she turned her back and began trying again to get her fire going.

Her sick husband continued to look at the ground. After a minute or so, he said, "I am actually from Mi Hung, but we moved to Ben Suc six months ago, after Mi Hung was bombed."

I asked how long he thought he would be made to stay in the camp.

"I don't know. I was just put here. I can't do anything about it. I can't speak English. How should I

know what they are going to do next? I can't understand what they are saying. Many of the old women
were weeping when they were taken away."

At another place, addressing myself to a mother
holding a baby, I was immediately surrounded by three
mothers. They all wore rolled-up black pants with
white or blue shirts—dirty now, since the camp had no
washing facilities. At first, only one replied when I
asked how they liked life at the camp.

"Everybody was taken away from Ben Suc," she
said. "We couldn't bring our rice, and we brought only
a few possessions. We ran into the bomb shelters when
the bombing started."

When I asked the women about their husbands, they
all began talking excitedly:

"My husband was out plowing, but I don't know
where he is now."

"We don't know where they are."

"They were taken away."

"I don't know if he is still alive or not."

"I saw people dead in the fields, but I didn't know
who they were."

One of the women moved forward, and the others
grew silent. "We want to go back, but they are going to
destroy everything." She was not supposed to know this
yet, but she looked at me evenly as she said it.

I asked her whether she was from Ben Suc.

"I am actually from Yao Tin, and was at Ben Suc
only for the harvest, to help my parents. I left all my

money and things at Yao Tin. I couldn't even go back to my parents' house after coming to the center of the village. My sister is still at Ben Suc, I think."

Having heard that Vietnamese villages often rely on a group of elders to make decisions on village matters, and thinking that it would be interesting to talk with them, I asked the three women if they could tell me who the village elders of Ben Suc were. As this was translated, a hint of mischievous amusement appeared on the face of one of the women, and with sudden cheerful recklessness she declared, "We didn't have any village elders." Her little smile was contagious, and the three women exchanged conspiratorial glances, like schoolgirls with a secret. Emboldened, the first speaker added, "Nobody was important. Everyone was equal." All three watched my face closely to see how I would react to this gambit.

I asked if anyone had collected taxes.

"No, there were no taxes," another of the women answered. "We used what we grew for ourselves."

The first then said, "There was no government. And no government troops." All three struggled with suppressed amusement.

I asked them how they had liked having no government and no government troops.

At this, they all broke into girlish laughter, hardly even trying to cover their smiles with their hands. No one answered the question. Instead, one of them said, "Anyway, now we must be protected by the government and the American troops." She still could not wholly suppress her rebellious smile. As though to say something calculated to please me even more, she added, "Last year, government troops and Americans came just to give out medicine, and no one was killed."

Another woman said, "This time, many were wounded, killed, or taken away."

In one compartment, an old man sitting on a mat told me, "I was born in Ben Suc, and I have lived there for sixty years. My father was born there also, and so was his father. Now I will have to live here for the rest of my life. But I am a farmer. How can I farm here? What work will I do? There were many killed, but luckily I came safely with my three daughters. They have given us rice here, but I can't eat it. The American rice is for pigs. And we have no cooking oil." (After the first handout of rice, in several places around the camp I noticed pigs with their snouts deep in piles of American rice that had been dumped out by the Vietnamese. Like most East Asians, the Vietnamese are extremely particular about the color, texture, size, and flavor of their rice. Rice also has ritual meanings for them that go beyond matters of taste and nutrition. The Vietnamese welcomed the long-grained, brownish, American-grown rice about the way an American would welcome a plate of dog food—as a dish that was adequately nutritious, and perhaps not even bad-tasting, but psychologically repellent.)

The old man had an idea for his future. "I have

relatives in Phu Cuong who will help me and my daughters. Won't you let me go out of here and build a new house in Phu Cuong, where I can farm?"

Once more I tried to explain that I was not from the government. The old man obviously didn't believe me.

In the morning of the fourth day, there was a high wind, which blew clouds of dust so thick that you couldn't see from one end to the other of the aisles between the canopies. Under one of the canopies, an old man with a wispy goatee and a mild, gracious smile sat on a mat, holding a baby in his arms, in the lee of a pile of possessions and several mats that his family had hung from the bamboo framework to protect themselves from the wind and dust. He smiled down at the baby as it played with a twig. Answering my questions, he said, "I have two sons, but I don't know where they are now. They went into the government Army, and I haven't heard anything about them for several years. Now I live with my daughter." The baby became agitated, beat its arms, and threw away the twig. Shifting the baby into one arm, the old man drew a tobacco pouch from his pocket and gave it to the baby to play with. In the pouch, along with a small box for tobacco and paper for roll-your-own cigarettes, was his newly issued identification card, which already had a slight tear in the center. The baby's interest lit on the I.D. card, and, grasping it tightly in both hands, it widened the tear until the card ripped in two and it was left holding a piece in each hand. The old man, who was delighted with everything the baby did, laughed warmly at its latest deed and smiled at the people around him. Then he put the two pieces back in the pouch and put the pouch in his pocket.

Meanwhile, a little girl who had her hair in a single long, black braid and was wearing golden rings in her ears had approached to watch me, curiosity overcoming fear.

"How old are you?" I asked.

"Eleven."

"What's your name?"

"Ngai."

"What do you do all day?"

"Nothing."

"Nothing at all?"

"I help my mother cook."

"What do you like best here?"

"I like my dog." She hoisted up a black puppy for me to see. "My friend gave it to me."

"What do you like least here?"

"It's too hot and crowded. I like my aunt's house."

"Why?"

"It's cool. It has walls."

The old man laughed in agreement.

As I stood up to leave, I saw that Ngai was wriggling with inner conflict and staring at me with a smile of determination and excitement. Then I saw that she was holding her hand out, palm upward but close to her body, in an irresolute play for a gift of candy from the American, but almost as soon as she had mustered the courage she lost it and turned away from me in embarrassment.

Under another canopy, a woman with a blank, lonely gaze sat holding a tiny baby. She hardly seemed to notice me as I approached her. When I addressed her, she talked as though she were thinking out loud, and didn't answer any questions directly. She said, "The helicopters came early in the morning while I was on my way to the field. My husband is in Saigon now. I think he's in Saigon. The loudspeakers came overhead, but how could I hear them? The bombs were exploding everywhere. My father is deaf, so how could he hear the voices from the helicopter? Now I don't know where he is. All I could bring was my children and my clothes. My father is very old. Maybe he is dead."

The demolition teams arrived in Ben Suc on a clear, warm day after the last boatload of animals had departed down the river for Phu Cuong. G.I.s moved down the narrow lanes and into the sunny, quiet yards of the empty village, pouring gasoline on the grass roofs of the houses and setting them afire with torches. Columns of black smoke boiled up briefly into the blue sky as the dry roofs and walls burned to the ground, exposing little indoor tableaux of charred tables and chairs, broken cups and bowls, an occasional bed, and the ubiquitous bomb shelters. Before the flames had died out in the spindly black frames of the houses, bull-

dozers came rolling through the copses of palms, up-
rooting the trees as they proceeded and lowering their
scoops to scrape the packed-mud foundations bare.
When the bulldozers hit the heavy walls of the bomb
shelters, they whined briefly at a higher pitch but
continued to press ahead, unchecked. There were very
few dwellings in Ben Suc to make a bulldozer pause.
The bulldozers cut their own paths across the back-
yard fences, small graveyards, and ridged fields of the
village, ignoring the roads and lanes. When the demolition teams withdrew, they had flattened the village, but
the original plan for the demolition had not yet run its
course. Faithful to the initial design, Air Force jets sent
their bombs down on the deserted ruins, scorching
again the burned foundations of the houses and pulverizing for a second time the heaps of rubble, in the hope
of collapsing tunnels too deep and well hidden for the
bulldozers to crush—as though, having once decided to
destroy it, we were now bent on annihilating every
possible indication that the village of Ben Suc had ever
existed.

THE
MILITARY
HALF

AN ACCOUNT OF
DESTRUCTION IN
QUANG NGAI
AND QUANG TIN

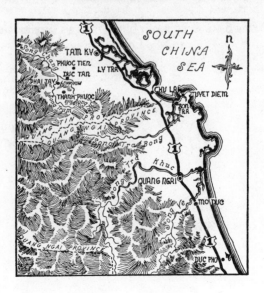

I OFFER THIS BOOK with love to my brother
Orville, who, against everyone's better judgment,
suddenly dropped out of his junior year in college
to set out for the Far East as third cook—
or vegetable peeler—on a Norwegian
dynamite freighter,
and thus set the basic style for the
many impulsive, unlikely trips East
we have both made since.

I WOULD LIKE TO EXPRESS my gratitude
to Ngo Long, who gave me great help
in preparing some
sections of this book, and shared
with me his
amazingly thorough and deep
knowledge of his country
and his people.

This book is about what is happening to South Vietnam—to the people and the land—as a result of the American military presence. I shall not discuss the moral ramifications of that presence. I shall simply try to set down what I saw and heard first-hand during several weeks I spent with our armed forces in South Vietnam last summer. What I saw and heard had to do mostly with the destruction that was going on in South Vietnam, but at the same time I found that the peculiar character of this war tended to be defined for me by how the men in our armed forces reacted to the various special conditions of the war: the immense disparity in size and power between the two adversaries, the fact that Americans are fighting ten thousand miles from home, the fact that the Vietnamese are an Asian and non-industrialized people, the fact that we are bombing North Vietnam but the North Vietnamese are incapable of bombing the United States, the fact that our bombing in South Vietnam can be met only by small-arms fire, the fact that it is often impossible for our men to distinguish between the enemy and friendly or neutral civilians, the anomalousness and the corruption of the Saigon government, the secondary role played by the South Vietnamese Army we are supposedly assisting, the fact that the enemy is fighting a guerrilla war while we are fighting a mechanized war, and, finally, the overriding, fantastic fact that we are destroying, seemingly by inadvertence, the very country we are supposedly protecting. Like many Americans, I am opposed to the American policy in Vietnam. As I came to know the American men who were fighting there, I could feel only sorrow at what they were asked to do and what they did. On the other hand, I could not forget that these men, for the most part, thought they were doing their duty and thought they had no choice, and I could not forget, either, that they were living under terrible stress and, like fighting men in any war, were trying to stay alive and hold on to their sanity. If our country stumbled into this war by mistake, the mistake was not theirs. If our continuing escalation of the war is wrong, the guilt is surely not theirs alone. If one disaster after another is visited upon the Vietnamese people, these disasters are the inevitable consequence of our intervention in the war, rather than of any extraordinary misconduct on the part of our troops. Thousands of Americans, of course, have lost their lives or been wounded in Vietnam, many of them in the belief that they were fighting for a just cause, and some of the men I came to know in Vietnam will lose their lives or be wounded in that same belief. Some of our men have been brutalized by the war, just as I might have been brutalized if I had been fighting beside them, and just as men on both sides of all wars have been brutalized. Yet some of them have done the job assigned to them without losing their compassion for the noncombatant Vietnamese, or even for the enemy in combat. In this article, however, I am not writing, essentially, about the men in our armed forces. I am writing about a certain, limited segment of the war—about the destruction by the American forces, as I observed it (mostly from the air), of a particular rural area of South Vietnam. All of us must share the responsibility for this war, and not only the men who bear arms. I have no wish to pass judgment on the individual Americans fighting in Vietnam. I wish merely to record what I witnessed, in the hope that it will help us all to understand better what we are doing.

In the spring of 1967, the United States Military Assistance Command in South Vietnam formed a new force, called Task Force Oregon, by assembling the 196th Light Infantry Brigade, the 3rd Brigade of the 4th Infantry Division, and the 1st Brigade of the 101st Airborne Division in Quang Ngai Province, which is the fifth province south of the Demilitarized Zone along the coast of the South China Sea. The creation of Task Force Oregon, which was to operate under the command of the 3rd Marine Amphibious Force, freed elements of the 3rd Marine Amphibious Force, which had been conducting operations in Quang Ngai since May of 1965, to move north to help combat increased activity along the Demilitarized Zone. The Annamese mountain range swings close to the sea in Quang Ngai Province, and between the mountains and the sea is a strip of arable flatland eighty kilometres long, twenty-five kilometres across at its widest point, and ten kilometres across at its narrowest point. The Allied Forces divided this strip, which supports more than eighty per cent of the province's population, of approximately six hundred and fifty thousand, into four Tactical Areas of Responsibility, of roughly equal size, and assigned one each, from north to south, to the 196th Light Brigade, to a brigade of Korean Marines that had landed in Quang Ngai in the summer of 1966, to a brigade of the Army of the Republic of Vietnam (abbreviated as ARVN and pronounced "Arvin" by the Ameri-

cans), and to the 3rd Brigade of the 4th Division. The 1st
Brigade of the 101st Airborne Division was reserved as a
roving force that could be flown anywhere in the province
by helicopter to launch surprise attacks on enemy units.
The principal mission of the troops that formed Task
Force Oregon was to find and kill soldiers belonging to
what are called main-force units of the Vietcong (or V.C.,
or National Liberation Front) and to the Army of North
Vietnam who were operating in Quang Ngai Province. In
order to break up any fixed patterns of operation that
might help the enemy to predict their movements, elements of Task Force Oregon sometimes went outside
Quang Ngai, carrying their operations into Quang Tin
Province and Binh Dinh Province, which are adjacent to
Quang Ngai on the north and on the south.

Task Force Oregon's area of operation was part of a
mountainous coastal region of South Vietnam that
stretches south from the city of Hué to Binh Dinh Province, and had traditionally been known for its natural
beauty and its poor, proud, and hospitable people. Because
even the narrow strip of flatland that lay between the
mountains and the coast in this region was too sandy for
good crops, a large proportion of the villagers long ago
took up other occupations, such as fishing in the South
China Sea and lumbering in the mountains. Many took up
home crafts, and the area became famous for silk and for
mats woven of reeds that grew on the banks of the local
rivers. Predominantly a rural people, the natives of these
mountainous provinces spoke with a broad, flat accent that
had a simple, country ring to the ears of a Vietnamese
from Saigon. They were also reputed to be shorter than
most other Vietnamese, and to have plain, clear features,
square jaws, and bold, frank natures. As late as 1964, most
of the primary schools in the area adorned their walls with

the traditional Vietnamese motto "Though your clothes may be soiled, keep your honor unspotted." Perhaps because the land was too poor to provide an adequate base for large fortunes, wealthy people in these provinces were particularly conscientious about giving their children the best education possible. Before the country was partitioned in 1954, the academic standards in most parts of what is now South Vietnam were far below the standards in the North, but students from the mountainous coastal provinces were noted for giving an excellent account of themselves at Hanoi University, which was regarded as the best in the country at that time. A large number of Vietnam's most popular writers were born in the region, including the late novelist Nhat Linh, who attacked the colonial French and corrupt Vietnamese officials in novels of social protest, and later became a hero to young people in Saigon when he led a movement of scholars and students against the regime of President Diem. The mountainous inland regions of the northern provinces were populated by primitive tribes known to the French as Montagnards, who lived by burning away patches of the forest, cultivating the cleared land until the soil was exhausted, and then moving on to another site.

Historically, the people of the region were rebellious and aggressive. It was from the provinces of Quang Ngai and Binh Dinh that the rulers of the Nguyen dynasty, in the sixteenth century, launched their long drive southward; when the French began their subjugation of Vietnam, in the late nineteenth century, it was in Quang Ngai and Binh Dinh that armed resistance to French rule was strongest; and it was in these provinces, again, that peasant rebellions first broke out, in the nineteen-thirties, against Vietnamese officials who served the French. After the Second World War, when the Vietminh, the anti-colonial

predecessor of the National Liberation Front, launched
the revolutionary campaign that eventually expelled the
French from Vietnam, Quang Ngai became a principal
center of revolutionary activity, and French troops never
succeeded in entering the province in force. In 1948, for
purposes of fighting the revolution, Ho Chi Minh divided
the nation into military zones of four types, which he
called "free zones," "guerrilla bases," "guerrilla zones,"
and "occupied zones," and he designated the provinces of
Binh Dinh, Quang Ngai, and Quang Nam (north of
Quang Tin) as free zones, meaning that those areas were
to be considered already freed from the French and
from the Emperor Bao Dai. The town of Duc Pho, in the
southern part of Quang Ngai Province, became one of the
largest rest centers in the country for Vietminh soldiers.
The women of Duc Pho had always been famous for their
beauty and their fiery, independent spirit, and there was a
ditty that warned the "fighting man" who came to Duc
Pho to be faithful to his jealous Duc Pho girl friend or risk
losing his manhood at the girl friend's hands. In 1954,
when many of the Vietminh soldiers and political organizers withdrew to the North, enough of them stayed behind in Quang Ngai and the provinces adjacent to it to
insure that the influence of the government in Saigon
would not penetrate beyond a few of the region's larger
towns. By the early nineteen-sixties, a whole generation of
young people in rural areas had known no government
other than that of the Vietminh and the National Liberation Front. Not only had they learned to read and write in
Vietminh and National Liberation Front schools but they
had also learned to sing revolutionary songs, accompanying themselves on the guitar or mandolin, in the course of
a drive by the Front to teach young people to play musical
instruments. In early 1962, because these provinces were

known to be National Liberation Front strongholds, the government in Saigon launched its Strategic Hamlet Program with particular vigor there. The program was intended to separate the people from the Front soldiers and organizers who lived among them, and as a means of accomplishing this the government ordinarily forced the people to leave their villages and to construct fortifications and new habitations at another site. Under a *corvée* system it had devised, it made each man responsible for constructing a certain yardage of wall around the strategic hamlet. If a family refused to move to a strategic hamlet, troops of the South Vietnamese Army might burn its home and its fields; by the end of 1962 parts of Quang Ngai—particularly areas near the mountains—were dotted with the ruins of burned houses. In Quang Ngai, as in other parts of the country, this program aroused hostility toward the government in Saigon, and within two years it was abandoned, to be reconstituted later as the New Life Hamlet Program. Usually, when the government succeeded in constructing a strategic hamlet, the Front quickly reëstablished—or simply maintained—contact with the villagers at their new site, and, consequently, in almost every case the strategic hamlets themselves were under the control of the Front. Supporters of the Front often wrote mottoes on the gates and walls of the strategic hamlets. One inscription, a couplet from the classical Chinese, appeared with particular frequency. It read, "How long can the Great Wall stand/When its base is not the heart of the people?"

At the end of August, 1967, after four months of military operations, Task Force Oregon announced that it had killed, and counted the bodies of, thirty-three hundred enemy soldiers, had "detained" five thousand people, and had captured eight hundred firearms in caches or on or near the dead. It also announced that two hundred and eighty-five Americans had been killed and fourteen hundred wounded. During that August, I travelled as widely as I could in Quang Ngai Province, in order to talk with military people and civilians, and to observe what the effect of the Allied military operations had been, and I also observed several of the military operations themselves, as they were being carried out by Task Force Oregon in the northern part of Quang Ngai and just across its northern border, in Quang Tin. During my travels in Quang Ngai Province, I learned from civilian officials that since the Marines arrived, in 1965, military operations had swelled the number of people in government "refugee camps" by over a hundred thousand, bringing the official count of these people to a hundred and thirty-eight thousand around the middle of August. The American and Vietnamese officials who managed the camps estimated that about forty per cent of the province's population had passed through the camps during the preceding two years. Over the same period, the Marines, the Army, the Korean Marines, and the ARVN had destroyed approximately seventy per cent of the villages in the province—which means seventy per cent of the houses. I first became aware of this destruction when I spent several days in early August flying, as a reporter, in the back seat of one or another of several two-seat, single-propeller Cessna O-1 Forward Air Control planes (abbreviated FAC, and pronounced "Fac") that flew daily visual-reconnaissance flights over the entire heavily populated coastal strip of the province. (The FAC planes, throughout South Vietnam, were always flown by Air Force pilots.) Some of the planes flew over single districts once a day for several weeks at a stretch, and the pilots became very closely acquainted with the terrain. Whenever it was possible, I checked my estimates of the percentage of houses destroyed against their estimates. In several districts, I was also able to check my estimates with the local ground commanders, although no figures of this kind were kept officially. From the FAC plane's prescribed flying altitude, which was fifteen hundred feet, I found it difficult to distinguish people, unless they were wearing their large brown conical straw hats, but I could easily distinguish houses and the remains of houses. The houses in Quang Ngai had been loosely grouped in groves of trees that stood out like dark-green islands in an expanse of lighter-green or yellow rice fields. From the air, the roofs of houses that were still standing appeared as dark-brown squares; the ashes of houses that had been recently burned appeared as gray squares; and the rain-washed clay foundations of houses that had been destroyed more than a month or so earlier appeared as red or yellow squares. When houses had been burned by troops on the ground, their walls—of clay-and-bamboo or stone—were usually still standing, but the walls of houses that had been bombed or bulldozed were flattened, or strewn over the rice fields. The pattern of destruction was roughly the same throughout the densely populated area of fields and villages lying between the mountains and the sea. Villages remained standing in a long belt a few kilometres wide bordering Route 1, a partly paved two-lane road running the full length of the coastal strip and approximately bisecting it. The rest—with certain exceptions, which I will mention—had been destroyed.

In Binh Son, the northernmost district of Quang Ngai Province, beyond a belt about two kilometres wide along the road, the houses that had stood on the flatland to the west of the road had been destroyed all the way down to the Song Tra Bong ("*song*" is a Vietnamese word for "river"). In the Song Tra Bong Valley, which had formerly been cultivated as far as about fifteen kilometres inland, between the mountains, the houses on the north side of the river had been destroyed as far as about ten kilometres inland. Beyond this, deep in the mountains, the town of Tra Bong, which had a population of several thousand and was also the site of a large Special Forces camp, remained standing. The Special Forces camp stood apart from the village, on a small hill. Bare of trees and grass, the camp was ringed by several rows of barbed wire, outside which were fences of sharpened bamboo poles, with rows of zigzagging trenches outside these. Inside all this was a cluster of low, heavily sandbagged huts with tin roofs. To the east of Route 1, in Binh Son District, beyond the belt of undestroyed houses along the road, seventy or eighty per cent of the houses had been destroyed all the way to the sea. South of the Song Tra Bong, in Son Tinh District, which was the Tactical Area of Responsibility of the Korean Marines, the situation was much the same. Along the south side of the Song Tra Bong, there was a Revolutionary Development project near the village of An Diem, about five kilometres west of the road, and the houses remained standing along this stretch of the river, although, as I have noted, the houses right across it on the north side, in the Tactical Area of Responsibility of the 196th Light Brigade, had been destroyed. On the coastal side of Route 1 in Son Tinh—again excepting the belt of a few kilometres along the road—from eighty to ninety per cent of the houses had been destroyed all the way to the sea. Along the Song Tra Khuc, which marks the southern border of Son Tinh District, the houses remained standing as far as ten kilometres away from the road on the mountain side, but beyond that, starting at the point where the river valley begins to wind between the mountains, they had been destroyed. Within one wide bend of the river, which described a full horseshoe, I could see networks of trenches that had been built by the National Liberation Front running down the center of many villages, and sometimes linking two or more of them. Throughout the province, I saw the black entrances to caves and networks of tunnels, which the entire population used as bomb shelters, and which the N.L.F. used as bunkers, hiding places, and escape routes, but in this bend of the river they were particularly numerous. Still deeper in the mountains, the village of Phuoc Tho remained standing, next to a Special Forces camp on a hill. All the houses of the village were crowded together in a square a hundred metres on a side, which was surrounded by a trench, and single houses out in the fields had been razed. This indicated that Phuoc Tho had been converted into a strategic hamlet. Like most of the province, the valley of the Song Tra Khuc was spotted with craters of all sizes. Craters from artillery fire, which were a yard or two wide, peppered the rice fields and the former villages, and craters from delayed-fuse bombs, which were as much as thirty feet across and seven feet deep, and many of which had filled with water, dotted the landscape with little ponds. Anti-personnel bombs, which explode on contact, had made shallow craters that spread out in rays across the fields, like giant yellow aster-isks, and napalm strikes had blackened the fields in uneven splotches. What had formerly been dense woods on the mountainsides that rose up from the cultivated valley in a series of delicate ridges were just as badly torn up.

The two districts to the south of the Song Tra Khuc— Nghia Hanh and Tu Nghia—which were the ARVN's Tacti-cal Area of Responsibility, were the least heavily destroyed of Quang Ngai's districts. Quang Ngai City formed the center of a large undestroyed pocket that extended east-ward all the way to the coast and, in places, extended westward along the south bank of the Song Tra Khuc almost all the way to the mountains. In the southern half of Nghia Hanh District, however, there had been considerable destruction near the mountains. To the south of these two least heavily destroyed of the province's districts, and divided from them by the slow-moving Song Ve, are Mo Duc and Duc Pho Districts, which were the Tactical Area of Responsibility of the 3rd Brigade of the 4th Division and were the most heavily destroyed of the province's districts. Except in four small areas, from ninety to a hundred per cent of the houses in these two districts had been destroyed, along Route 1 as well as away from it. The less heavily destroyed areas consisted of an intact stretch about four kilometres in diameter around the village of Mo Duc; a strip about seven kilometres wide extending north from the town of Duc Pho along the western side of Route 1 for about five kilometres, where about half the houses remained standing; the southernmost fifteen kilometres of the coastline, where, again, about half the houses remained standing; and, finally, a region three or four kilometres long and wide around the Song Tra Kau—a small river just north of Duc Pho—and near the mountains, where about sixty per cent of the houses remained standing. As I flew over the coast of Mo Duc District, where over ninety per cent of the houses had been destroyed, I asked the pilot about the people who had lived there, and he answered, "All the personnel that were down there were pretty much V.C."

The villages had been destroyed in many ways and in a great variety of circumstances—at first by our Marines and later by our Army. In accordance with the local policy of the 3rd Marine Amphibious Force, a village could be bombed immediately and without the issuing of any warning to the villagers if American or other friendly troops or aircraft had received fire from within it. This fire might consist of a few sniper shots or of a heavy attack by the enemy. Whatever the provocation from the village, the volume of firepower brought to bear in response was so great that in almost every case the village was completely destroyed. A village could also be destroyed if intelligence reports indicated that the villagers had been supporting the Vietcong by offering them food and labor, but in such a case the official 3rd Marine Amphibious Force rules of engagement required that our Psychological Warfare Office send a plane to warn the villagers, either by dropping leaflets or by making an airborne announcement. Because it was impossible to print rapidly enough a leaflet addressed to a specific village and specifying a precise time for bombing, the Psychological Warfare people had largely abandoned leaflet drops as a method of warning, and had begun to rely almost completely on airborne announcements. There was no official ruling on when troops on the ground were permitted to burn a village, but, generally speaking, this occurred most often after fire had been received from the village, or when the province chief had given a specific order in advance for its destruction. In some cases, the villagers had been removed from an area in a big-scale operation and then the area had been systematically destroyed. By the beginning of September, there had been two large Army operations of this kind. Five thousand inhabitants of the valley of the Song Ve were made to leave their homes. In Binh Son District, along ten kilometres of coastline south of the former village of Tuyet Diem, five thousand people were "extracted." But for the most part the destruction occurred sporadically and piecemeal, without a guiding plan. Although most of the villages in the province had been destroyed, the destruction of villages in large areas was not ordinarily an objective of the military operations but was viewed as, in the words of one official, "a side effect" of hunting the enemy.

When I attempted to find a record of what the Marines had done in Quang Ngai during their two years of operation before Task Force Oregon arrived, I met with very little success. The Information Officers of the units in Task Force Oregon were unable to name any operations that had been conducted by the Marines, and they did not possess any record of casualties, enemy or friendly. Several times, in August, while I was flying over areas where the remnants of fields, forests, and villages were densely pockmarked with half-overgrown craters from the days of Marine operations, I asked the Forward Air Control pilots what operations had been launched in the areas, but they were unable to tell me when, or why, the areas had been bombed.

I met one man who had worked as a Psychological Warfare Officer with the Marines when they first arrived in Duc Pho. He said that for the first month they had been unable to travel five hundred yards beyond their camp without running into heavy enemy fire. After receiving reinforcements, they had moved out farther but had still been unable to penetrate many areas. When the Marines had developed a system in which they took reprisals against the rural people by bombing villages that were thought to be giving support to the National Liberation Front, Leaflet No. 244-286-67 announced this system to the villagers. Its title is listed in a catalogue of Psychological Warfare leaflets used by the Marines and by Task Force

Oregon in Quang Ngai as "Marine Ultimatum to Vietnamese People," and its target is listed as "Civilian Population." The text of the leaflet, like that of all such leaflets, is printed, of course, in Vietnamese. On one side there are two cartoon drawings. The first shows several soldiers of the Vietcong setting up a mortar position near a thatch-roofed house while another soldier leans out of a window firing an automatic weapon. A woman holding a child by the hand stands next to the house. Under the picture, a caption reads, "If the Vietcong do this . . ." The second picture shows an Air Force jet pulling out of its dive over the house. An explosion in front of the house has thrown the soldiers and the woman and her child to the ground, and the house is aflame. In the foreground, a man lies on the earth, clutching his chest. Streams of blood flow from his eyes, nostrils, mouth, and ears. The rest of the pamphlet is in black and white, but this blood is printed in red ink. The second caption, completing the unfinished sentence of the first, reads, ". . . your village will look like this." On the other side is a text reading:

DEAR CITIZENS:

The U.S. Marines are fighting alongside the Government of Vietnam forces in Duc Pho in order to give the Vietnamese people a chance to live a free, happy life, without fear of hunger and suffering. But many Vietnamese have paid with their lives and their homes have been destroyed because they helped the Vietcong in an attempt to enslave the Vietnamese people. Many hamlets have been destroyed because these villages harbored the Vietcong.

The hamlets of Hai Mon, Hai Tan, Sa Binh, Tan Binh, and many others have been destroyed because of this. We will not hesitate to destroy every hamlet that helps the Vietcong, who are powerless to stop the combined might the G.V.N. and its allies.

The U.S. Marines issue this warning: THE U.S. MARINES WILL NOT HESITATE TO DESTROY IMMEDIATELY, ANY VILLAGE OR HAMLET HARBORING THE VIETCONG. WE WILL NOT HESITATE TO DESTROY, IMMEDIATELY, ANY VILLAGE OR HAMLET USED AS A VIETCONG STRONGHOLD TO FIRE AT OUR TROOPS OR AIRCRAFT.

The choice is yours. If you refuse to let the Vietcong use your villages and hamlets as their battlefield, your homes and your lives will be saved.

Peaceful citizens, stay in your homes. Deny your support to the V.C.s.

After a reprisal bombing had been carried out against a village, the Marines sometimes showered it with Leaflet No. 244-068-68. Its title is listed as "Your Village Has Been Bombed," and its target, again, as "Civilian Population." The second picture on the leaflet entitled "Marine Ultimatum to Vietnamese People," which shows the house aflame and the people dead, occupies one whole side of this leaflet. The caption reads, "THE VIETCONG CAUSED THIS TO HAPPEN!" On the other side, the text reads:

ATTENTION VILLAGERS:

1.—Your village was bombed because you harbored Vietcong in your village.

2.—Your village was bombed because you gave help to the Vietcong in your area.

3.—Your village was bombed because you gave food to the Vietcong.

4.—We warned you about the bombings because we did not want to hurt innocent villagers.

5.—Your homes are damaged or destroyed because of the Vietcong.

6.—Your village will be bombed again if you harbor the Vietcong in any way.

7.—You can protect your homes by coöperating with the G.V.N. and the Allied Forces.

8.—Tell the G.V.N. and the Allied Forces where the Vietcong are, so they can protect you.

9.—The G.V.N. and the Allied Forces will drive the Vietcong away from your villages.

10.—The G.V.N. and the Allied Forces will help you to live in peace and to have a happy and prosperous life.

Both the Marines and, after them, Task Force Oregon had originally envisaged a system in which warnings would be issued to the villagers before bombing their village. Most officers I spoke with said that they delivered such warnings whenever they could. The fourth item in the above leaflet and similar passages in many other leaflets concerned with bombings refer to warnings that would allow "innocent villagers" to flee the village. But in practice, of course, when such warnings were delivered, any of the enemy who might be in the village also took the opportunity to leave or to hide underground. And if the enemy had left the village, the bombing became exclusively a reprisal against houses, with no military objective. Rather than carry out a bombing of this kind, which had virtually no chance of killing any enemy soldiers, the American forces often took the course indicated in the "Marine Ultimatum to Vietnamese People," and bombed "immediately," to increase the chance of killing some of the enemy—even if it also increased the chance of killing

villagers—and of thereby preserving the partly military
character of the target.

Another leaflet, No. 244-055-68, which was ordered by
the 1st Marine Regiment, and, like the others, had as its
target "Civilian Population," shows a photograph of a field
of rubble with a few blackened poles protruding from the
earth at odd angles in the foreground. The caption reads,
"IF YOU SUPPORT THE VIETCONG . . . YOUR VILLAGE WILL
LOOK LIKE THIS." The text on the back reads:

> The U.S. forces have joined with the forces
> of South Vietnam to rid your villages of Viet-
> cong agents and protect your lives. The
> Vietcong hide among innocent women and
> children in your villages to fire upon troops
> and aircraft. If the Vietcong in this area use
> you or your village for this purpose, you can
> expect death from the sky. Do not let your
> lives and your homes be destroyed. Do not let
> the Vietcong be the reason for the death of
> your loved ones.
>
> Report all Vietcong locations immediately.
> Once the Vietcong are eliminated, peace will
> come to South Vietnam. Help the G.V.N. help
> you!

In preparation for some of their ground operations, the
Marines dropped Pamphlet No. 44-65, whose title is
"Marines Are Friends of Civilians." One side shows a tall
Marine shaking hands with a small Vietnamese peasant.
The caption is "The U.S. Marines are the friends of the
Vietnamese people." The text on the other side reads:

> The Marines are here to help you. Do not
> run from them! If you run, they may mistake
> you for a Vietcong and shoot at you. Stand

still and the Marines will not harm you. Tell
this to your friends.

At least once, the Marines announced to the press the
accidental bombing of what they called a "friendly" village, but they did not mention the intentional bombing of
any "unfriendly" villages. The New York *Times* ran the
following story on September 28, 1966:

> Two United States Marine Corps planes
> bombed a friendly village in South Vietnam
> by mistake yesterday, killing 28 mountain
> tribesmen and wounding 17, a Marine spokes-
> man said today.
>
> The bombing also destroyed about 100
> houses in the village, which is in Quangngai
> province about 350 miles north of Saigon.
>
> The village was under the control of the
> South Vietnamese Government, the Marine
> spokesman said, and was outside the target
> area for the attack mission to which the two
> Marine planes had been assigned.
>
> Marine evacuation helicopters went to the
> village and evacuated the wounded to a Gov-
> ernment hospital in the nearby city of Quang-
> ngai.
>
> The victims were montagnards—the no-
> madic hill people who furnish large numbers
> of fighters to help the allied cause.
>
> The Marine spokesman said the village also
> contained some Government soldiers and their
> families. . . .

An air strike is not over after a single large explosion
that covers the whole target; rather, it involves eight or
nine low passes by several fighter-bombers and usually
takes from ten to fifteen minutes to complete. Because the

pilots of the small propeller Forward Air Control planes observe every pass and help the fighter-bomber pilots adjust for inaccuracies, it is virtually impossible for the full ordnance of an air strike to land on a village simply through poor aim. It may be stated that the accidental bombings that are reported in our press have occurred either because a strike intended for an "unfriendly" village was mistakenly delivered on a "friendly" village or because the Army misjudged the "friendliness" of the village actually bombed. In the case of the bombing reported in the *Times,* the presence of the ARVN soldiers gave incontrovertible proof that the bombed village had been in the "friendly" category.

Task Force Oregon continued the Marines' practice of dropping leaflets threatening to destroy villages that supported the Vietcong. Leaflet No. 244-279-67 uses the two-frame cartoon of a house being bombed, with the caption "If the Vietcong do this . . . your village will look like this," that appears on the "Marine Ultimatum to Vietnamese People." The text on the back reads:

> The military forces of the G.V.N. and the free world have no desire to harm the innocent people of Vietnam who are willing to live in peace. However, if the criminal Vietcong are allowed to hide in your house, both they and your house will be destroyed.

Another leaflet shows a soldier of the Vietcong on his knees, in the foreground, being shot at simultaneously by six jets, two helicopters, two artillery pieces, a tank, and four infantrymen. The caption is "WE MUST DESTROY THE VIETCONG TO HAVE PEACE." The back reads:

> The U.S. forces have come to help the G.V.N. rid your village of the Vietcong who

enslave you. If you allow the V.C. to hide in your hamlet, you can expect destruction from the air from mortars and artillery. Do not let your hamlet be destroyed. Point out the V.C. who bring death and destruction to you and your home.

Other leaflets that were available to Task Force Oregon for adaptation to its area publicize and condemn damage caused by the Vietcong. Leaflet No. 244-492-67, whose title is "Message to the V.C. from the Citizens of Phong Dien District," shows a photograph of a building with half its roof blown off. The caption reads, "The Buddhist school at the Phong Dien Refugee Center lies in ruin following a senseless V.C. attack on the 15th of May, 1967." The text on the back reads:

> A MESSAGE TO THE V.C.:
> We the citizens of Phong Dien District will never be won over to such a cause as yours. A cause that advocates the murder of our people and your people. We the citizens of Phong Dien beg each of you who have been duped by the V.C. propaganda to think of the sorrow you have created and forsake this alien cause. Would it not be better for you to join with us in building our great fatherland under the peaceful flag of the G.V.N.?
>
> THE CITIZENS OF
> PHONG DIEN DISTRICT

The citizens of Phong Dien first became aware of this message when airplanes dropped it by the tens of thousands over their district.

A number of leaflets issued very detailed instructions to the population just before an operation began. On one side of Leaflet No. 244-099-68, which is titled "Instructions to the Citizens of Binh Son District," there is a map consisting of a single line, which represents a five-kilometre stretch of road, and four dots, which represent the villages of Tan Hy, Long Ve, Dong Le, and Phuoc Hoa, from left to right along the road. A red line forms a long, narrow rectangle enclosing the area between the villages of Tan Hy and Phuoc Hoa, which are at opposite ends of the map. The instructions on the back read:

> ATTENTION CITIZENS OF BINH SON DISTRICT:
> The area framed in red on this map is a danger zone. No one may be in this area except on the road. You may not leave the road inside this area. Enter and leave this road outside of the danger zone. Anyone caught within 300 metres of the road between Tan Hy and Phuoc Hoa may be fired upon.
> You must follow the instructions of the G.V.N. The G.V.N. cares about the welfare of the people. The G.V.N. does not want you and your loved ones to be hurt. Obey the laws of your G.V.N.

One almost decisive disadvantage of using leaflets such as this one was that, even if the instructions were coherent and clear, only a tiny minority of the peasants were literate enough to read them at all, and virtually none of the peasants could read maps. When the American Psychological Warfare Officers composed leaflets that told the peasants to flee Communism and come to Saigon government camps, or told them, as one leaflet did, to reject "the Chinese Communist master of the Vietcong," or ordered them to make a choice between the National Liberation Front and the Saigon government, or advised them to boil water before drinking it, it was easy for these officers to forget that, although the enemy was tough and experienced and smart, the majority of the peasants—particularly the women, the children, and the aged—were people who had spent their lives almost wholly within tiny farming communities, and who had no knowledge of the Saigon government's system of camps, of the Chinese Communists, or of the rules of modern hygiene that were described in the leaflets. Often, in addition to assuming literacy and a familiarity with world conflicts on the part of the peasants, the leaflets took it for granted that the peasants shared with the authors of the leaflets a broad range of assumptions about such things as the legitimacy and benevolence of the Saigon government and the criminality of the National Liberation Front.

In late August of 1967, I spent several days in Quang Ngai's southernmost districts, Duc Pho and Mo Duc, which were the Tactical Area of Responsibility of the 3rd Brigade of the 4th Division. First, I visited the brigade headquarters at the Duc Pho base to ask the officers and men of the 3rd of the 4th what resistance they had met from the enemy and how effective they judged their operations to have been, and to ask what had become of the two hundred thousand people who had lived in the two districts before the villages had been destroyed. In a briefing, an officer told me that although few American units had suffered heavy casualties in any single battle, they had suffered heavy casualties over a period of months in hundreds of small encounters with the enemy. He said that from the twenty-second of April to the middle of August a force of eight hundred combat troops directly exposed to enemy fire had suffered six hundred and ten casualties, including a hundred and twenty killed in action. Another officer present put in, "A platoon sergeant can pretty much expect to get hit within three or four months." The briefing officer told me that in the same period the 3rd of the 4th had killed eighteen hundred and seventy-five of the enemy, and captured five hundred and sixty-six firearms. For a month or so, the brigade had kept a tally of what it called "military structures destroyed," but then it had apparently lost interest in these figures, for it had let the statistic of "3,128 military structures destroyed" stand for over a month on a chart in the commanding officer's briefing tent, without bringing it up to date. "We just stopped keeping track after the first month," the briefing officer said.

A high-ranking officer expressed deep concern over the situation in Duc Pho and Mo Duc Districts. When I asked him what had happened to the people living in the two districts, he told me, "We estimate that there are a hundred thousand people living in Duc Pho. We have about twenty thousand living in refugee camps and twenty-eight thousand more living in towns along Route 1; these are our safe areas. That means that we have about fifty-two thousand people still living in zones that we send harassment-and-interdiction fire into through the night. And there has been no attempt to provide security for any of the villages there. We pull out of a village a few hours or days after we go in. Except for the towns of Mo Duc and Duc Pho and the strip of coastline that stretches south from here—it's only about one-half destroyed—these districts are pretty well torn up. The question is: Where do we go from here? ARVN troops are supposed to be doing the Pacification—to go into a village after we have gone through it—but they just can't do it. They aren't here. But, I mean, don't get the idea that we are the only people doing this. Have you been down in Binh Duong Province? The 1st Cavalry Division has wiped out every village it got sniper fire from down there. We're so damned stuck on this body count. If only people could get their minds off that for a while and look at the four hundred defectors, which are the really important thing. But I'll tell you one thing: We haven't been winning any hearts and minds out there, that's for sure. And, you know, the ARVN—they don't care what you destroy. General Hoang Xuan Lam, the commander of I Corps, came down to look at these districts, and when he saw how the place was torn up, he just said, 'Good! Good! They are all V.C. Kill them!' " The officer made a dour face and shook his head. "We sometimes call off strikes because women and children are there. As far as I'm concerned, this idea that women and children are V.C. just doesn't go. A few months ago, we moved a lot of people out of their villages in helicopters before we burned the places, but when we got those villagers to Duc Pho the refugee people said they just couldn't handle them, because they already had too many people for the amount of food and tin roofing they had, so they released the people we'd moved in, and those people went back out there to live underground."

I asked the officer whether he thought the 3rd of the 4th had found an effective way of furthering American war goals in South Vietnam.

Instead of answering, the officer returned the question to me. "What would *you* do with this mission, and this size force in this area?" he asked.

A Psychological Warfare Officer who had worked with the 3rd of the 4th related, "You'll think I'm pulling your leg, but sometimes when we'd planned an air strike on a village, the day before, or the week before, or something, the FAC would be flying over there and notice *people* walking around. You see, that was an area where there wasn't *supposed* to be any people. They wasn't *supposed* to be there. So we would go up there on a chopper an hour before the strike and tell the people to *didi* on out of there." "*Didi*" is Vietnamese for "get out," and is a stand- ard word in American pidgin Vietnamese. "And you'd see 'em puttin' their little sticks on their shoulders, and gettin' their buffalo, and *didi*-in' out. It worked. The 3rd of the 4th was real good about that. Sometimes it don't happen that way. A lot of units will just say 'Unpopulated area— screw it!' and put in the air strikes. But, like I say, the 3rd of the 4th was real good—understandin' the people, and all. The rule is that you have to send a Psy War plane over a village before you hit it unless you get fire, and then you can hit it right away, without askin' anybody. Of course, every once in a while the guys on the ground might burn a couple of hootches that they wasn't supposed to, but that happens everywhere." "Hootch" is military slang for a Vietnamese house. "When they been out in the field a while, they get a little short-tempered, if you know what I mean. You can hardly blame them. This is the toughest damn war we ever fought. In most wars, you could just walk through the place and shoot up everything, but here you can't tell. You just don't know who's with you and who's against you."

One night, I visited the 3rd of the 4th's Fire Direction Center, and learned that on the Duc Pho base alone the brigade had three batteries of six howitzers each and one battery of two eight-inch guns and two 175-mm. guns. A major who was on duty that night told me that there were several ways of deciding on targets. Ground troops could call for artillery fire at any time, and these requests were given the highest priority. But by far the most frequent type of fire was that known as harassment-and-interdiction fire, or h.-and-i. fire, which the major described to me as "a kind of intelligence fire." He went on to explain, "It's not really worthwhile blasting the place through the night. So we just put a shot in now and then. Sometimes we'll get a specific target for h.-and-i. fire, but just as often they'll give us a block five or ten kilometres on a side. At one time or another, we've had these blocks just about everywhere in the district, except along Route 1 in places." The major also told me, "We don't have any unobserved fire. We can put a round through the window of your house if we want to. And I want you to know that we clear everything we fire with the province chief."

I asked what the procedure for obtaining clearance was.

"The province chief marks out the areas where we can't fire without his special permission," he answered, speaking the words "province chief" with extreme gravity. Then he guided me over to a map of Duc Pho and Mo Duc Districts and directed my attention to three strips along Route 1, each about three kilometres wide, that were circled in red. Together, they constituted about forty-four square kilometres of a total of approximately five hundred square kilometres of densely populated flatland between the sea and the mountains that was within the range of guns in the two districts. "Here's the thing that's really important— here's the thing that I want you to see," the major said. "These are the areas for the protection of the friendly Vietnamese civilians. Unless our troops receive fire, we can't shell these areas without specific permission from the Vietnamese province chief.'"

Black circles on the map showed the outer limits of each battery's range of fire. The circles overlapped to cover the entire populated area. Little green dots, designating targets for harassment-and-interdiction fire, were speckled over the whole map except for the three no-fire zones. There were several large green squares, indicating blocks to be "covered" by harassment-and-interdiction fire over a period of days. There was one red box, about two kilometres wide and four kilometres long, around an area consisting of rice fields along with several villages. The major explained that this was a "free-fire zone." Most officers referred to areas that were hit regularly by harassment-and-interdiction fire as "free-fire zones," but at the artillery center, since almost the entire populated territory in the two districts was being hit by harassment-and-interdiction fire, the men had recently restricted the application of this term to a few isolated areas. In its new, narrower definition, it meant simply a harassment-and-interdiction zone where the target was considered particularly "lucrative," and was therefore to be hit quickly with a particularly heavy volume of fire.

I had observed artillery fire from a FAC plane, and had seen that the first few rounds were usually from two hundred to three hundred metres off target. I asked the major about this.

"Yes," he said. "The first few rounds are about two hundred or three hundred metres off, but then the forward observer tells us how far off we are, and we can adjust it to a pinpoint."

I asked what the margin of safety for ground troops was, in average circumstances.

"A thousand metres," he answered. "In tight situations, we'll put it in as close as four hundred or six hundred metres, but that's real hairy. That's the real danger zone."

A chart on the wall listed eight types of fire and the number of missions that had been fired in the three and a half months since the 3rd of the 4th had arrived in Duc

Pho and Mo Duc Districts. (A mission averaged nine shells.) From top to bottom, the chart read:

TYPE OF FIRE	NUMBER OF MISSIONS
Registration	266
H & I	6266
Destruction	7
Prep	30
TOT	109
WA	66
Defensive concentration	328
Others	44

I asked the major to explain the differences between the types of fire.

"Registration fire is to check the accuracy of the gun," he replied. "We pick a spot that's easily recognizable both on a map and from the ground or air. Then we set our guns to what *should* be right, and when we see how far off the shells land we adjust the gun's aiming device to correct any inaccuracies. Junctions of streams provide good, clear targets for registration fire. So do road junctions, but we sometimes have trouble getting clearance for those." He laughed. "H.-and-i. fire can originate with just about anyone, and we just make a general clearance check for that. That is, we check to see if there are any friendlies in the area." By "friendlies" he meant United States or Korean or ARVN troops. He continued, "Destruction fire is when someone says 'I want that bunker.' A specific point on the ground. Some kinds of fire are considered on target within about three hundred metres of the coördinate. 'Prep' is preparation fire. It's the fire we put on a landing zone before the troops go in. 'TOT' fire means 'Time on

Target' fire. It's a kind of artillery surprise attack. We set all our batteries on the same target, decide on a time, and then fire them all out at once. 'WA' means 'Will Adjust.' This is fire where they want to make sure where it goes, so they have a forward observer, or someone else, who actually observes where the shells are landing, and tells the battery how far off they are."

I asked the major whether this meant that other types of fire went unobserved.

"When I said that all fire was observed, what I meant was that someone always sees the target sometime before it's hit," the major answered, and he went on, "Defensive concentration fire is put down all around the company when they are bedding down for the night. First, we put in some check rounds to get the fire on target, and then, if there is trouble later at night, the gun is already adjusted and the fire is there."

In the three and a half months since the 3rd of the 4th had arrived, the batteries at Duc Pho alone had fired 64,044 shells into the populated flatlands of Mo Duc and Duc Pho Districts. (This figure does not include shells fired by the Navy from the South China Sea, or shells fired from batteries taken out into the field to supply direct support to operations.) Another chart listed the number of enemy "KIA" (for "Killed in Action") and "WIA" (for "Wounded in Action") credited to each of the batteries. "We just keep this count for ourselves," the major explained. "Actually, we don't get any credit for the kills. The ground troops get all the credit for the kills." He said that the most commonly used shell, the 105-mm., would kill anything within a radius of thirty-five metres on unobstructed flat ground, and the largest shell, the 8-inch, would kill anything within a radius of seventy-five metres under the same conditions.

An article in the August 16th edition of the *Screaming Eagle,* the weekly newspaper of the 1st Brigade of the 101st Airborne Division, gives an indication of the freedom with which artillery has been used in Duc Pho District. The headline is "RED LEGS CELEBRATE ON ENEMY" ("Red Leg" is the radio call sign for "artillery") , and the article reads:

> DUC PHO (2/320-IO)—What began as a ceremony to fire its 250,000th round turned out to be a fire mission for the 2nd Bn., 320th Arty. recently.
>
> On a mountain-top overlooking the Song Ve river valley, B Btry. was poised for the ceremony. Lt. Col. Andrew Bolcar, Knoxville, Tenn., stood near the 105 howitzer, lanyard in hand. Nearby the color guard stood at attention, flags blowing in the breeze. The ceremony was about to begin.
>
> Then a message came up from the fire direction center. B Co. of the 2nd Bn., 327th Inf., had made contact with the enemy and needed artillery support. Commands were given and adjustments made on the gun sightings. Colonel Bolcar pulled the lanyard and the 250,000th round was on its way to enemy positions.
>
> "There couldn't have been a better way to fire a milestone round than at the enemy," said Bolcar.

The *Screaming Eagle* does not say where the two-hundred-and-fifty-thousandth round was headed before the decision was made to fire it at the enemy.

That same night, to make further inquiries about the estimated fifty-two thousand people who still lived in areas that were being shelled with artillery fire in Duc Pho, I visited Captain Converse B. Smith, who was in charge of the 3rd of the 4th's Civil Affairs Office. Captain Smith, a tall, blond, heavy-boned ex-professional boxer, told me that the Marines had "generated ten thousand refugees" in Duc Pho before the 3rd of the 4th arrived, and that operations of the 3rd of the 4th had swelled the number to twenty thousand. "We haven't been able to do any resettling yet," he said. "The district doesn't have enough troops. We can't secure areas yet. The trouble is that we weren't included in the plan for Pacification and Revolutionary Development for 1967. When Task Force Oregon came, the money wasn't available at the provincial level. They didn't think that we would be ready for it yet. But these districts are ready now for a tremendous Pacification Program. Those people who are still out there had a choice. If they want to come into the secured area, they can come in."

I asked him about the people who had been brought into the camps and then released again.

"We never turn away anyone who says that he *wants* to stay," he answered. "But what are we going to do? When our boys get into a fight, we can't just let the women and children get killed out there, so we bring them in. They are taken to the police and talk to the refugee people, but some of them are inevitably ticked off, and take their sticks on their shoulders and go on back. A lot of times, villagers will allow the V.C. to fight from their village, but they are released again after they are taken and interrogated, even though we *know* that they are V.C. A couple of times, we took the same people out of the same general area three or four times, but they didn't lock them up. We *know* they are all V.C., but the interrogators let them go back again."

I asked Captain Smith whether he expected the villagers to support our Army.

"It boils down to this—they've got to make a decision, one side or the other," he said. "We're here to support the government of South Vietnam, and they are the citizens, and if they want to end this war and get the V.C. killed *they've got to decide*. They can tell us when the V.C. come into the village. They have to stop giving the V.C. food and letting the V.C. fight from their villages. Many Vietnamese get apathetic. This is a feeling that unfortunately many people have in this country. We've got the same problem back in our country. We're spilling blood over here, but a lot of the people don't seem to care."

I asked Captain Smith how he expected a villager to inform on the Vietcong to our soldiers when we could not protect him in his village afterward.

"We have a secret informing system," the Captain replied. "We have many secret contacts. The V.C. don't know about it. And the people have had a chance to come to the government-controlled areas if they wanted to. It is up to them to tell us."

The commonest tactic of large-scale American military operations in Quang Ngai was to suddenly lift troops in on all sides of a reported enemy unit in an attempt to close a trap on it and destroy it. By the end of August, the 1st Brigade of the 101st Airborne Division had attempted three times in Quang Ngai, and also once in Quang Tin, to trap a large enemy force in this way—first in Operation Malheur I, next in Operation Malheur II, then in Operation Hood River, and, finally, in Operation Benton, this last being in Quang Tin—but in each case the trap had closed empty, and the brigade had had to measure the success of the operation by the amount of small-unit fighting it encountered, which was often considerable. In Duc Pho and Mo Duc Districts, the 3rd Brigade of the 4th Division had been fighting on a different principle. Instead of conducting large sweeps according to a detailed plan, it had been sending many company-size units into different parts of the field simultaneously and maneuvering them according to day-to-day assessments of the situation in each small area. On the briefing maps, the paths of a half-dozen units twisted, turned, and doubled back on each other. By the end of August, all the units were operating in an area where most of the villages had already been destroyed, and a great part of their effort consisted in searching for the enemy in networks of tunnels that honeycombed the area.

This area included the region in which it had been estimated that there were still some fifty-two thousand people living, and because these people used the tunnels as their dwellings, and also hid in them when air strikes, artillery fire, or ground fire alerted them to the approach of American troops, the greatest problem that the 3rd of the 4th faced in conducting tunnel warfare was to distinguish enemy soldiers from civilians. Furthermore, the reprisals against the villages had impelled a number of women, old people, and children to take up arms against our troops. Many Vietnamese of the district threw their lives away in desperate, impossible attacks on our troops— attacks that were apparently motivated by pure rage. I heard one officer tell wonderingly of two old men who had rushed a tank column carrying only rifles. "That's when I stopped worrying about shooting the old men," he added. A G.I. told me that he had discovered an old woman trying—and failing—to fire a machine gun at his unit while two small children attempted to guide the ammunition belt into the firing chamber. In the mountain valleys, there had been several cases of attacks with bows and arrows.

Of the civilians in general, an officer related, "We've had tremendous difficulty in hunting them out of the tunnels. We usually try to persuade them with loudspeaker teams to come out, but they just won't. So sometimes we pump tear gas into the tunnel and then blow the place up. I remember once there were several people in the tunnel and we sent down two V.C. defectors in front of our tunnel rat." "Tunnel rat" is a nickname given to American soldiers—usually small soldiers—who have been chosen to enter the tunnels to search for supplies and for the enemy. "After they had gone down about two levels, someone in there fired on them. They came out and we talked some more with loudspeakers, but whoever was down there wouldn't come out. We must have blown half of that hillside away."

After the teller of the story said this, another officer, who had been listening, leaned over the table and said hurriedly, "Of course, we knew that there were some hardcore V.C. down there with those people."

The first officer continued, "Often the local V.C. will be armed with only one hand grenade. Once, we made an announcement into a tunnel and a grenade flew out and killed one of our soldiers. Then a kid about fourteen years old ran out, and we shot him. The grenade was all he had. But I guess he had completed his mission. He had killed an American."

In the *Screaming Eagle,* which relates each week's most dramatic combat stories, there appeared on August 30th an account of one of the 1st of the 101st's tunnel-warfare

episodes during the period when this brigade was conducting Operation Malheur I. Under the headline "CONG
YANKS CONG," it read:

> In a day-long hide and seek contest, para-
> troopers of the 101st Airborne matched Com-
> munist resistance with American determina-
> tion and won the prize—feet first. . . . Spec. 4
> Donald R. Kinton, Kreole, Miss., entered the
> cave and the quartet began enlarging the hole
> in the cave floor.
>
> Once the hole was expanded, Kinton, armed
> with a lighted torch, crawled into the tunnel.
>
> He saw a VC about to pull the pin on a
> grenade. Kinton thrust the burning torch into
> his face and scrambled out of the tunnel.
>
> The grenade was a dud.
>
> Disgusted with the stubborn enemy, the
> paratroopers dropped several grenades into
> the tunnel opening.
>
> When the smoke and dust cleared away, one
> VC crawled out of the hole and surrendered.
> . . .
>
> Legari [Pfc. Vito Legari, West Islip, Long
> Island, New York] decided to enter the tunnel
> for a look around. An enemy bullet zipped by
> his head.
>
> The paratroopers pulled back to map new
> strategy. Third Platoon joined them in sug-
> gesting tactics they hoped would force the
> stubborn enemy to surrender.
>
> A Claymore [a mine that can be aimed to
> project steel pellets in a given direction] was
> set off in the tunnel opening.
>
> The VC responded by throwing out a gre-
> nade.

Another dud.

The prisoner was sent back to the tunnel opening where he tried to talk his comrades into surrendering.

Nothing happened.

In contempt, Staff Sgt. James A. Ross, Canton, Ohio, dropped another grenade into the tunnel and brought the prisoner back again to persuade them to surrender.

One of the hesitant VC responded, bringing two weapons with him. He explained there was one Viet Cong left in the tunnel and two dead.

Apparently, the report of one remaining stubborn VC was too much for Mr. Pham Minh Cong, interpreter working with "A" Company.

In anger, Mr. Cong threw his helmet to the ground, went into the tunnel and came back dragging the last VC by his heels.

It had taken nearly all day to capture the three prisoners, but it was worth it. The platoon had captured an area VC commander, his assistant, 70 pounds of documents, more than 700 pounds of rice, a typewriter, and medical supplies.

In conversations and in the *Screaming Eagle* I found very little hatred for the enemy expressed. More often, I heard expressions of respect, especially when the enemy was compared to the Vietnamese we were supporting and working with. Nonetheless, most officers spoke of very high morale among our troops. The August 16th edition of the *Screaming Eagle* ran an article on the high morale of some veteran troops which gives a picture of an attitude that the

101st's leadership regarded as a good one for the troops to have toward their work and the war. The article reads:

> DUC PHO—Three paratroopers of the 101st Airborne have the unusual distinction of serving two continuous years in the same unit under seven different commanders. Each has extended his tour of duty in Vietnam a minimum of two times.
>
> Staff Sgt. James Howard, Detroit, Staff Sgt. Pablo Gonzales, San Antonio, and Spec. 4 Roger W. Drought, Janesville, Wis., have been with Troop A of the 2nd Sqdn. (Abn), 17th Cav. since the 101st arrived in Vietnam in July, 1965.
>
> "We sailed over on the USNS General Leroy Eltige," said Drought. "The trip took 22 days and, as I recall, we ran out of fresh water."
>
> The three men have been everywhere in Vietnam the 101st has been sent. They agree the stay at Tuy Hoa, one of the 25 locations occupied by the Screaming Eagles, was the best.
>
> "Tuy Hoa was great," said Drought. "There was a nice beach, a nice town, and plenty of action in the field."
>
> The constant moving doesn't bother them.
>
> "It's just another day's work," said Gonzales. "I've been doing it now for 20 years."
>
> "You get used to it," added Drought. "You even begin to look forward to the moves."
>
> Each paratrooper has seen seven troop commanders come and go. "They've all been good commanders and we have a great unit," said Gonzales. "But then we're prejudiced, having been in it for two years."

Why do men extend tours in Vietnam? The three paratroopers each had their reasons.

"Work here is better than the spit and polish of stateside duty," said Drought. "Here you can see more results of your work."

Howard believes soldiering in Vietnam to be more realistic. "When you go on alert here," he says, "it's the real thing."

Gonzales, close to retirement, thinks Vietnam is the place for a career soldier to be. "I just felt I should finish my Army career here," he said.

The three paratroopers have seen friends leave and return.

"Right now there are guys back in the brigade who have come back," said Drought. He plans to extend again and, perhaps, again.

"I encourage a man to stay if it can benefit his career," said Howard, whose tour is up in August, but [who] is considering staying. "But then no one has ever really tried to talk me into going home," he smiled.

Most of the American soldiers I met in Vietnam supported the war effort as a whole, but I also met a number who expressed doubts. One evening in late August, at the Duc Pho base, I joined a group of four draftees who had entered a small shack to get out of a heavy rain that had continued all day and was turning the base into a sea of mud. They were engaged in a lively argument about the war. Two were deeply disturbed by the war, one was doubtful about certain aspects of it, and one supported it enthusiastically. The conversation was being carried on principally between the two men who were most deeply disturbed—Brandt and Sproul, I will call them. The man who supported the war—I will call him Dehlinger—only looked up occasionally from a pistol he was cleaning to interject a few remarks. The fourth man, whom I will call Jackson, also had comparatively little to say.

"When I got here, some of the villages were wiped out, but quite a lot were still there," said Brandt, a private from California. "Then every time I went out there were a few less, and now the whole place is wiped out as far as you can see. The G.I.s are supposed to win the people's confidence, but they weren't *taught* any of that stuff. I went through that training, and I learned how to take my weapon apart and put it back together again, and how to shoot, but no one ever told me a thing about having to *love* people who look different from us and who've got an ideological orientation that's about a hundred and eighty degrees different from us. We don't understand what they're thinking. When we got here, we landed on a different planet. In Germany and Japan, I guess there was a thread of contact, but even when a Vietnamese guy speaks perfect English *I* don't know what the hell he's talking about."

"No one has any feelings for the Vietnamese," said Sproul, a private from Texas. "They're lost. The trouble is, no one sees the Vietnamese as people. They're not people. Therefore, it doesn't matter what you do to them."

"We interrogate our prisoners in the field, and if they don't coöperate, that's it," said Brandt. "Our prisoners are usually people that we have just picked up in a hamlet that should've been cleared. But there are insufficient facilities for the people in the refugee camps, so they come back, and they're automatically considered V.C. Then we give it to 'em."

"Those V.C.s are hard to break," said Sproul. "One time, I seen a real vicious sarge tie a V.C. upside down by the feet to the runners of a chopper and drag him three thousand feet in the air, swinging out over the paddies. When he came down, hell, he was blabbering it. Another time, I seen them get a bunch of V.C.s in a chopper. They push out one first, and then tell the others that if they don't talk they go out with him. And they talk."

I asked Sproul what he was going to tell people about the war when he returned to the United States.

"Maybe when I go home I'll just crawl back inside myself, and not say a word," he answered. "Things are so violent nobody would believe it. And I don't want to die of frustration trying to convince them."

(The remark "They wouldn't believe it back home" was one that I heard almost every day in Quang Ngai, from the many who supported the war as well as from the minority who did not. While I was riding in a jeep at the Chu Lai base, the driver, who had spent time in the field, suddenly turned to me and said, "You wouldn't believe the things that go on in this war."

"What things?" I asked.

"You wouldn't believe it," he said, with finality.

"What kind of things, then?" I asked.

"You wouldn't believe it, so I'm not going to tell you," he said, shaking his head to show his determination not to tell me. "No one's ever going to find out about some things, and after this war is over, and we've all gone home, no one is ever going to know."

I could not persuade him to elaborate.)

In response to what Sproul had said, Jackson, who was from Georgia, spoke up. "I know. I've seen all that stuff. I've seen the G.I.s out in the field get angry and beat people up—women and all—but I just turn myself off. I know it's wrong, but I just don't say anything about it."

The conversation in the shack turned to the question of whether we should be in Vietnam at all. Sproul thought we should not be. Brandt was unhappy with the war, but he was afraid that we might have to fight another war somewhere else if we didn't fight this one. Jackson thought we should drop nuclear bombs on North Vietnam, and on China, too, if necessary, rather than continue to fight what he saw as an unwinnable war in South Vietnam.

When Communist China was mentioned, Dehlinger looked up to say, "They killed a Red Chinese at Kontum."

"How do you know he was a Chinese?" Brandt asked.

"They can tell by the way they look."

"Well, how did they know he was a *Red* Chinese?"

"Any old Chinaman comes from China, doesn't he?" Dehlinger answered, and he went on to say, "I've seen about forty dinks get zapped in the field, and I can tell you that I want to get out there and pop some more dinks!" The four soldiers all laughed at this sudden resolute declaration.

A few minutes later, Brandt said, "Yesterday, I was out on a Medevac"—a Medevac is a helicopter that carries the wounded from the field to hospitals—"and three civilians had got shot up real bad. There was a little boy and two women. One of them was really messed up. She had three or four major bandages. But they were just chuckin' her onto the helicopter like cordwood. There was a strap hanging down from the ceiling of the chopper with a buckle on it, and it slapped the woman in the face as they tossed her in. Now, some G.I. could have pushed that buckle aside and *then* put her in, couldn't he? And her blanket blew off, leaving her sort of half naked. Now, you'd think that some G.I. would have put that blanket *on* again. But no. I remember once, when I was on a ski slope, I broke my leg. It was excruciating! I remember when the guy came along to take off my boot he was real careful not to cause me any more pain, and I really remember that.

You really remember kindness when you're really suffering. Like if someone does something nice for you when your mother dies. That's when you really remember it. They drop those millions of leaflets, but they won't put on the blanket."

On August 19th, I flew in a "bubble," or OH-23, helicopter over the northern twenty kilometres of the coast of Duc Pho and Mo Duc Districts, and had a chance to view at first hand the areas I had seen on the Duc Pho artillery maps and had been discussing with the men of the 3rd of the 4th for the last several days. The OH-23 seats two people inside a clear-plastic bubble that affords a view in all directions except through a small steel plate underfoot and through the seat backs. The engine sits, uncovered, directly behind the bubble, and supports the long rotor blades on a metal shaft; behind the engine a thin, sticklike tail supports a small rear rotor. The machine rests on narrow metal runners. Originally, the Army had brought the OH-23 to Vietnam strictly for reconnaissance flights, but the 3rd of the 4th had converted it into a gunship by dangling an automatic weapon by a piece of wire in the open doorway on one side of the bubble. The OH-23 pilots, who were Army men, went out daily over the destroyed, but still inhabited, areas on what they called "squirrel-hunting missions," to find the enemy and either kill them with the dangling machine gun or call for artillery fire. They informed me that in the course of three months their body count had reached fifty-two, which was more than the larger Huey gunships of the 3rd of the 4th could claim for that period. "The Huey has to start its run on a target from much farther away than we do, and has to pull off sooner, and it can't fly low at all," a young pilot told me while I was talking with a group of OH-23 pilots.

I asked whether they considered everybody who remained in the destroyed areas to be one of the enemy.

"They've had a chance to get out," the pilots' commanding officer answered. "But they're not *all* V.C., I guess. Sometimes they just go back to their fields. But anyone of military age is a pretty sure bet as a V.C. It's definitely a V.C.-controlled area. We've got shot at in that area ever since we got here. A lot of times, you see a guy taking a shot at you and a woman and kid are standing right nearby. I used to hesitate to call artillery strikes on them, but I'm getting over that now."

The purpose of the flight I went on was only to convey me from the Duc Pho base to the city of Quang Ngai, but the pilot offered to take me on a detour over the areas where he and his fellow-pilots hunted the enemy. Since there was go gunner aboard, it would not be possible to fire on anyone the pilot might identify as a Vietcong soldier during our flight. We left shortly after five o'clock— about half an hour before sunset. Flying in the bubble gives one an entirely different sensation from flying in any other aircraft. In contrast to the Huey helicopter, a ten-passenger craft that takes off and lands slowly and hesitantly, like a boat leaving or approaching a pier, the bubble seems to leap effortlessly into the air, like an elevator in a modern office building. Aloft, you find that as you face forward or to either side no part of the helicopter is visible except the control panel at the front, the tiny floor, and the edge of your seat, which sticks out several inches beyond the edge of the floor. Most helicopters fly over the landscape, above the treetops and house roofs, but the bubble flies *within* the landscape—often among the trees and level with the houses, when they are not too close together. Above rice fields, it easily skims along at an altitude of six or eight feet. Flying in this tiny, agile craft, with all the machinery out of sight behind you, you feel a tremendous freedom to go wherever you please—as though you could alight on a tree branch, like a bird, or fly right in at the door of someone's house and then out through a window.

As we flew east toward the coast, I saw that the destroyed area began on the outskirts of the base. Tracks made by tanks, bulldozers, and armored personnel-carriers criss-crossed the red-earth foundations of the houses; not even the ruins were left standing. We soon passed beyond these former villages and arrived over a wide belt of rice fields lying between Route 1 and the coast. The fields were covered with craters but were still cultivated; people wearing the loose black garment of the Vietnamese peasant were bent over at work in the rows of rice. The fields were littered with scraps of paper, which covered the field divides and had sunk into the shallow water between them. The pilot explained that these were Psychological Warfare leaflets. (An average of a million leaflets were being dropped on Quang Ngai Province every day.) We crossed a tree line at the eastern edge of the rice fields and entered an area where the homes of between twenty and thirty thousand people had been loosely grouped in villages along a coastal strip that was about twenty kilometres long and four kilometres wide. The houses along this strip had been destroyed almost without exception. In the coastal area of Duc Pho District, approximately two-thirds of the houses had clay-and-bamboo walls with thatched roofs, and the rest had stone walls with red tile roofs. Where soldiers had set fire to a house on the ground, the back-yard garden and fence, the well, the hedge, the stone gateposts, and the surrounding palm glade or bamboo grove remained standing, but the house that had provided a focus for this setting, and had received the shade of the trees, was missing; only a square of ashes and debris remained on the foundation. In places where the villages had been shelled, bombed, or strafed, the destruction had not been so selective. "General-purpose" bombs had sent out hails of steel fragments and shock waves, and, near their craters, the upward force of the blasts had torn off the leafy tops of the palm trees, leaving only the trunks standing, with their shattered tips pointing at the sky. Shrapnel had cut down many trees halfway up their trunks, or lopped off their branches, or, in places, thrown whole trees fifty or a hundred yards into adjacent fields. In places where napalm had been used, the yards and fields were blackened and leafless in large splotches. Many artillery and bomb craters were partly filled with leaflets that had been carried across the fields by winds. It did not appear that the destruction had been carried out systematically. The ruins of most of the villages displayed the marks of many methods of destruction. Knowing that the artillery often simply "covered" large areas several kilometres on a side with harassment-and-interdiction fire over a period of days, I found the senseless-looking pattern of craters— dotting the open fields as well as the tree lines and the villages—more understandable. Tanks and armored personnel-carriers had cut their own roads through the landscape. Apparently, the drivers had chosen to travel through the fields rather than use the existing roads, which were likely to be mined.

The families who had returned from the camps, or had just stayed on in the area, lived underground. The dark mouths of their caves dotted the tree lines of the back yards. As we flew overhead, whole families sitting in the yards of destroyed houses tilted their heads up and froze in position to watch us out of sight. It was nearly six o'clock now, and many families were crouching around fires, cooking their dinners. Pots, bedding, and a few pieces of furniture lay out in the yards. In some places, the spindly frames of tiny huts had appeared. Everywhere there were mounds of hay about three feet high, and I later found out that these were small, wall-less individual sleeping shelters consisting of straw thatching mounted on sticks. Some people had built their straw shelters out in the center of the fields, away from trees and bunkers—perhaps because they knew that our Army, believing all bunkers and caves to have been constructed by the Vietcong as fortifications, treated them as prime military targets. Firewood, most of it beams from the destroyed houses, lay about in piles. Children played in the dust, and generally there were far more children, women, and old people in sight than men. Small boys were riding in from the fields on the backs of water buffalo. The pilot noticed artillery shells sending up puffs of whitish smoke in several spots near one edge of these fields, and took care to skirt the area by about a kilometre. The people below continued to work outside their shelters and did not show any sign of noticing the artillery shells that were exploding nearby. The pilot flew the bubble out over the rice fields, and we raced across them at a height of fifteen feet. He pointed out a few scraps of twisted metal and machinery lying in a scorched circle in one of the fields and said that his helicopter had been shot down there a month before. He and his gunner had landed without injury. Once they were on the ground, guerrillas had shot at them from a tree line, and they had fired back. Fifteen minutes later, they had been rescued by another helicopter. A minute or so after he'd pointed out the spot where he crashed, he performed one of the bubble's many aerial stunts. He raced toward the tree line and then, when it seemed that we would crash into the trees, suddenly brought the helicopter sharply upward and arrested its forward motion, so that it rolled up over the trees and house ruins and came to a stop in the air as though it had been caught head on by a blast of wind. As we floated slowly just above the half-destroyed trees, the pilot exclaimed, "Look! There's one!" In a rising tone of tense excitement, he continued, "See? See? He's hiding!" I looked down and saw a youth crouching on a path next to a line of trees. The pilot wheeled the bubble and headed it back toward the youth, who then stood up and began to chop at a log with an axe. "See? Now he's pretending to be working!" the pilot said. An instant later, he cried out, "Look! There's another. She's hiding! See how she's hiding?" I looked down and saw that as our bubble drifted in a slow arc a woman in black edged carefully around a thin tree, always keeping on the opposite side of the trunk from the bubble.

We flew inland to the other side of Route 1, where the villages had also been destroyed. Rushing low across the darkening landscape, we passed over a field of tall grass, and the pilot said, "I killed four there. They ran for a bunker, but they didn't make it." We came to a destroyed village that had stood in the shade of rows of trees. A line of smoke rose from an orange dot of flame in a thicket, and the pilot said, "There's a V.C. havin' his supper. There shouldn't be anyone down there. He shouldn't be there." We began to fly a meandering seaward course down the Song Ve, which marked the boundary between the 3rd of the 4th's Area of Responsibility and the South Vietnamese Army's Tactical Area of Responsibility. A naked boy stood washing a smaller naked boy in a broad bend of the river, which was clear, with a sandy bottom. The two froze and watched as our helicopter passed over them. The spans of two bridges lay twisted in the river. On the south bank, where the 3rd of the 4th had been operating, piles of bricks and ashes and skeletons of blackened poles stood on the foundations of houses, and the fields were brown or black, or had gone wild, but on the north bank, where the South Vietnamese Army had been operating, the trees and fields were full and green—it might have been a different season there—and the houses remained standing, next to their vegetable gardens, yards, and palm trees. As we returned toward Route 1, we crossed over to the north bank. Smoke from supper fires rose from dark courtyards. People carrying loads on shoulder poles walked homeward down the sides of the road, and girls glided down other roads on bicycles. When the pilot set me down on a small helicopter pad within the American Advisory compound on the edge of Quang Ngai City, night had fallen. Inside the compound, all was American, and there was nothing to indicate that I had not magically been set down within the United States itself.

The buildings of the compound were of white clapboard, and neatly ordered, and the busy sound of conversation floated out of a brightly lit dining hall, where food was being served buffet style. Soldiers and civilian advisers with fresh shirts and neatly combed hair laughed and chatted as they entered an air-conditioned movie theatre. I went into the officers' bar and sat down next to a table of officers who were singing as they drank. Their voices were loud and unrestrained, and they banged their glasses on the table to keep time. The lyrics of one of the songs—a song that was apparently meant, in part, to ridicule the idea that civilians are unnecessarily killed by our air strikes, and one that I was to hear again, in many variations, during my stay in Quang Ngai—went:

> Bomb the schools and churches.
> Bomb the rice fields, too.
> Show the children in the courtyards
> What napalm can do.

In June, while the 3rd Brigade of the 4th Infantry Division was operating in Duc Pho District, the men of the 1st Brigade of the 101st Airborne Division, whose motto is "No slack," moved to the northwest to launch Operation Malheur II. (The 1st of the 101st named this operation and its predecessor Malheur after a town in Oregon, and not because the word means, in French, "misfortune," or "woe.") Operation Malheur II was the first of a series of three operations in which the 101st moved progressively northward through the three large river valleys that open out into the coastal lowlands of Quang Ngai. (Operation Malheur I had been in Duc Pho.) By killing enemy units in this area, and turning it into a harassment-and-interdiction-fire zone, the 101st hoped to impede the flow of supplies and men between the guerrillas in the lowlands and the guerrillas in the mountains. Malheur II was launched in the valley of the Song Ve, which winds between the mountains for ten or fifteen kilometres. The first step was to move some five thousand people living in the valley to sites nearer the coast, where camps were to be built. The villagers were transported by helicopter, and they were permitted to bring whatever possessions they could carry in their arms.

As in all operations in which American troops evacuated large numbers of civilians from an area of operation, the 101st was faced, in Malheur II, with the task of rapidly categorizing each person according to his estimated degree of involvement in the National Liberation Front. The categories, from the most suspect to the least suspect, were "confirmed V.C.," "V.C. suspect," "V.C. supporter," "detainee," "refugee," and "defector." But in conditions like those prevailing in Malheur II—with the Army Intelligence people working with no more than a half-dozen interpreters and having only a few days to sort out more than five thousand people in an area where the South Vietnamese government had maintained no presence for over a decade and had no knowledge of the people, and where women, children, and old people had been known to take up arms with the N.L.F.—it was virtually impossible, in most cases, for the Army to determine a person's involvement in the N.L.F. It is fair to say that in most cases the Army decided what category a person was to be put in on the basis of what the Army was doing to him at that moment or had just done to him. When the troops entered a village and rounded up the villagers for evacuation, they categorized the villagers as "V.C. supporters" or "V.C. suspects," and categorized the village as "100 per cent V.C.," but when the same villagers were removed to a camp the Army categorized them as "refugees." By the same token, a Vietnamese who had been shot by our troops was almost invariably categorized as a "confirmed V.C." (The soldiers had a joke that ran, "Anything that's dead and isn't white is a V.C.") The practice that had grown up of judging the guilt of a Vietnamese by what we happened to do to him could be clearly seen in the Army's use of the category "detainees." A "detainee" was theoretically a person whose degree of participation in the N.L.F. was unknown and who had been detained simply for interrogation. But in Malheur II the 101st listed the number of "detainees" (there were six hundred and thirty-one) along with the number of enemy killed and prisoners of war taken, as though by detaining them the Army had proved them to be members of the N.L.F. Matters were further confused by a wide overlapping of terms, and extreme ambiguity in their usage. The terms "detainee," "V.C. suspect," and "refugee" could all refer to the same person, depending on how the local commander chose to see him, although the terms were kept separate on statistical charts that were sent to Saigon. In Malheur II, all the "refugees" could certainly be said to have been "detained," and while they were in their villages their area was considered hostile and they were considered to be "V.C. supporters." In the field, the terms "V.C. suspect" and "V.C. supporter" were often used interchangeably. When a man was deemed to be a particularly suspicious "V.C. suspect," the usual procedure was to tie his hands behind his back, tie a sandbag over his head, and send him to an interrogation center. Finding him in this prisonerlike condition, the next people who dealt with him tended to treat him as a confirmed supporter of the enemy, and he was lucky if he escaped torture and imprisonment.

While Malheur II was going on, the 101st organized a project that appealed greatly to the men's sense of humor— a cattle drive. They rounded up more than a thousand head of cattle and water buffalo and began to drive them down the valley toward the camps to which the people had been moved. The project took much longer than had been expected, however; after six days the cattle had travelled only sixteen of the twenty kilometres to the camps. Sick of cattle driving, the 101st turned the herd over to a unit of South Vietnamese local-defense soldiers, or Popular Forces, who stole about two hundred of them and drove the remainder to the stockades near the camps. Some days later, the theft was discovered, whereupon American troops returned and shot many of the stolen cattle.

A brigade press release recounted the evacuation and cattle-drive phases of the operation as follows:

> More than 5,000 residents of the Song Ve River Valley west of here regained their identity with the Republic of Vietnam government as Vietnamese and American military units concluded the largest civil affairs operation ever launched in Quang Ngai Province. . . .
>
> As the villages were evacuated, the joint military force collected cattle and livestock, initiating the second phase of the operation by driving the herd to Nghia Hanh. While helicopters whisked the villagers to Nghia Hanh, paratroopers began the cattle-drive. They dubbed the overland route "The Chisholm Trail," and cries of "head 'em up; move 'em out" echoed through the valley. The Vietnamese forces sang folk songs; the paratroopers replied with western tunes. Private First Class Gary M. Nichols, Wynne, Ark., a dozen hours away from a degree in veterinary medicine, administered to the herd and calves born during the trip.

For release to the press, the brigade selected a photograph that showed soldiers herding the cattle through large paddy fields where young, recently transplanted rice shoots were showing only a few inches above the water, and supplied it with a caption that read, "Rice paddies, not plains." In conversation, officers of the 101st often displayed warm amusement and delight at the idea of transplanting such a typically American thing as a cattle drive into a Vietnamese setting of rice fields.

Several weeks after the completion of Operation Malheur II, I flew over the Song Ve Valley in a FAC plane, and observed that all the houses there had been destroyed. The pilot told me that troops of the 101st had destroyed them after the people had been evacuated. He also pointed out that the fields had turned uniformly brown, and explained that Operation Ranch Hand—the organization that carries out defoliation—had sprayed the valley.

A few days later, I asked the Information Officer of the brigade how the destruction had taken place.

"I'm afraid you've got your information wrong there," he answered. "We didn't destroy that valley."

I told him that I had just flown over the area and had observed that it had been destroyed.

"I don't know about that, but we didn't destroy the valley," he said.

I asked how he accounted for its destruction.

"Well, when we left the valley, it was standing," he said. Then, after a long pause, he added, "We had no *plan* of destroying the valley. But then Charlie went back in there, and we had no choice about it, so we inserted two battalions back into the valley, and then it got destroyed in the process of denying it to the enemy."

The Information Officer at the Task Force Oregon headquarters expressed complete astonishment when he heard that the villages in the valley had been destroyed. "That's a new one on me," he said.

I often found that American officers tended to ignore some of the results of their operations—such as the destruction of the villages in a large area—or even to deny them, if these results hadn't been envisaged in the original optimistic plans they had made for the districts they were operating in.

When the villagers from the Song Ve Valley were landed at the empty lots in Nghia Hanh, where shelter was theoretically to be provided soon, they became part of what was at that time an officially registered population of a hundred and twenty thousand dispossessed people in Quang Ngai Province—people whose minimum needs of shelter and food had not yet begun to be met. In late June, Mr. Ernest Hobson, who held the civilian post of provincial adviser for refugees in Quang Ngai, under U.S. AID, had written in the monthly *Statistical Annex to the Special Joint Report for the Province of Quang Ngai:*

> The most significant problem in the area of refugee service this month was brought about by the military operation of Task Force Oregon, in which the Refugee Service was called upon to specifically support a military action. . . . The mounting problems of inadequate staff, both VN and American, Logistics, and funds cannot be met without substantial emergency assistance from both regional and national headquarters. . . . The aforementioned military action has exceeded camp construction for new refugees. 500 additional units are needed in Nghia Hanh alone.

At the time the people from the Song Ve Valley arrived, there was a severe shortage of emergency rations, and, because of an administrative mixup, the Army did not release until almost a week later some sixty-two tons of rice it had collected in the valley. After four days without food, a number of people who had been placed in a field directly beside one of the storehouses of captured rice attempted to break into it at night. The Army responded with tear-gas grenades, and two twelve-year-old boys were killed. At the end of August, two thousand families in the camps, some of them from the Song Ve Valley, were still without shelter of any kind. In early August, Deputy Ambassador Robert Komer was alerted to the situation by television and newspaper reports, and he wrote a letter, dated August 15th, to Dr. Nguyen Phuc Que, the Saigon government's Commissioner for Refugees. The letter was copied and distributed to some officials in I Corps. (I Corps is the military designation of the five northernmost coastal provinces of South Vietnam.) It read:

> I am sure you agree that the refugee situation in I Corps is serious.
>
> At least one half of the refugees in South Vietnam are in I Corps. There is an intense concern in the U.S. and particularly in our Congress about the details of the situation in I Corps. There have been several newspaper stories and TV reports during the past week in the U.S. on the I Corps situation. I am afraid that the refugee problem in I Corps is outstraining G.V.N. capability to deal with it. There is a shortage of aluminum roofing and other shelter material accentuated by inadequate airlift capability. There is critical need for emergency rice rations. We are told that

less than 50% of the refugees have received Temporary Relief Payments; less than 25%, Resettlement Assistance; and that the special commissariat on refugees is seriously hampered by lack of interest on the part of many province officials.

The Ambassador went on to suggest a system in which a high priority would be given to the transportation of supplies for dispossessed people in I Corps.

Dr. Que, in turn, placed the responsibility for the crisis on the United States Army. On October 13th, a U.P.I. dispatch reported Dr. Que as saying that at some of the camps in I Corps "the food shortage is so severe starvation is a threat." The dispatch continued:

> Dr. Que complained that he frequently gets only a day's advance warning when U.S. military operations suddenly create thousands of refugees.
>
> He said he can make no arrangements for receiving the refugees—sometimes in groups of 10,000 at a time—when he is not told beforehand.
>
> He said 14 military operations so far this year have generated about 300,000 refugees.
>
> "Only at the last moment—maybe a day or two before—do I receive a phone call: 'Dr. Que, there will be 10,000 refugees for you tomorrow at such and such a place.'"

From the "Refugee Relief Operational Handbook," which lays down the countrywide rules for dealing with the dispossessed in South Vietnam, I learned that the term "temporary relief payment" referred to food and money that were supposed to be given as an emergency provision to people who had arrived at the camps. The handbook states, "The official rate of temporary relief payment, regardless of age and ethnic origin, is VN $10 [about eight cents] per refugee a day. Temporary relief allowances may be paid either wholly in cash or partly in cash and partly in rice." In short, Deputy Ambassador Komer's statement meant that, as of August 15th, over half the people in government camps in I Corps, who numbered more than a half million, had received no food from our government, or the Saigon government, since their arrival in the camps. After the letter had been sent, some emergency assistance was given to I Corps. But between June, when Mr. Hobson wrote his emergency plea, and the end of August the number of people dispossessed by military operations had increased by 31,888 in Quang Ngai alone, and the crisis had become more acute. To help relieve the food shortage in the camps in Duc Pho District, the 3rd Brigade of the 4th Division collected as much as half a ton of leftovers from its mess halls several times each week and distributed this food at nearby camps.

In speaking of the people in the camps, American officials usually avoided any direct reference to the manner in which these civilians were dispossessed, and referred only to "refugees generated," or "refugees from Communism," or "people freed from V.C. domination." The slogan "Two million refugees have voted with their feet for the G.V.N." has become one of the clichés of the war, and the American Office of Civil Operations includes many of these camps in its reports on the number of "secure hamlets." In his August report, Mr. Hobson stated the problem in different terms:

> From June 13, 1967 to date, we have received a total of 31,888 new refugees as a direct result of allied military operations.

Most of these new refugees were in fact
evacuees. The meteoric rise in the number of
refugees severely taxed the G.V.N.'s capa-
bilities to deal with the situation. There exist
serious shortages in rice, U.S. commodities,
and roofing material. Region and Saigon find
themselves hard-pressed to overcome the critical shortage in roofing material before the
onset of the rainy season. Presently there are
approximately 2,000 families without adequate housing of any kind.

The June sheet of a mimeographed report called *General Refugee Situation in Province,* which is put out by the
South Vietnamese provincial government, classified some
80,000 of 122,680 "refugees" as "scattered," which meant
that they had not received shelter within the camps. This
sheet stated that there were 122,680 people in or around
the camps and that they had been supplied with 573
latrines, 33 schools, and 27 medical dispensaries, or 1
latrine for every 214 people, 1 school for every 3,000
children (calculating the number of children as roughly
two-thirds of the "refugees") , and 1 medical dispensary for
every 4,543 people. These facilities were not evenly distributed among the camps. Out of 68 camps, 50 had no
schools, 46 had no latrines, and 42 had no medical dispensary. Of the 573 latrines, 471 were in camps in Son
Tinh District, with the remaining 102 distributed over all
the other districts.

An estimated fifteen per cent of the people in the sixty-
eight camps were able-bodied men. There were a few jobs
available to the women of the camps, mostly on American
bases. A number of women became waitresses in the American mess halls, and a number were employed to fill and
carry sandbags for the construction of fortifications. All

these women were paid a salary. At both the Duc Pho base and the Chu Lai base, prisoners of war also filled sandbags, and were made to labor on fortifications. On the bases, it was a very common thing to see a gang of Vietnamese women out in the sand dunes, filling and carrying sandbags in the hot sun, while an American soldier sat near them holding an M-16; once, on the Chu Lai base, a mine was discovered built into a wall of sandbags that a gang of these dispossessed Vietnamese women had constructed near an ammunition depot. A number of the young women of the camps became part of the population of prostitutes who catered to the Americans. (A town that was right in front of the gates of the Chu Lai base was considered so insecure that the servicemen visited its bars and its prostitutes only between eight and eleven o'clock in the morning.) The few able-bodied men in the camps could find occasional work breaking rocks on the bases. All jobs on the bases were filled according to a daily-pickup system, and workers were hired or laid off as the Army's construction needs changed. Another small group of people from the camps made baskets or curios for the G.I.s to buy as souvenirs. However, all these kinds of work occupied, at most, only a few hundred of the people. The rest remained idle.

Shelter in the camps consisted, typically, of long parallel rows of barrack-shaped, unwalled, floorless frames made of poles and roofed with tin. The people listed as "scattered" slept under low roofs of thatching propped up on poles, or out in the open. Some people built shacks of cardboard boxes, on which the same markings would be repeated again and again. (The walls of several houses read "COMBAT MEAL COMBAT MEAL COMBAT MEAL" from top to bottom.) Because food was a greater necessity than shelter, some of the camp dwellers sold their allotment of tin roofing to people in Quang Ngai City in order to get money for rice, whose price had risen enormously as a result of the sudden increased demand from the camps and the concomitant drop in local production following the abandonment of the land. Provincial and district officials also stole a considerable quantity of tin and sold it in the towns. The main streets of Quang Ngai City glittered with illegal new tin roofs. It was these new tin roofs that alerted American refugee advisers to the fact that much of the tin was not being used in the construction of shelters for the people in the camps. The best-developed camps were some that, in coöperation with American and Vietnamese authorities, were run, and also financially assisted, by the Cao Dai sect of Buddhists. As in the other camps, the shelters were laid out in straight, barracklike rows with treeless aisles running between, but here they usually consisted of clay walls on bamboo frames, and no one slept uncovered. The people in these camps, unlike the rest, had been supplied with a small amount of government land to farm.

The "Refugee Relief Operational Handbook" outlines standard procedures that officials in the Refugee Division of the Office of Civil Operations in Saigon had devised for dealing with the people in the camps. In the handbook's plan, two stages are outlined—Temporary Camps, and Resettlement. Section I-B of Chapter 3 of the handbook lists a number of facilities as "mandatory" for every hundred families in the temporary camps—twenty latrines, one classroom, and two wells, for example. Section I-C of the same chapter lists several temporary-camp activities, including "collective activities, civic action, and civil operations, solidarization of refugees, orientation in democracy," and "vocational training," but in Chapter 4, entitled "Resettlement," the report notes, "Under no circumstances will the construction of vocational training centers be permissible. Arrangements should be made to use government or private housing . . . to avoid unnecessary budget drain." Section II, which is headed "Refugee Registration Procedure," requires that a specialist take fingerprints and photographs of all "unidentified persons." Section IV of Chapter 3 specifies that the temporary relief payment of ten piastres a day may be given for one month, and that an extension of one month may be made "in case local insecurity still prevails, or the construction of resettlement centers has not been achieved in time." Section IV-B lists people in the following categories as eligible for temporary relief payments:

> 1. Refugees from insecure areas and regrouped in temporary camps.
> 2. Non-native applicants for temporary shelter [who] should be interrogated for background data and home province-leaving reason. Details of previous relief status should be obtained via a cable from the province of origin for assessment and action. Meanwhile, they are granted provisional shelter at a refugee camp and commodity support only.
> 3. Dependents of cadres . . . and Popular Forces elements . . . coming from insecure areas. . . .
> 4. Dependents of V.C. elements, for humanitarianism's sake; however, the local authorities should keep track of their whereabouts for possible subversive activities.

Although payments to people in the temporary camps are supposed to last only two months, at the longest, the handbook notes that in what are termed "old temporary camps" additional wells and latrines may be needed.

In the second stage outlined in the handbook—"Resettlement"—the people in the temporary camps are en-visaged as returning to a normal existence in new villages, with jobs, proper houses, and an effective system of security to protect them from Vietcong influence. Several methods of resettlement are listed. Of "Return to Village," the first method mentioned, the handbook states, "This is the best resettlement formula. However, the home village should be completely pacified and absolutely secure to eliminate the chance of a second exodus." If the displaced people are from another province, the "host province" may give them temporary relief payments only if it has received confirmation from the original province of "the honesty of their escape from Communism." A second method of resettlement is titled "Resettlement in Temporary Camps." The handbook says, "If there are no locations favorable to resettlement in a given province or Autonomous City, refugees will be resettled at their temporary camp. In this matter, the temporary housing unit they have occupied to date now becomes their own and the local administration is excused from paying them VN $5,000 resettlement housing allowance." Chapter 4, Section II, Paragraph 2 specifies that resettlement sites "should have easy access by surface and a vast potential which will endure a flourishing economy."

At several points, the handbook makes it clear that people who have been victimized by the Vietcong are to be treated more generously than people who have been victimized by American military operations or natural disasters. In Chapter 5, which concerns "disaster relief assistance," the handbook specifies that if a person over eighteen is killed "By V.C.s" his family is to receive four thousand piastres, but if he meets his death in any other way—and the handbook lumps all other ways together under the heading "Caused by Carelessness"—his family is to receive only three thousand piastres. At the end of this chapter, the handbook states, "The above assistance is only applicable to refugees who have been receiving temporary relief or been permanently resettled for a period of less than one year. In excess of this time limit they are considered as having recovered a normal life."

Late in August, I spoke with Mr. Hobson, a stocky Negro administrator who holds an M.A. in business administration and who before coming to Vietnam as the provincial adviser for refugees had spent several years as a parole officer in the United States and had worked on youth projects in Harlem. "We have completely dropped the ball on these refugees," he told me. "These people have been neglected or abused since they arrived. Right now, I have five thousand people with no roof over their heads. We just don't have the manpower and supply. Of course, these are the worst camps. Our two best camps are supported by the Buddhist sects. Most camps have situations where ten families live in the space for one. And the people have no jobs. Eighty-five per cent of the refugees are women, children, and old people. If they get any land to farm, it's usually the worst land, because government land is always the worst. We've been trying to get a job-training program going, but the basic problem is that this is not an industrial country and there just plain aren't any jobs for these people. You can't take some hundred and twenty-five thousand people off their land in an agricultural province and expect them to make a decent life for themselves around the towns. In the Song Ve Valley operation, for the first time, we got a little bit of Psy War in, so at least the people had a faint idea of what was coming, but that was only because of our insistence. Before that, there was *nothing*. Those people didn't know *why* they were getting kicked out, *where* they were going, or *what* was

going to happen to them. You wouldn't believe the con-
tradictions in the situation here. If I told people about this
back in the States, they'd say I was lying. And every
situation is different. No two camps are the same and no
two operations are the same. And every one is being
carried on separately from the others. The Army suddenly
just tells us that five thousand people are going to arrive,
with no possessions and no food. It's like a band where
everybody's trying to play a solo at the same time—you
know what kind of music that makes."

Later, I saw one of the Psychological Warfare leaflets
that had been dropped over the Song Ve Valley. On one
side is a photograph of a man and his wife, each holding a
small boy. All four members of the family are smiling at
the camera. The caption reads, "I, Trinh Su, and my
family have resettled in the Nghia Hanh resettlement
camp, where we have received sufficient aid from the
G.V.N. I advise you to follow instructions of the U.S. Army
in Nghia Hanh and you will live in safety, as we do." On
the back, the text reads:

> People of the Song Ve Valley, the G.V.N.
> urges those of you that are still living in the
> mountains to come down and move to Nghia
> Hanh. There you will be protected and cared
> for by the G.V.N. and Allied Forces. Your
> friends who have moved to Nghia Hanh have
> received food and medical care. At Nghia
> Hanh you will be safe. There will be shelter
> for you and your family. Those of you who
> choose to remain in the area will be considered
> hostile and in danger.

Eventually, I talked with one of the men who took
photographs for such leaflets. He was an American private
about six feet four inches tall and very stout. "We make

funny faces and kind of horse around to get them to laugh or smile," he told me. "We were trying to get one old buzzard about sixty years old to laugh, but he just stood there without cracking a smile, no matter what we did. But then I was climbing up a stepladder to shoot a picture, and I kind of slipped and fell off it, and you should have seen the old bastard laugh then!"

Before I left Mr. Hobson, he explained to me that one of his greatest problems was finding out which foods were suitable for preparation in the camps. After rice, the principal staple in the American relief supply was bulgur wheat. Mr. Hobson had discovered, however, that the people in the camps, even when they were hungry, sold the wheat to pig farmers—partly because they disliked the taste of wheat gruel but mainly because it took too much firewood to cook the wheat. There was a great scarcity of firewood, particularly in the camps, and to use several days' supply of grass and twigs to prepare one meal of bulgur wheat spelled hunger as surely as using up a week's supply of rice in one day. Mr. Hobson said, "It's hard for us Americans to tell what is good for the Vietnamese. For instance, it's hard to tell the difference between a rich man and a poor man. They don't have any washing machines or fancy houses. The difference might just be a motor scooter out front. So to the G.I.s everyone looks poor."

Mr. Hobson credited his continuing education in Vietnamese customs to his assistant, a Mr. Te, for whom he expressed high respect. "Mr. Te is going to make a real Vietnamese gentleman out of me someday," he said, half to me, half to Mr. Te. "And the first thing that's got to go is my loud laugh. I've got a loud laugh, and Mr. Te says that's the No. 1 problem. But I've got to be myself, so I'll have to become a gentleman *with* my loud laugh." He gave his loud laugh.

Later in our talk, he said, "I ask you, if we can't win the allegiance of a captive audience in these camps, how are we going to win their hearts and minds out in a hamlet way off in the boonies somewhere? The big shots want to move everyone all around. They say, 'The Montagnards gotta learn to live in the lowland, the farmers gotta learn to live in the towns.' The trouble is, they have no heart. They just plain have no heart."

I said I had noticed that statistics on refugees in the province listed tens of thousands of people as having been "resettled."

Mr. Hobson explained that this had all taken place under the "Refugee Relief Operational Handbook" provisions for "Resettlement in Temporary Camps." "All that resettlement is just paperwork," he said. "We're supposed to give each family five thousand p's"—that is, piastres—"as a resettlement housing allowance, so they can build a new house, but what we do is say, 'O.K., this place we've built for you is now *permanent,* it's *yours,* so you don't get the five thousand p's.' Another way of doing it is to put in a village chief and give the camp a *name.* Then it can be treated as a village or a hamlet. Of course, the place has to meet certain criteria, but basically it's paperwork. What it means is that the place goes out of the hands of the Special Commissariat for Refugees and into the hands of the Ministry of Social Welfare—which is *also* me!" Mr. Hobson again gave the laugh that was holding him back from becoming a Vietnamese gentleman. But he quickly became silent, and shook his head. "I don't have time to find out where they're coming from," he said. "All I can do is try to get them some food and put roofs over their heads, because otherwise they haven't got a damn thing going for them."

On October 6th, a British physician who had worked in Quang Ngai's civilian hospital—there is just one in the entire province—for over three years wrote in a report that health conditions in the camps "differ from camp to camp," explaining:

> More established [camps] are a little better. They usually have a pseudo nurse, toilet, and well. Disease, poverty, and malnutrition common.
>
> New camps: poor water and toilet facilities, little money, little food, housing poor, cold, and again disease and malnutrition common.
>
> Recent camps: hovels, no housing, tents, camp in the open, no water, no toilets, no money, no food, diseases like dysentery, malaria, malnutrition, infectious hepatitis, plague an everyday occurrence. Many people die— average 2 to 3 a week—from any of the above causes. Now with the rainy season starting their immediate future is terrible indeed. Of this category there are approximately 5,000– 10,000 in the province.

At the beginning of 1967, American officials in Vietnam, both military and civilian, commonly expressed the view that the "generation of refugees" was an unfortunate but unavoidable consequence of conducting effective military operations. By August, most officials were declaring that the removal of people from their original homes and villages was in itself a valuable tactic in the struggle against the National Liberation Front. Military men, in particular, were fond of quoting Mao Tse-tung's dictum that in guerrilla warfare the guerrillas are the fish and the people are the water. They argued that they could catch the fish only by drying up the water. I heard Mao Tse-tung's metaphor mentioned in this connection on at least five occasions in Quang Ngai. In an article titled "The Cause in Vietnam Is Being Won," which appeared in the issue of *The New York Times Magazine* of October 15, 1967, General Maxwell D. Taylor, former chairman of the Joint Chiefs of Staff and former United States Ambassador to South Vietnam, explains the logic of population control and, without naming the camps as such, describes the advantages to the South Vietnamese government of having from three million to four million of the country's population of roughly seventeen million in or around government-controlled camps:

> As an indicator of progress in pacification, there has been an encouraging increase in Government control in rural areas in recent months. Indeed, since mid-1965, there has been an increase of some 3 million people in rural areas clearly under Government control. About 1,200,000 of this increase has occurred in the last six months. Concurrently, the Vietcong-controlled population has decreased by more than a million since 1965, the remaining Governmental gains having come from contested areas. In that year, it was estimated that 26 per cent of the total population (including the cities) was under Vietcong domination; now it is down to 14 per cent. If one includes the cities, the total population under secure Government of Vietnam control has increased from 6.6 million in mid-1965 to 10.8 million in mid-1967. . . .

> Population liberated from Vietcong control
> is a double asset from our point of view. Not
> only are these people freed from the tyranny
> of Vietcong domination, but they are with-
> drawn from among the human assets so neces-
> sary to support the guerrilla movement. The
> Vietcong are necessarily parasitic upon the
> rural population from whom they drew re-
> cruits, porters, food and other forms of help.
> Without this rural support, the local guerrilla
> movement risks atrophy and progressive at-
> trition.

I met a young American lieutenant colonel in Binh Son
District who was discouraged by the current situation in
the province but thought that things would improve
greatly if a sweeping plan he had in mind should be put
into effect. After talking for over a year with Vietnamese
whose command of English was poor, the colonel had
developed a very slow, careful style of enunciation and had
come to employ a minimal basic vocabulary. This way of
speaking had become such a habit with him that at times
he used it even with Americans, especially when he was
trying to elucidate difficult points. His slowness of speech
was accompanied by strong emphasis on every important
word and a tense, passionate gesticulation with his fists that
expressed his total dedication to his work. Sometimes he
would expend so much energy explaining an idea about
the future of the province that he would have to slump
back in his chair with a weak smile of exhaustion when he
had finished.

While I was with the colonel, I heard him tell an
observer from the American headquarters for Pacification
in Saigon, who had come to evaluate the "potential" of the
province for Revolutionary Development, which is the

South Vietnamese government's response to the Vietcong's political-indoctrination program, and is usually abbreviated as revdev, or R.D., "Look, the V.C. get their people to support them. They *organize* the people. Those people are *alive;* they are highly *motivated*. But the people who are supposed to be on our side are just *blobs*." He screwed up his face in chagrin and clenched his fists in front of him. "The refugees sit around all day doing *nothing,* and *we are doing nothing about it,*" he continued, coming down hard on every word. Then he outlined his plan for reconstruction. "We've got to get these people out where they can get killed," he said, then stopped himself, smiled, and added, "Don't get me wrong. I don't want them to suffer any more than they are suffering now. They've suffered too much already, but what I mean is, we've got to give them some *reason* to support the government. We have to give them some motivation to defend themselves. Now they don't have any jobs, or houses, or anything that they can get excited about, and I don't blame them for being apathetic. Look at the camps. *Anybody* would be apathetic." The first requirement for reconstruction, as he saw it, was security, and for this he envisaged a vast, superbly conducted training program for the local young men, who would learn a new self-confidence and the will to defend their villages against the National Liberation Front. Next, the villages would have to be physically rebuilt—"preferably by the villagers themselves." He said, "The Vietnamese have to do it themselves. We always try to do it for them, to give it to them. I know what a tremendous temptation it is to give candy to kids. It makes you feel good inside. You're No. 1. But for every piece of candy you give a kid, you're destroying the kid's faith in his father, who can't give him any candy. I have seen so many cases of Americans who want to play Santa Claus and feel warm all over, but this kind of thing is only corrupting, and it destroys the people's pride. If only we could learn that!" The next part of the plan involved the creation of a democratic village government, chosen by the people themselves and responsive to their aspirations. Finally, the change at the local level would be accompanied by the total abolition of corruption at the provincial level, and the beginnings of a nationwide changeover to civilian rule. In short, the colonel wanted to see a vigorous, democratic, prosperous, happy, entirely new and changed society rise from the ashes of Quang Ngai to resist the National Liberation Front because the local villagers felt a spontaneous love for their new life and a deep enthusiasm for a wholly reformed government of South Vietnam.

I pointed out to the colonel that approximately seventy per cent of the villages in the province had already been destroyed, and asked if he saw this as a serious obstacle to the realization of his plan.

"I know it," he said. "In the fifteen-kilometre stretch of coast of our area of operation there are just *two* villages still standing, and if anyone tells you there are more they are liars. One thing is that the Vietnamese can rebuild their houses very quickly, with very little trouble at all." He then patiently described to me in detail how the thatch-roofed houses that had made up about eighty per cent of the homes in the province were constructed. "The thing is, we've got to change the population patterns," he went on. "It's these widely dispersed *population patterns* that allowed the V.C. to get going in the first place. So we won't necessarily move the people back to their original villages. If we could change the population patterns, getting people consolidated into tighter areas, we could put up defenses, and the government could control them more easily. We could check them every night for I.D. cards, and in that way keep the V.C. from infiltrating."

When the colonel had concluded his remarks, the observer from Saigon said that he would like to spend a day and a night in a village of the district with his Vietnamese interpreter, to judge for himself whether conditions were ripe for a Revolutionary Development Program, and he asked the colonel to recommend a village. Clapping a hand to his forehead, the colonel laughed in dismay, and said, "You can't sleep in a village. I couldn't let you do that. We don't have any villages an *American* could spend the *night* in."

After completing Operation Malheur II in the Song Ve Valley, the 1st Brigade of the 101st Airborne Division took another hop in its drive northward and launched Operation Hood River in the Song Tra Khuc Valley. The hope was to trap a large unit of the enemy by landing on the hills above the valley and sweeping down into it from all sides, but, as in the two earlier operations, the trap closed empty. Sporadic contact with the enemy was common during these sweeps, but this time it was lighter than usual. The official figure for enemy killed during the two weeks of the operation was seventy-eight, and the figure for American casualties was three killed and thirty-eight wounded. The troops, and the artillery and aircraft that supported them, did, however, destroy most of the villages in the river valley and on the coastal plain at its mouth.

In mid-August, when I first arrived at the Chu Lai base,

which is situated just north of Quang Ngai Province, in the southern part of Quang Tin Province, and which was the headquarters for Task Force Oregon at that time, I was given a briefing on the composition of the enemy in Quang Ngai Province by the head Information Officer for the task force, Major Patrick H. Dionne, who is a portly man with a round face and a smile that appears, along with an outstretched hand, as soon as someone enters his office— a greeting that seems to say, "We're going to get along fine!" (Throughout my stay in Quang Ngai, I was given perfect freedom to see whatever I wanted, and was encouraged by Major Dionne and other Information Officers to fly in FAC planes and accompany operations on the ground as often as possible.)

"We're here to sell the government of South Vietnam to the people in this province," Major Dionne said. "The trouble is, they don't *want* to have the government sold to them, so what we are really doing is cramming the government down their throats. This place has been V.C. ever since the Japanese, so they've never really had any contact with the government." Picking a pink card out of a desk file for reference, he continued, "There are from seven hundred thousand to a million people in Quang Ngai. About half of these are under G.V.N. control and a quarter are V.C. supporters. We've got quite a large number of refugees in the province. They fled the V.C. or left their area because of combat, and now the G.V.N. controls them. We've got both local V.C. and N.V.A. units in the province. The 3rd N.V.A. Division is based in Duc Pho District."

I asked if these North Vietnamese Army soldiers had infiltrated into South Vietnam recently.

"Actually, these are the ones that came down in 1954 and stayed, and they organized the local people to support

Hanoi," Major Dionne said. "You might say that the people are North Vietnamese–oriented–living on this side of the D.M.Z. The N.V.A. here are the old Vietminh who stayed on. They have their families down here and don't really have too much to go back to up North. Then, there's the V.C.–the local-force guy and the main-force guy. The local-force guy lives at home and is poorly armed–a squad might have two rifles and six hand grenades–but he's highly motivated, and does the political cadre work. As opposed to the N.V.A., the local V.C. is a loner–with a lot of other loners. They feel pretty sure that they are going to succeed. The main-force guy is organized in units and roves around. He's better armed."

When I spoke with American officers about the civilians who were sometimes killed in our bombings of villages judged to be hostile, they often brought up the fact that the Vietcong also mistreated and killed civilians in *their* operations. During my month in Quang Ngai Province, two incidents of this kind figured heavily in Army press releases, in battalion newspapers, and in Psychological Warfare posters and leaflets. On August 9th, the Vietcong had attacked a village along Route 1 that was supposed to be protected by Popular Forces stationed there. The Popular Forces had fired at the Vietcong, but without venturing outside their fortified positions, and the Vietcong had destroyed a dozen houses with satchel charges and killed and wounded several villagers; they had, however, left the medical dispensary, which was financially supported by Americans, untouched. Army photographers arrived the next morning to take photographs of civilians wounded or killed in the attack. Later, these photographs were printed on propaganda posters and were also released to the press. The other incident was the discovery of two men that the Vietcong had held prisoner for several months. The August 16th edition of the *Screaming Eagle* reported the discovery as follows:

> Duc Pho—"God, they were a mess," said one paratrooper. "They looked like something out of those World War II prison camps." The 101st Airborne trooper was shocked at the physical condition of two South Vietnamese soldiers liberated from a Viet Cong prison camp near here during Operation Malheur II. The prisoners were emaciated, haggard and beaten. Eyes and cheeks were sunk into their gaunt faces and their voices weak and inaudible due to lack of strength. Both suffered from malnutrition and exhaustion.
>
> "They were in pretty bad shape," said Lt. Corky Boswell, Chico, Calif. "The VC had beaten them, used them for laborers, and fed them just enough to keep them alive. And that wasn't very much, as you can see. . . ." The two former prisoners, exhausted, and limited in their knowledge of enemy movements, were of little help. "We can't help you," said Xuan. "We just dug tunnels. They watched us carefully all the time and never talked in front of us."

Major Dionne expressed deep disgust with the Vietcong for attacking the village on Route 1. "O.K., so maybe one of our artillery rounds goes astray and hits a friendly village every once in a while," he said. "But I don't know." Major Dionne's expression became disturbed. "With a hidden device—a V.C. mine . . . I mean, *I* get paid to wear the uniform, so if something happens to me it's not so bad. But these poor old buzzards don't get paid for that. I don't know . . ."

Every few weeks or so, the Vietcong overran another village along Route 1 that was supposed to be under the protection of the Popular Forces. In October, I asked U.S. AID officials in Washington how many village officials had been assassinated by the Vietcong in 1967 in Quang Ngai Province. When AID or any other government agency gives statistics on "village officials" killed, these may include officers of the Popular Forces and members of the Combat Youth—these are both lightly armed groups of villagers recruited to defend their own villages against the Vietcong—and Revolutionary Development workers, Civic Action cadres, interfamily chiefs, security agents, and a great variety of other types of individuals. For the period from January 1st to October 1st, AID listed a total of eighteen "village officials" as having been killed by the Vietcong in Quang Ngai. They consisted of three Revolutionary Development workers, three hamlet chiefs, two Youth Cadre members, one Civic Action cadre, four Popular Forces officers, one Combat Youth member, one chief of a rehabilitation center, one former village security agent, one village security agent, and one former interfamily chief. Usually, the Vietcong were careful to bomb only the houses of government employees, and several Americans expressed horror at the coldblooded premeditation of these assassinations. "We may have accidents," said one, "but we never set off a mine or shoot a bullet with some specific guy's name written on it in advance."

Major Dionne told me that Task Force Oregon's proudest nonmilitary achievement was the opening of Route 1 to traffic. When the task force arrived, it found that the Vietcong had blown up almost all the bridges on the road. Task Force Oregon engineers rebuilt the bridges and then opened the road to public traffic in a big ceremony, with several high-ranking officers of Task Force

Oregon and the province chief present. Several times each week, American teams swept the road for Vietcong mines, finding an average of two a week. A light traffic of bicycles and motor scooters began to travel between certain towns, although other stretches were still unused.

Later on, Major Dionne told me, "When I get to wondering what this war is all about, I take a trip up to the base hospital. You know—a guy smilin' at you, saying that he's going to be up in a few weeks, when what he doesn't know is that he's lost the use of his legs and is crippled for life. And when I see what these boys are willing to sacrifice, that really makes me see what it's all about over here."

I also spoke briefly with an Intelligence captain assigned to the FAC control desk about the character of the enemy. "They have a parallel structure," he told me. "The orders originate in Hanoi and go to COSVN." He pronounced it "Cosvin" and explained that it meant the Central Office of South Vietnam.

I asked if he would tell me what he meant by a parallel structure.

"O.K., let's take a look at Communism—at North Vietnam, the U.S.S.R., and China," he said. "They all have a front organization that tells the people that the government has moral objectives that are sound. All these countries have that in common."

"What does the front organization consist of?" I asked.

"It's the fact that they have a President."

"How does this apply to the National Liberation Front?"

"I don't know precisely how the front and the real government are related, but the front is the organization that tries to tell them that Communism is a good deal."

"If there is a parallel structure, what is parallel to what?" I asked.

"The Front is one—the National Liberation Front—and

the other . . . Oh, hell, I can't think of the other. Did you read Allen Dulles' book about intelligence?"

I said I hadn't.

"It's described in there. There's the apparatus that spreads Communism. But I forget what they call it here." (That night, the captain came in to tell me he had done some research and had found the name that had eluded him earlier—it was the People's Revolutionary Party.)

Conversations in Vietnam tend to become muddled because many meanings are attached to a few favorite terms, as in the above conversation, in which the Intelligence captain often failed to make it clear when we meant "front" in the sense of the National Liberation Front and when we meant it in the sense of a cover, or front, organization. Later, I was talking with the same captain about "the V.C. infrastructure," and I suddenly realized that this term, which he had used at the beginning of the conversation to mean the political organization of the Vietcong at the local level, had changed as we talked to mean the wood-and-packed-mud "infrastructure" of the Vietcong's tunnels and bunkers. "Parallel structure" is another of the favorite terms, and it can apply to the Vietcong governmental apparatus, which "parallels" the South Vietnamese government, or to the American advisory system, which also "parallels" the South Vietnamese government, or, as in my conversation with the captain, to the "parallel structure" of all Communist governments, including the National Liberation Front. (The word "structure" is itself a favorite in Vietnam. The military refer to all Vietnamese houses as "structures.")

After completing Operation Hood River, the 1st Brigade of the 101st Airborne Division was to move north once again and launch Operation Benton, in the southern part of Quang Tin Province. I flew over the Song Tra Khuc Valley in FAC planes—assigned by the Air Force to the 1st Brigade of the 101st Airborne Division—during the last two days of Operation Hood River. FAC pilots had two duties. The first was to fly over specified areas noting anything that seemed suspicious to them and choosing targets to recommend for air strikes. The targets were not further examined at first hand, and unless they were found to be near friendly troops or in "no-strike zones" they were bombed. Some FAC pilots flew over a certain area every day for several weeks at a time, acquainting themselves with it as thoroughly as they could from the air with the aid of maps. Other pilots would be assigned to the brigade, and would fly over the brigade in all its operations, wherever it went. The FAC pilots' second duty was to guide fighter-bombers to their targets. Air Force spokesmen were always careful to stress the point that a FAC pilot could not, on his own authority, call planes to bomb a target—that the Army had to give its clearance in every case. In practice, this meant that when a FAC pilot spotted something he wished to have bombed he would radio its position to the DASC (Direct Air Support Center) office for his military corps area and enter a request for a flight of fighter-bombers. DASC would weigh the urgency of the mission against other requests made for fighter-bombers at that particular time, and decide which of the requested targets should be bombed by the limited number of planes that were aloft or "on hot pad alert," ready for immediate takeoff. The Air Force divided all air strikes into two categories, which it termed "pre-planned strikes" and "immediate strikes." A pre-planned strike was scheduled anywhere from twenty-four hours to two weeks in advance of the time of the bombing, and an immediate strike was carried out within a few hours, at most, of a call from ground troops or from a FAC pilot who had spotted what he judged to be enemy activity. In conversation with a FAC pilot, I once said "planned strike" instead of "pre-planned strike," by mistake, and was swiftly corrected. When I asked what the difference between the terms "planned" and "pre-planned" was, the pilot answered, "*All* our strikes are *planned*. We *have* no *unplanned* strikes."

At the Danang airbase, I received a briefing from a major on the role of FAC pilots in I Corps. When I asked what kinds of targets were usually hit by pre-planned strikes, he answered, "In the mountains, just about anything that moves is considered to be V.C. We've cleared most of the people out of there, and anything that's left has got to be V.C. No one else has got any reason to be there. We go after enemy base areas and V.C. r.-and-r. centers." The Army refers to the overnight way stations where Vietcong soldiers are believed to sleep as "r.-and-r. centers," after the Army's own practice of sending its troops for one week of "rest and relaxation" each year in a foreign capital, like Bangkok, Tokyo, or Sydney. "Most of the action is in the lowlands," the major continued. "There we hit mostly the bunkers and fortifications. The V.C. hide in there, and store their supplies in there, too. Of course, we can never hit *all* the bunkers. Also, we hit fortified villages. In some of these villages, the lines of trenches and bunkers are amazing. It looks like World

War I. These fortified villages are all known to be enemy installations. I mean, they've been shooting at people and harboring the V.C. But before we hit any place we send a Psy War craft in to warn the villagers to escape. We used to drop warning leaflets, but they didn't do much good, so now we've switched over to announcing. We give the people at least a good ten or fifteen minutes to get out of there before we put in a strike. But it's the immediate strike that gives the best results. That's where you get your K.B.A.s." The initials stand for "Killed by Air." "Of course," the major added, "enemy troops in the open are the kind of target that we all like the best."

I asked him what was involved in getting clearance for an air strike.

"First, we check the area for friendly troops, and then, when the request goes in to DASC, the province chief has to give his O.K.," he said. "We *never* put in a strike without first getting permission from the province chief. He's a Vietnamese, and he knows the local conditions, so he's the man in the final analysis who knows who's friendly and who's unfriendly. And, after all, it's their country, so they ought to know what's going on." (Later, I asked Province Chief Hoang Dinh Tho, of Quang Tin Province, about the specific steps that were usually taken in securing his clearance, and learned that at the beginning of each operation in his province he designated certain regions—typically, those surrounding district capitals—as no-strike zones, and gave the ground commanders of the operation a free hand in deciding which targets to bomb in the rest of the area of operation.)

The major explained that the Vietnam Air Force (or VNAF, pronounced "Veenaf" by the Americans) had its own organization, separate from the United States Air Force but flying out of the same bases. VNAF supported

ARVN with A-1 propeller-driven fighter-bombers—a type of plane that was last used by our Navy in the Korean war. "VNAF has its own FACS," the major told me. "They work just the way we do. One-half of the base is for VNAF and one-half for us."

I asked what VNAF FACS did, mostly.

"VNAF FACS usually cover convoys," the major replied. "They're pretty much tied up with that. But it's a very necessary function—to cover those convoys. VNAF uses one side of Danang. We built the facilities just the same as the American facilities, but separate. But they don't know how to take care of something nice. You go over there now, and it's a stinking mess. You know what one of the first things they did was? They unscrewed the taps and spigots in the bathrooms and took them into town and sold them."

I asked whether American FACS guided the VNAF fighter-bombers to their targets.

"Those old A-1s that VNAF uses are a lot slower than our planes, and more accurate, so they don't use any FACS for that," the major answered.

I learned that ideas for targets of the American fighter-bombers were gathered mainly from the recommendations of ground commanders, FAC pilots, and "agent reports"— the name given to most other sources of information. Occasionally, a province chief would order a town burned or bombed. All targets were described to DASC in terms of their coördinates on a military map, and DASC would relay these coördinates to the FAC pilot who was guiding the air strike. The FAC pilot would locate the target point on a similar map that he carried with him in the plane. The maps were crosshatched by a grid. The horizontal lines, spaced two centimetres apart, were numbered from 01 to 99, and the vertical lines were similarly spaced and numbered. Each square formed by the lines represented one square kilometre on the ground. The coördinates were given in six figures divided into two groups of three—691 873, for example. The first two digits of the first group of three designated a vertical line, and the first two digits of the second group of three designated a horizontal line. The third digit of the first group indicated a distance, in hundreds of metres, east of the vertical line on the map, and the third digit of the second group indicated a distance, in hundreds of metres, north of the horizontal line. However, the hundred-metre intervals were not drawn on the map, so the pilot had to estimate for himself what one hundred, or three hundred, metres along the lines amounted to. And even if the pilot estimated accurately, the smallest area that could be designated by this system was a hundred metres square. (Everything within the hundred-metre square northeast of the coördinates 691 873 was designated by those coördinates.) On about half the missions, DASC would give the FAC pilot a description of the type of target that was to be located in the hundred-metre-square area designated by the coördinates. Some of the official descriptions, such as "bunkers," "military structures," and "enemy hamlet," referred to targets that could sometimes be spotted from the air, but other descriptions, such as "V.C. r.-and-r. area," "suspected enemy troop concentration," and "infiltration route" did not, and in these cases the pilot had to rely entirely on his coördinates. Once the pilot had found the target area on his map, he would plot its position on the ground by using as reference points prominent topographical features that showed on his map; in the mountains he would use the configurations of the ridgelines as reference points, and in the flatlands he would use rivers, roads, and villages. After finding the target on the ground, he would relay the coördinates by radio to the fighter-bombers when they came overhead.

Just before the strike, he would "mark" the target by hitting it with a phosphorus rocket, which sends up a highly visible cloud of white smoke and also splashes burning phosphorus over a twenty-yard area. Then, using the smoke as a guide, the fighter-bombers would fly over the target, dropping their bombs or cans of napalm, or hitting it with rockets or strafing fire. The FAC plane meanwhile circled slowly nearby, watching the strike and telling the pilots of the fighter-bombers by radio how far from the target they were hitting. Usually, there were two or three fighter-bomber planes on a mission, and each plane flew two or three passes, depending on what armament it was carrying. When the strike was completed, the FAC pilot would fly over the area again and make a Bomb Damage Assessment Report—usually called the B.D.A. Report—to DASC and to the fighter-bomber pilots. The B.D.A. Report included the percentage of "Bombs on Target" and the percentage of "Target Destroyed." The pilot would also report any "Military Structures Destroyed." When there were friendly ground troops in the area near the target, the ground commander would radio the coördinates of their position to the FAC pilot, who would relay the information to the pilots of the fighter-bombers. The FAC pilot would make contact with the commanders of nearby artillery batteries, too, to check the trajectory of artillery shells being fired at that moment, so that he would be able to avoid them. A FAC pilot told me that one in twenty FAC pilots was killed during 1966, but he explained that he and his fellow-pilots felt less fear than many G.I.s on the ground who had a smaller chance of being hit. In the air, you didn't know when you were being shot at until a bullet came very close to the plane, or actually hit it, the pilot said, and he described a bullet passing close by as making a snapping sound, "like someone closing an ashtray in the back seat of your car." The fighter-bomber pilots made no decisions about targets themselves. A fighter-bomber pilot who was based at Danang told me, "We are going four or five hundred knots, and we can't see much ourselves. I've never seen a body or a person yet, and I've been on over a hundred missions. It's virtually impossible to see any movement on the ground. The FAC is the expert. We're only experts on delivery."

In August, there were six FAC pilots detailed to the 1st Brigade of the 101st Airborne Division. During Operations Malheur I and Malheur II, they had flown out of Duc Pho, but as the brigade moved north for Operation Hood River and Operation Benton, the FAC pilots shifted their base of operation north to Chu Lai. While the brigade was conducting an operation, the FAC pilots always kept one plane aloft over the area of operation during daylight hours. Each pilot usually flew a three-hour shift each day, though occasionally, when an emergency called for it, each would fly a six-hour shift. From August 10th to August 21st, I flew with the FAC pilots attached to the 1st of the 101st almost daily, lived with them in their quarters, and ate my meals with them on the base.

On August 10th, the next-to-last day of Operation Hood River, I flew in the early morning with a FAC pilot from Texas who had a thin face and a slight frame and was about thirty years old. I shall call him Captain Reese. The standard FAC plane was a Cessna O-1 Bird Dog. It seated two, one in front and one in back; had a single propeller; and was armed with four tubes containing phosphorus rockets, two tubes being mounted under each wing. It could fly as slowly as forty miles an hour, and could hold an extremely tight corkscrew turn when the pilot wanted to look at one small area of ground for a sustained period.

Before climbing into the plane, Captain Reese picked up a flak vest, a helmet, a submachine gun, and a survival kit, the last two for use in case the plane was hit and had to make a forced landing. On the flight line, where the planes sat enclosed by steel walls to protect them from shrapnel in mortar or rocket attacks, three young mechanics lounged shirtless in the heat, waiting to refuel O-1 planes or repair their engines. Although it was against the rules, the pilots occasionally let the mechanics climb into the pilot's seat and taxi the planes across the fifty-yard stretch of asphalt between the fuel pump and the protective walls.

Just before our plane went out on the runway, one of the mechanics, who was pulling safety rods from the rocket tubes on the wings, asked Captain Reese, "You gonna get any of 'em today, Captain?"

"I dunno," answered Captain Reese.

The mechanics often asked the pilots about their missions, but they rarely got answers any more revealing than this. During most of the day, the mechanics sat on wooden boxes around a soft-drink cooler that was protected by a canvas roof, and read back issues of *Stars and Stripes,* or looked for the hundredth time through a few thumb-greased copies of *Sir!* and *Escapade* magazines. Beyond their little spot of shade stretched a landscape of hot asphalt, shimmering corrugated metal, and airplanes. Part of their job was to assemble phosphorus rockets and load them under the wings of the FAC planes. The rockets were about a yard long and came in three pieces, which the mechanics had to screw together. I once asked a mechanic who had just dumped a case of four rockets on the asphalt whether a rocket would explode if he tossed it up in the air and let it fall onto the runway. He picked up a front section, which was marked "Warhead," and, dangling it about five feet off the ground, said, "It would go off if I dropped it from here. If it gets on you, it'll burn right through you for days and it won't go out with just water. You have to put it out with a special chemical we've got over there in the shed." The mechanics did not learn about any military operation that the FAC planes supported until four or five days after it had been launched, when a copy of the Task Force Oregon mimeographed *News Sheet* might reach them, and they could read, for example, "The infantry units mounted a three-pronged attack, and in the ensuing ground action tallied 44 enemy killed, bringing the body count to 65 for the action north of Duc Pho," or "Two Chinese mines were discovered by the airborne-infantrymen as they searched for the enemy in heavy jungle west of Quang Ngai City. One detainee, suffering a bullet wound in the back, was turned over to authorities. The paratroopers captured three enemy weapons and one and one-half tons of rice." Every once in a while, one of the mechanics would get a word or two out of a FAC pilot about a current operation, and he would relay the information to the other mechanics with studied nonchalance, as though he always had an inside line on what was going on. But usually the mechanics just fuelled the planes, watched them disappear in the sky, read old magazines, and listened to the day-long thunder of bombs on the other side of the mountains.

When Captain Reese and I had strapped ourselves into our seats, a young mechanic waved us forward onto a siding of the runway. Captain Reese had to wait for an F-4 fighter-bomber to take off ahead of us. The F-4 was mottled with green and brown camouflage paint and had a heavy, sharklike body with stubby wings, downward-slanting tail fins, and a drooping black nose, which was just rising off the runway as the plane crossed our bow. For a few seconds, the deep roaring of its engine filled one's head completely, overpowering thought. In a quarter of a minute, the orange-tipped blue flames of its afterburners were vanishing in the distance as it rose at a steady steep angle.

Captain Reese taxied onto the runway, and our small plane lifted off the asphalt after running only a hundred yards or so down the runway, which was two miles long and stretched out of sight in front of us like a turnpike in a desert. As soon as the plane was off the ground, Captain Reese turned southwest and started a climb to fifteen hundred feet. According to regulations, the FAC pilots were not supposed to fly below that altitude, but almost all of them frequently broke this rule, and sometimes they went down as low as a hundred feet. ("As soon as I heard that rule, I knew that it was one of the rules made to break," a FAC pilot once said to me. "You can't even see people from one thousand feet. You can't see anything unless you go down there.") Captain Reese guided the O-1 over the brown, abandoned rice fields and blackened ruins of the villages in the western part of Son Tinh District. There was a heavy, high gray overcast.

Using a headset and a microphone wired for the back seat, I asked Captain Reese what types of target were most common and what the targets of the present mission were.

Speaking through a microphone the size of a lima bean that reached around on a small metal arm from the side of his helmet almost into his mouth, Captain Reese answered, "Oh, usually we get a V.C. base camp, burn off a village, or hit a supply depot. Today, we're going to hit a suspected enemy troop concentration at 324 733." (All figures given for coördinates in this account have been changed.)

I asked how it had been decided to bomb this target.

"I don't know. An agent reported it, or something, I guess," he said.

We crossed a small ridge of hills and came out over the Song Tra Khuc Valley. The cultivated fields were pale green, and the forests on the mountain slopes were a vivid deep green under a sky that was darkening before rain. Several miles to the west, where the valley vanished into the mountains, curved plumes of rain trailed down from the cloud cover, and to the east more plumes of rain descended into the sea. The air below the clouds seemed oddly clear, and tall, bluish mountains were visible far to the west, above the delicate ridges of nearer, smaller mountains. The line between the sea and the sky was lost in a uniform grayness, and a large blue island, clearly visible twenty or more kilometres offshore, seemed to be floating in the sky. The tops of four or five of the low mountains on the north and south sides of the valley were bald and blackened. Captain Reese explained that intensive bombing and machine-gun fire were usually directed at hilltops—often starting forest fires—in order to kill anyone there before our troops made a landing. In the valley, the cultivated fields were marked with craters of all sizes. Five or six thin, straight columns of smoke rose from the valley floor. "They're burning off some hootches. This is a solid V.C. area," Captain Reese told me. He circled lower, for a closer look. In that part of the valley, widely separated clusters of houses stood along a line of trees bordering a small stream. Troops were advancing across a rice field and entering a courtyard that was surrounded by three houses. A minute later, as they reappeared in a field on the other side of the yard, a spot of flame began to spread on the roof of one house, then on the roof of another, and soon all three roofs were collapsing in flames. Captain Reese brought the plane back to fifteen hundred feet and headed southwest again, toward his target area. Below us, the gray squares of freshly burned houses dotted the ground. Arriving over the target area, Captain Reese found that the hundred-metre square designated by the coördinates included a wooded ridge and a small ravine lying halfway up a mountain about three thousand feet high. The side of the ravine across from the ridge was lined with rows of crops stretching up the steep mountain slope.

"They want us to hit that ravine," Captain Reese said. "That's the target."

At eight-forty-five, the flight commander of three F-4 fighter-bombers radioed to say that they had arrived over the general area.

"Tell me what ordnance you've got, and all that jazz," the Captain said.

"We've got six napes, six seven-hundred-and-fifty-pounders, and six two-hundred-and-fifty pounders. Can you use it?" the flight commander answered.

"We can use all that. I'll mark the target for you," the Captain replied.

Throughout most of the strike, the pilots communicated in relaxed, genial voices and with a perfectly flat intonation, which came across the headsets with a nasal, buzzing quality, perhaps because the pilots placed their lips against the tiny microphones as they talked. Captain Reese spotted the three F-4s through the clear roof of the cockpit as they cut under the clouds above us. Wheeling his plane over the target, he went into a sharp dive, and threw a switch to fire a phosphorus rocket from a tube under his wing. The rocket did not fire. "Damn. Won't fire today," he said. He banked around again, brought the plane into another dive, and threw another switch. Once more, the rocket failed to fire. On his next pass, he dropped a smoke grenade by hand out the window, and it failed to explode. He dropped three more grenades in succeeding passes, and these, too, were duds. The fifth grenade trailed a thin line of smoke from the plane down to the top of the ridge, and a large puff of white smoke soon appeared over the trees. "I want it right down in that valley. You can come in from the east and break west," Captain Reese told the flight commander, and then he began to fly in a tight circle a few hundred yards from the target. As the O-1 was closing its second full circle, he lined up the first fighter-bomber in his front windshield, and he held it in view while it went into a low dive over the cleft. The bombs travelled diagonally earthward and landed on the wooded ridge. A visible shock wave sprang outward from the point of impact, and a cloud of brown smoke shot up several hundred feet above the woods. The fighter-bomber pulled up at a sharp angle, presenting its belly, with the bombs grouped under its stubby wings, to our view. "Real fine!" exclaimed the Captain. "That's right in there! Next time, try to get it fifty metres south, down in the valley." The next plane, diving from the same angle, landed its bombs farther up the ridge. "That's real fine," said the Captain. The third plane sent two silver canisters of napalm toppling down, end over end, and they also landed on the wooded ridge. A pillar of black smoke, with a thick column of orange fire boiling briefly at its core, puffed up over the trees, and red globs of burning jelly splashed outward over the jungle. The next two loads were also napalm, and they also hit the top of the ridge. After the third napalm strike, the flight commander asked, "Do you want it down pretty much in the ravine?" and Captain Reese answered, "Yes, right down there in the ravine." The next three passes put bombs in the ravine, filling it with brown smoke. With that, the strike was over, and the Captain flew back across the target area. Large brown holes had been opened up in the woods, with blasted trees lying in pieces around the edges. Globs of napalm still burned in patches on the ground and in tree branches. At the bottom of the ravine, two bombs had landed directly on a tumbling stream. Above the trees, a flock of birds flying in tight formation wheeled swiftly in circles. One bomb had landed on the cultivated side of the ravine. "I don't see anything," the Captain observed to me, in a tired voice. Then, to the flight commander, he reported, "A hundred per cent of Bombs on Target. Fifty-per-cent Target Coverage. Thank you very much, sir. I've never marked this area before, and I don't seem to mark it very well."

"Not at all," answered the flight commander. Throughout this strike, as in most of the strikes I accompanied, the FAC pilot and the flight commander addressed each other in polite, almost humble tones.

I asked the Captain who had cultivated the fields.

"That's just Montagnard farming. You'd be amazed at the places they farm," he said.

Captain Reese headed the plane back eastward over the Song Tra Khuc Valley. The line of smoking houses along the river was now a kilometre long, and led away from the river into the fields, where two flaming houses marked the troops' advance units. Since the Captain had no further need to talk with the flight commander, he listened in on fragments of conversations on the ground. Communications between ground units crackled into our ears between bursts of static.

"We've captured one Charlie, but we haven't interrogated him yet," said a voice.

"Did he have a weapon?" asked another.

"He had on the black pajamas, short type, but he didn't have a weapon," the first voice replied. "Most likely he hid it somewhere. We found him four hundred metres south of where we were last night."

To me, the Captain said, "Yesterday, five of them ran

into a hole, and came out shooting, and got killed. All the villages around here have foxholes and bunkers under them. This place is almost entirely V.C.-controlled, or pro-V.C."

I asked whether the bunkers did not also serve as bomb shelters for the general populace.

"No," he said. "The V.C. build them—or force the people to build them—strictly for the V.C.'s own protection."

Below us, the lines of smoke from the burning houses had mingled to form a thin haze, which drifted eastward down the valley. DASC at Chu Lai radioed to say that the fighter-bombers assigned to the second target had been diverted to a more urgent mission and would not be coming.

"Well, we'll have to hit it tomorrow, or something," Captain Reese remarked to me.

I took advantage of the lull to ask him about the bombing policy—that is, the policy on the bombing of villages—that he, as a FAC pilot, helped carry out.

"We've got two kinds of strikes—pre-planned and immediate," he answered. "The pre-planned strikes are when we say, 'O.K., you people have been bad now for two or three months, and we haven't been able to talk you into being good, so we're going to wipe you out. You've got twenty-four hours to get out.' Usually, we give them twenty-four hours. That's the pre-planned. Then there's the immediate strike. Now, when there's an Army unit near the village, and they get fire from the village, they say, 'O.K., you people quit shooting or we're going to hit you now—right now.' Of course, that would be in a case where almost everyone in the village is pro-V.C. Technically, the village doesn't have to be warned of a strike when we are flying in conjunction with an operation, like we are now."

While we were talking, we had reached the entrance of the valley, where the river flowed out onto the coastal plain. Here, also, smoke was rising from a roadside, and houses were aflame. The lines of smoke were spreading westward, toward the troops of the 1st Brigade of the 101st, who were moving eastward as they burned more houses. "Those guys down there burning off those hootches are Civilian Irregular Defense Forces," Captain Reese said. "They're Montagnards trained by the Special Forces."

A single main road ran the length of the valley, following the meanderings of the river. Between the villages being burned by the Civilian Irregular Defense Forces and the villages being burned by the 1st Brigade, the road was crowded with cattle and with people carrying double loads on shoulder poles. Near the road, a Special Forces camp had been dug into the bald summit of a round hill that stood alone on the valley floor, overlooking a large village where houses were jammed together inside a small fortified square. Captain Reese said he thought that the village was probably a "new-life" hamlet and would be spared destruction.

As we turned westward again, I asked him about his aerial-reconnaissance duties, and how he distinguished houses and trails used by the enemy from those used only by civilians.

"You look for changes—something that's different," he said. "Normally, you're at fifteen hundred feet, searching for trails and tree lines, and looking for hootches. It's almost a fact that anything out in the open is friendly, so anything you see in the trees you suspect is unfriendly, because it might be V.C. We report hootches that are hidden in tree lines."

I pointed out that, except in the "new-life" hamlets, almost all the houses were built in the shade of tree lines.

"Yeah, they'll be built in the tree lines," he said. "But out in the sticks, if you spot a hootch with no fields around, it's probably V.C. Maybe a rice-storage house."

I asked who lived in the mountains.

"Just the Montagnards and a lot of Vietnamese," he said. "They've taken most of the people out of the mountains, so nobody has any business being here except the V.C. Even the Montagnards here are kind of coöperating with the V.C. We watch for trails up in the mountains, too."

I had noticed that many of the hilltops were cultivated and that most of these were laced with webs of foot trails, and I inquired about the trails.

"I'll look real close at the trails," the Captain said. "If someone walks through one, the grass gets bent."

I asked whether he could spot freshly bent grass from his airplane.

"Oh, yeah, you can tell," he said.

DASC called again, to say that a flight of two fighter-bombers had not expended all its bombs in a previous strike and had been looking for a target for the rest, so DASC had suggested Captain Reese's second target.

To get to the second target, we headed south and crossed a thousand-foot ridge into a small, high abandoned valley, where the rice fields—thickly terraced ones—had already gone wild and the house foundations were half overgrown. Four straight, mile-long avenues of craters from B-52 strikes crisscrossed the valley. The path of craters from one strike began on the ridge on the north side of the valley and marched across the fields and a stream, straight up the southern hillside, and out of sight beyond. The coördinates described a hundred-metre square in a wide stretch of woods on the southern hillside. "We're going to hit a place the troops were in a week ago," Captain Reese said.

"They found some hootches and burned them off. Then, yesterday morning, a FAC pilot spotted some smoke comin' out of there. There wasn't supposed to be any smoke comin' out of there, so we're going to hit it today." Then, looking at his control panel, he exclaimed, "Hell, I forgot to pull the safety switch on the rockets! *That's* why they wouldn't fire." He went on, "You can see that they've hit this target before." He indicated scores of bomb craters and irregular splashes of brown and black from napalm strikes that scarred the woods in the target area. "It's a V.C. base area," he said. "It's got a number. All the base areas have got numbers."

The fighter-bombers for the second strike arrived over the valley and radioed that, all told, they were carrying six five-hundred-pound bombs and four tubes of rockets, with nineteen to a tube. Captain Reese brought the O-1 into a dive, and there was a sharp metallic explosion as a phosphorus rocket fired off our right wing. This was followed by the appearance of a pillar of white smoke rising from the woods. The Captain instructed the flight commander that the F-4s should land their bombs forty metres west of the smoke. Two bombs sent down in the first pass hit a hundred metres east of the smoke. The bombs sent down in the second pass landed fifty metres east, and in the third, and final, bombing pass the bombs landed within thirty metres of the white smoke. The strike continued with four volleys of rockets. Each volley spread over sixty or seventy metres of the woods, sending up puffs of brown smoke, and the rockets were all on the target or within thirty metres of it. Afterward, Captain Reese guided the O-1 into a descending tight spiral over the bomb craters to observe the damage. At the edge of one hole in the woods he saw a pile of debris that he judged to be the remains of a hut, and in his Bomb Damage Assessment Report he mentioned one

"Military Structure Destroyed." At eleven o'clock, he headed our plane back to Chu Lai.

The Chu Lai base had expanded steadily since it was founded, in 1965, and by August of 1967 it was about ten miles long and five miles wide, and occupied what must be one of the world's most beautiful stretches of coastline. A wide beach of pure-white sand runs the length of the base in a gently curving crescent, and the water of the South China Sea is a bluish green, even on cloudy days. Along parts of the shore, a warm surf rolls evenly toward the beach across long sandbars; a mountain island lies off the coast. The area occupied by the base had once been heavily populated. A three-mile-long hilly promontory forming the northern tip of the base had been the site of a dense conglomeration of fishing villages. As the base expanded, leaflets were dropped on these villages announcing that they were going to be destroyed in order to make room for the base. (In the catalogue of leaflets used by the Marines and Task Force Oregon I saw several leaflets of this kind.) The people were evacuated, the villages were bulldozed away, and the Americans laid out their installations on the stretch of bare earth.

Upon landing, Captain Reese started back to head-quarters in a jeep. The twenty-minute drive from the FAC flight line to the Task Force Oregon headquarters led through several miles of bulldozed fields of sand and dirt dotted with warehouses, munitions dumps, and repair sheds, and then ran along the beach for a mile or so. The sky was still overcast, and the beach was empty. Beer cans were strewn on the sand around simple canvas roofs on pole frames, which served as canopies for evening cook-outs. (When the sun was out, the waves were usually dotted with heads and with men riding the surf on air mattresses, and the beach was usually covered with suntanned soldiers in bright-colored boxer-style bathing trunks.) Beyond the beach, the road continued up a hill and out onto the rocky promontory at the northern tip of the base. At the top of the promontory, Captain Reese turned right and drove into the command complex of Task Force Oregon. In the center of a dirt parade ground that was surrounded by low, tin-roofed barracks, the American flag and the South Vietnamese flag (three horizontal red stripes on a yellow ground) flew at exactly the same height on two flagpoles standing side by side. Two gaily painted Buddhist shrines, each about ten feet tall and adorned with Chinese characters, also stood on the parade ground. These were the only traces of the Vietnamese villages that had once stood on the site of the base.

Captain Reese had a light lunch and then went to his quarters for a long nap. At just about any time of day after eleven in the morning, two or three of the six pilots could be found sprawled on their beds, asleep in the breeze of an electric fan. The pilots took turns standing by at a central control desk, which was in one of the barracks on the parade ground. It was in constant communication with DASC and with the FAC pilot who was aloft. Although the FAC pilots almost never flew after dark, one of their number helped supervise, from the central control desk, any bombings carried out at night, and coördinated night flights of AC-47s (this was the military version of the DC-3, and was nicknamed Spooky) that supported troops on the ground with heavy fire. On nights when the fighting on the ground was particularly intense, a pilot would have to stay up all night at the control desk and sleep the next day.

Except when the FAC pilots were flying missions, they lived entirely within the confines of their base. It would have been perfectly possible for any one of them to pass his entire one-year tour of duty in Vietnam without ever talking to a Vietnamese or setting foot inside a Vietnamese village or city other than Saigon. Except for their r.-and-r. trips to foreign cities, and occasional expeditions in the FAC planes to the Danang airbase to buy beer and soft drinks, on what they called "the soda-pop run," the pilots' daily lives revolved solely around their missions, their quarters, the central control desk, and the dining halls, bars, and movie theatres in the officers' clubs. The FAC pilots' quarters, which they called the Hootch, consisted of one of the several rows of tin-roofed barracks, which had mosquito netting serving as the upper half of the walls. The barracks was partitioned into three rooms, containing four beds each, and the beds were separated by tall metal clothes cabinets. Most of the pilots had decorated their walls with *Playboy* Playmates of the Month. On the wall next to one major's bed, Miss May of 1967, who is shown standing on a sun deck with her pink shirt open, dwarfed a dozen small snapshots of the major's wife, in one of which she was standing, arms akimbo, in a bathing suit on a beach, and of his eight-year-old son, shown standing beside a lake and holding a small fish up to the camera. On the major's desk were a can of spray insecticide, a Reader's Digest volume of condensed books (featuring President Eisenhower's book "At Ease," which is subtitled "Stories I Tell to Friends"), a can of Pepsi-Cola, a softball, a dozen loose bullets, and a life-size wooden carving of a fist with the middle finger upraised. The Vietnamese do not use the gesture of raising the middle finger, and this kind of sculpture had been developed especially for American soldiers looking for souvenirs of Vietnam. Sometimes the younger pilots played darts on a board that hung on one door, and they also occasionally played Monopoly. A refrigerator was kept stocked with beer and soft drinks.

Because of the heat, most of the pilots had at least two beers or soft drinks a day. Each was on his honor to put fifteen cents in a common refreshment fund in a box in the back of the refrigerator every time he took a drink, but someone who, it seemed, had not been wholly able to put his trust in an honor system had halfheartedly attempted to revise it by taping to the front of the refrigerator door a sheet of paper with everyone's name on it, on which each person was supposed to mark down the number of drinks he had taken and the number he had paid for.

Around the central control desk, and in other places where the pilots gathered, an atmosphere of perpetual low-keyed, comradely humor prevailed. There was a steady stream of light remarks. One man who was standing idly around said to another, with weary joviality, "It's a beautiful, beautiful war!" The second man said, "It's the only one we've got." A FAC pilot entered a room full of FAC pilots and said, "Here are our hard-working FAC pilots," in a tone that indicated neither that they were hard-working nor that they weren't. In this way, the FAC pilots rarely talked about the war directly, and yet never quite got away from the subject, either. The relaxed style of their humor was, I thought, caught quite precisely in their choice as their squadron's emblem of Charles Schulz's comic-strip dog Snoopy, who daydreams of fame as a First World War flying ace. On the outside of the door of the central-control-desk office, Snoopy was depicted, in a sketch, wearing goggles and a scarf that trailed out behind him as he went into a dive in a First World War Sopwith Camel biplane. Cartoon bombs exploded below him. (On a wall of the Duc Pho central-control-desk office, there was a large painting of Snoopy accompanied by a speech balloon that had him saying "Curse you, Charlie Cong!" The Task Force Oregon *News Sheet* reproduced one episode about

Snoopy in each of its issues, and the pilots of the 20th
Tactical Air Support Squadron in Danang carried calling
cards that depicted Snoopy in his biplane firing a machine
gun. On a wall of the squadron's office was a large color
poster that bore a reproduction of a painting of an American pilot walking sadly through a prisoner-of-war camp. A
vow not to give the enemy any information that was not
required by international law was printed below the picture. The pilots, who flew regularly over North Vietnam,
had pencilled a beard and mustache on the grave, pious,
spotlighted face of the captured American.)

At the Chu Lai officers' club for Task Force Oregon,
drinks were twenty cents each, and the pilots usually had
three or four rounds each evening before supper. One
pilot observed, "At these prices, you can't afford *not* to
drink." On the evening of August 10th, the FAC pilots
drove to the Marine dining hall, which was a favorite of
theirs among the base's many dining halls. Ham, chops,
steak, and chicken were served there. They were all prepared in the dependably appetizing style of an excellent
truckers' diner on a big American highway, and you could
have as much as you could eat. Some Korean officers sat
grouped together at several tables. Most of them were
enjoying the Korean version of r. and r.—a visit to an
American base like Chu Lai, where they were allowed to
eat in the American mess halls, shop in the American PX,
and swim on the safe stretch of beach occupied by the base.
Conversation at dinner usually revolved around matters
having to do with the flying life. Often, the pilots discussed
the day's events, sometimes criticizing or praising the accuracy of certain missions of fighter-bombers. They stuck
fairly closely to day-to-day events and to the technical
problems of bombing missions, such as what altitude is
best to bomb from and how to tell if a bomb is "hung" on

the wing after the bomb release has been triggered. This evening, they discussed an incident in which a pilot had spotted a man on the ground, had judged him to be a Vietcong soldier when he attempted to escape observation by running into a grove of trees, and had called in planes to bomb the trees. This incident, which in itself was quite ordinary, had one unusual aspect: the FAC pilot had been flying outside his assigned area, and the bombs had only just missed some American troops nearby.

Another pilot said that he, too, had spotted a Vietcong soldier and had later guided an air strike onto the woods the man had disappeared into.

I asked him how he had been able to tell that the man was a Vietcong soldier.

"Well, he walked real proud, with a kind of bounce in his gait, like a soldier, instead of just shuffling along, like the farmers do," the pilot answered.

During my stay with the FAC pilots, they never discussed the progress of the war as a whole, nor did they ever express any hatred for the enemy. They talked a lot about pensions and salaries, they complained about the administrative sloppiness of the promotion procedures, and they discussed the advantages of various cities for r.-and-r. tours (Thai women had good figures; Hong Kong had good cheap clothes, hi-fi equipment, and cameras). The pilots laughed when they read in the *News Sheet* that lectures on venereal diseases, and how to tell if you had any of them, were going to be given to the men just before they went on r.-and-r. tours. The armed services displayed a completely tolerant attitude toward the soldiers' patronage of brothels in Vietnam and in the Asian cities used for r.-and-r. tours. In Hong Kong, until very recently, the Army employed a prostitute of mixed Chinese and Portuguese parentage, who spoke understandable English, to brief the soldiers on how to pick up prostitutes among the city's bar girls without getting into fights or getting fleeced. The briefing was intended to minimize the ugly incidents that occur when a soldier is overcharged or misunderstands a girl's intentions. The pilots talked a great deal about the living conditions and the food on other bases. Once, at dinner, Captain Reese got into a long discussion about food with another pilot, and as he ate a plateful of ham, he gave a detailed description of a chicken dinner he had eaten at the Duc Pho base. Then, beginning on a piece of cake, he described to me the breakfast at the Marine dining hall in which he was eating at that moment. "They have terrific breakfasts here," he said. "Every day, they have eggs, bacon, pancakes with butter and maple syrup, toast, milk, raspberry jam, grapefruit juice, coffee, and tea—the works. Real fine breakfast."

Although the pilots never spoke angrily of the Vietcong, they often spoke disparagingly of the Army, compared to the Air Force; they called Army men "grunts." Their feeling about the Army seemed very much like one ball club's or college fraternity's feeling about a rival, but occasionally they expressed a bitterness that went beyond such friendly rivalry. One pilot told me, "The Army guys sometimes don't care what you have to do, so long as they get an air strike. But I'm not going to send men on an impossible mission to get killed like that. I'm responsible to the Air Force, too, and I've got to think of Air Force safety. Sometimes it's kind of hard, because you have to look a general in the eye and say, 'No, sir, I can't do that.' " I was surprised at the intensity of the rivalry not only between the services but between units in the same service. The men of the 1st Brigade of the 101st Airborne, who were extremely proud of their paratrooper training, referred contemptuously to all infantrymen as "legs."

Once, when I was driving inside the Chu Lai base on a cruelly hot afternoon with a paratrooper of the 101st, he refused to pick up a hitchhiking soldier, on the ground that the soldier was a "leg," and "no leg is worth picking up." High officers of the 101st and the 3rd of the 4th maligned each other, in my presence, by claiming that the other brigade's body count was falsified. "The 3rd of the 4th count the probables in their body count," an officer of the 101st told me. "We don't deal with probables. We only deal with confirmed kills counted by sight. That's the only way." On another occasion, an officer of the 3rd of the 4th made the same charge about the 101st, and added that the 101st's "weapons-kill ratio" was much worse than the 3rd of the 4th's, the implication being that the 101st was far less discriminating than the 3rd of the 4th when it came to deciding whom to kill. Men of both the Army and the Air Force made derogatory remarks about the Marines. One soldier of the 101st told me that the Marines were "no different from the Vietcong" in their handling of prisoners. I asked if he meant that they beat the prisoners. "Hell, *we* work 'em over before we talk to 'em," the soldier said. "The Marines are a lot worse than that. They're just like the V.C."

After dinner that evening, the pilots had a choice of two movies, one at an outdoor theatre on the beach near the Marine dining hall and the other up at the Task Force Oregon officers' club. The officers' club stood on the crest of a five-hundred-foot hill, overlooking a brushy meadow that swept down to the sea. A number of tables with chairs were arranged in a large, three-walled room under a broad, barnlike palm-leaf roof; the front was open to the ocean. In back, there was a long bar with a television set at one end, swivelling barstools, a dart board, and bartenders who wore gaudy Hawaiian shirts. Movies were shown in front.

The club commanded a view of the entire twenty-kilo-
metre crescent of beach. Even on the hottest, stillest day, a
fresh breeze blew in off the water. At night, out on the
ocean, the lamps that all local fishing boats were required
to keep burning after dark glowed from miles away. On
most evenings, the booming of artillery and bombing
sounded steadily, sometimes lighting up the night sky
down the coast. During some operations, flares, which are
fired by artillery or dropped from planes, and descend
slowly on parachutes, seemed to be hanging over the
mountains throughout the night. Two hundred yards from
the club, the helicopter landing pad for the base hospital
sat on a high ridge, from which there was a sharp drop to
the sea. Several times each day, a helicopter would fly up
the coast at full speed and settle rapidly onto the asphalt,
which was in full view of the front of the officers' club and
looked from there like a small black stage. Two figures
would run up to the helicopter and then run back to the
hospital, bearing a man on a stretcher. If the cloth over the
man covered him only up to his shoulders, the man was
wounded, but if the cloth covered his face the man had
died. Inside the club, the hospital landing pad was visible
only from a few front tables, and most of the officers did
not notice when a helicopter arrived, but when the officers
were standing in front of the club at their weekly outdoor
barbecue, tending their steaks in the charcoal pits, the
arrival of a helicopter at the hospital caused a brief
slackening in the din of conversation as the officers looked
up from their drinks and steaks to watch the two figures
bearing a wounded or dead man into the hospital.

Once every few weeks, on nights that did not precede
military operations or important pre-planned strikes, some
of the FAC pilots, I was told, would get together to get
drunk. One evening, Captain Reese and two other pilots,

whom I will call Major Nugent and Captain Leroy, returned to the FAC pilots' quarters from the officers' club
talking in booming voices and laughing loudly at everything any of them said. Major Nugent had apparently half-
seriously yielded to an Army officer's urging that he enter
airborne training school, and Captain Reese was snicker-
ing and teasing him about it. "Why would anyone want to
jump out of a perfectly good airplane? You must be out of
your gourd!" he exclaimed seven or eight times, provoking
a more uproarious laugh with each repetition. His idea
that you should stay in an airplane until it was shot down
reflected his loyalty to the Air Force and his contempt for
paratroopers. About midnight, when Captain Leroy was
on his way to bed, he tripped over someone's box of gear
and fell on the floor. Later that night, an unidentified
person threw a glass of water on another pilot as he slept.

On August 11th, the last
day of Operation Hood River, I flew on a FAC mission with
a pilot of about forty, whom I will call Major Billings.
Major Billings has slightly asymmetrical features, wide-
open, staring eyes, a somewhat hoarse voice, and a simple,
frank laugh from the belly which bursts forth suddenly on
one tone. He told me that he had flown in three wars and
had given up everything for the Air Force, including his
wife, who had divorced him because he was so rarely
stationed in the United States. He liked to tell the other
pilots, in his cheerful, straightforward manner, about his
problems with his girl friends back in the United States.
("They're all over fifty," he joked.) He told the other
pilots that he had been a Catholic until the Second World
War, but then had noticed that all the churchgoing pilots

seemed to be getting shot down, and had never gone to church since. He said that in civilian life he drove a sports car and always wore bright-red socks.

We took off in the early morning into a perfect blue sky. Major Billings had been assigned one pre-planned strike, and did not expect any immediate strikes to be called. Flying southwest from Chu Lai over the rubble and the abandoned fields that lay along the Song Tra Bong between Route 1 and the mountains, we soon reached the town of Tra Bong, which stood alone in the mountains, and then we turned south, crossed a ridge of mountains, and continued to a smaller ridge, which was indicated by the target coördinates. A few kilometres to the south of the target, in the valley of the Song Tra Khuc, Operation Hood River was coming to a close. To the north of the target, craters from a B-52 strike formed a line of yellow splashes on the flanks of many small, steep knobs and ridges in a high valley that looked from the air like a choppy sea. The top of the target ridge was covered for most of its length with fields cultivated by the Montagnards, but in one place, on top of a small cliff, there was a square patch of dense woods about two hundred yards on a side, and it was this that was the target. "A lot of Montagnard farming goes on up here," said Major Billings. "They grow rice and corn."

As we approached the wooded patch on the ridge, the Major pointed to a wisp of smoke that hung over the woods, and exclaimed, "Look at the smoke! See the smoke? That's Charlie having his breakfast!"

I asked him how he knew the smoke was from the fire of a Vietcong soldier.

"After a while, you get to know Charlie's habits," he said. "Now we'll leave the area, like we didn't know a thing. Even the Montagnards up here are under V.C.

control. We had troops in here a while ago, when Hood River began, but they've gone into the valley now. The Montagnards are a funny people. They live out in the open. Only the V.C. live under the trees. That whole hilltop is supposed to be a large base camp. I'll stay out of the area for an hour, until my flight comes in, so as not to arouse any undue activity on the V.C.'s part."

We turned north and began to circle over the town of Tra Bong. As we waited, a few snatches of conversation between ground units in the Song Tra Khuc Valley came over our radio. A voice said, "We were attacked by one Victor Charlie. He was an old guy, and he rushed our point man carrying a stick. The point man yelled at him to stop and then fired him up."

An answering voice laughed, and then said, "Sounds like a vicious attack," and laughed again.

The first voice said, "He seemed to be kind of doped up."

Major Billings remarked to me, "The V.C. often dope up their soldiers with marijuana before they go into a fight, so they won't be scared and will have good endurance. We've seen a lot of cases of that."

A minute later, a new voice on the ground said, "If you go much beyond that northernmost burning village, you'll be getting out of our area of operation."

"We picked up some weapons and a bunch of refugees," said another voice.

"We've captured two tons of rice," said yet another voice.

After we had circled for twenty minutes, three fighter-bombers reported their arrival in the area, and Major Billings immediately spotted them cutting across the sky above us. They reported that they were carrying, among them, six five-hundred-pound bombs and six canisters of napalm. Flying back to the target, Major Billings saw that the wisp of smoke was still hanging above the trees. "Oh, Daddy! This is the one I have been waiting for! They're *still* down here!" he exclaimed. Cutting back sharply, he bore down hard on the ridge, so that the woods filled the whole front windshield for five seconds or so, growing larger and larger. The rocket was fired off the wing with a loud explosion. Immediately, Major Billings pulled the craft's nose up sharply, thrusting both of us deep into our seats, and flew away from the ridge, leaving a puff of dense white smoke rising out of the trees about thirty yards south of the original wisp of smoke. "I want you to hit thirty yards above my smoke," he told the flight commander. Holding the plane in a continuous tight turn well below two nearby peaks, Major Billings watched the first fighter-bomber dive low over the patch of woods in a practice run. A second plane sent two bombs into the forest, and they struck about a hundred yards from the original wisp of smoke. "Oh, nice! Nice!" exclaimed Major Billings.

He told the flight commander, "Try to get those next ones up a little higher, right above my smoke there."

The next bomb load missed the forest completely and landed in a field of brush.

"I want you to get it right near my smoke," the Major repeated.

"Yeah, sorry," the flight commander answered.

The next plane sent its bombs onto the top of the ridge, within thirty yards of the first wisp of smoke.

"Nice, baby—beautiful. A good shot there," said the Major.

A plane sent two canisters of napalm onto the opposite side of the ridge, into some woods at the bottom of the cliffs.

"That's the wrong side there," said the Major.

A second load of napalm splashed into the forest about fifty yards west of the smoke from Major Billings' rocket, and a third, and final, load splashed about thirty yards south of his smoke.

We flew in and circled three or four hundred feet above the woods, banking so sharply that the ground seemed to be directly below the left side of the plane. Clouds of dust from the bombs and black smoke from the napalm rose from the woods. Unspent napalm was burning itself out in a few small patches, and the five-hundred-pound bombs had made gaps about eight feet across in the trees. A pungent odor of dust, seared leaves, and smoke reached us as we flew over the destroyed woods. After a moment or two, Major Billings pulled out of the dizzying corkscrew turn and, addressing the flight commander, said, "Where that smoke was coming from—there's nothing there. You got it real well. A real nice job. I'll give you eighty per cent of Bombs on Target, because of those two shots down the hill. Thanks very much. We'll see you another day."

To me, Major Billings added, "I don't know what kind of people were down there, but they're not there now."

Since it would be an hour before the next FAC plane came to relieve him, Major Billings decided to fly east to the entrance of the Song Tra Khuc Valley, where the 1st Brigade of the 101st Airborne was concluding Operation Hood River. "You can't see anything from fifteen hundred feet," the Major said, and as we passed out of the mountains and over the populated coastal plain, he swooped down to about a hundred and fifty feet and began to fly in a continuous S pattern, to make it difficult for snipers on the ground to take aim at the plane. Men of the 101st were burning the houses on the plain just north of the Song Tra Khuc. From a few hundred yards away and an altitude of under a hundred feet, the orange flames of the houses and the green moving figures of the men wavered wildly in heat waves billowing off the plain, and sometimes were almost blotted out by them. Major Billings continued his twisting, low-altitude explorations, and we suddenly came in view of a figure dressed in black, walking along a path that divided two fields and led into a shady grove where a house was still standing. The Major cut the plane sharply left and rushed low over the person on the path, who stopped walking and looked up. "Ah, it's just an old lady," he said to me. "She isn't *supposed* to be here. They were given twenty-four hours to get out, but they keep wandering back in. That's one of the big problems. You tell them they're not supposed to come into the free-strike zone or they'll get shot, and they keep coming back in. If they're men, they're just one of two things—draft dodgers or V.C."

I asked what the official policy toward people who left the camps and returned to their homes was.

"You can't always be sure what they are, but if a place is thoroughly infested with V.C. the province chief gives us permission to destroy the place," he said.

At that moment, we flew over a stream running through the fields, and Major Billings spotted three boys sitting naked in a little pool, taking a bath and looking up at our plane. "Look!" said Major Billings. "They're hiding down there! But this is out of our area of operation."

We had flown several miles north of the valley entrance. Here and there among the ruins, groups of houses remained standing. People walked along the paths near these, and children played in several of the courtyards, but few fields had been left unmarked by artillery and bomb craters.

I asked the Major how he distinguished members of the Vietcong from the rest of the population.

"If they run is one way," he said. "There are a lot of

ways. Sometimes, when you see a field of people, it looks like just a bunch of farmers. Now, you see, the Vietnamese people—they're not interested in the U.S. Air Force, and they don't look at the planes going over them. But down in that field you'll see *one guy* whose conical hat keeps bobbing up and down. He's looking, because he wants to know where you're going. So you make a couple of passes over the field, and then one of them makes a break for it—it's the guy that was lookin' up at you—and he's your V.C. So you look where he goes, and call in an air strike. You can split up the V.C.s and the innocent civilians that way. There are a hundred ways of telling a V.C. It gets to be second nature. Sometimes you see the V.C.s hiding by plastering themselves against the wall of one of those paddies. One trouble is, aside from these rockets, we don't have any weapons. But once I about ran a guy to death. I caught him out in the open, and I'd make a pass and he'd run for it, and then I'd make a pass in the other direction and he'd run the opposite way. Then he'd hide in some trees, and when I'd make a pass at him he'd make a break for it. I must have chased him for about an hour before I got some planes to put in a strike."

I said that this seemed to amount to a technique of sniping with bombs.

"That's it. You could say that," he answered.

Later, back at the FAC pilots' quarters, Major Billings told me, "I guess you can call it a kind of intuition. I think I can just about *smell* a V.C. from five thousand feet by now. Like everything else, some people have got the knack and some people don't. Some people wouldn't be able to tell a V.C. no matter *how* long they tried."

That evening, Operation Hood River came to a close, and the troops rested in the field for a day and received fresh supplies as they prepared for the new operation.

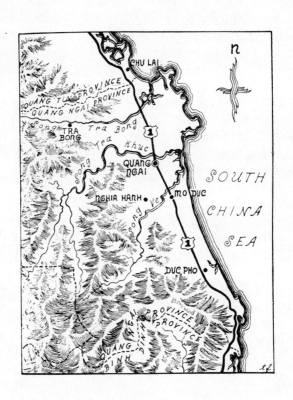

On August 13, 1967, two days after Operation Hood River came to an end, Task Force Oregon launched Operation Benton. In Quang Ngai Province I had seen the results of the American bombing, shelling, and ground activity but, for the most part, I had not seen the destruction take place. Now I was about to observe in detail the process of destruction as it unfolded in Operation Benton, in which Task Force Oregon went over the northern border of Quang Ngai into Quang Tin Province. I spent several days flying in FAC planes attached to the 1st Brigade of the 101st Airborne. On August 12th, I flew over the area where Operation Benton was to be carried out. This was a three-hour reconnaissance mission, with a pilot whom I will call Major Ingersol. Major Ingersol was a few years older than the other pilots, and he was more reserved. At the FAC pilots' quarters on the base at Chu Lai, he often read paperback mysteries or other novels while the rest of the pilots joked together. When he did enter into the conversation, he ordinarily spoke in serious, measured tones, which did not quite fit in with the usual light banter. Once, when the other pilots were sitting around drinking and discussing the figures of Thai bar girls, his contribution to the conversation was "I've heard that there are some exquisite restaurants in Bangkok." Another time, while chatting with a captain in the FAC central control room, he expressed a keen appreciation of the natural beauty of Quang Ngai. "It's a lovely countryside," he said. "One of my favorite activities is following

waterfalls up through the valleys. It's a shame we have to
destroy it."

While Major Ingersol and I were flying to the area of
the new operation, he described to me his method of
distinguishing Vietcong soldiers from the rest of the population. "You know that they are V.C.s if they shoot at you
or if you see them carrying a weapon. Those are about the
only two ways," he said. In the matter of trails through the
woods, he had subtler criteria. As we passed over the flank
of a tall mountain, he pointed out a trail, almost as wide as
a small road, that ran up the mountainside from the valley.
The trees were tall and dense, and the path was visible as
an occasional gap in the jungle foliage. About halfway up
the mountain, this large, clearly distinguishable trail began to get narrower. For a stretch, it apparently continued
under the dense foliage, because farther up the mountain
it became visible once again, but then it was lost to sight
altogether, "This is the kind of thing we look for," Major
Ingersol said. "See how that trail disappears up there?
That indicates to us that there is probably a base camp up
there. These trails that go up into the mountains and
disappear are often V.C. trails. Also, we look to see if the
trails have been freshly used."

I remarked that from fifteen hundred feet it must be very
difficult to tell whether a trail that was mostly covered by
dense jungle foliage had been used recently.

"Even then you can tell," Major Ingersol said. "You see,
the V.C. use water buffalo and other large animals to carry
their equipment around, and they leave marks. These
trails often get hit by artillery fire at night." As we flew
over a thirty-foot-wide crater that had eliminated one
section of a footpath, Major Ingersol commented, "Now
look down there. See how someone has built the trail

around the crater? This is the kind of sign you look for." He said that he also looked for bunkers to recommend as bombing targets. And, as still another example of the kind of suspicious sign he looked for on his reconnaissance missions, he told me that in one small field high in the mountains there was a small herd of water buffalo that disappeared from sight every few days. "We speculate that the V.C. use those water buffalo to carry things," he said.

Major Ingersol spent most of his three hours flying over a maze of little hills and valleys, for these were to be the scene of Operation Benton. The area of operation was a rectangle of about ten by twenty kilometres lying south-west of Phuoc Tien, a town in the southern part of Quang Tin Province. The 1st Brigade of the 101st was to launch the operation the next morning in an area ten kilometres on a side, and two days later some units of the 196th were to be lifted into an area of equal size to the east. I had decided that, within the area of operation, I would concentrate my attention on a somewhat smaller area, clearly discernible both on aviation maps and on the ground, and observe it from FAC planes on as many of the first few days of Operation Benton as I could, in order to see how bombings were carried out during a large military operation. Just southwest of Phuoc Tien, which lies in a valley of rice fields surrounded by foothills, two small rivers—the Song Tien and the Song Tram—join to form a single stream, called the Song Chang. (The Vietnamese word *"song"* means "river.") Within the fork of the rivers stands a small mountain, about a thousand feet high, called Chop Vum, and around its base there were at that time a number of villages and scattered houses. To the south of Chop Vum, a narrow dirt road ran east and west through thickly settled fields. I decided to observe an area six

kilometres square surrounding Chop Vum, and henceforth
I will refer to this as the Chop Vum area. It was bordered,
roughly, on the east by the Song Tien, on the west by the
Song Tram, on the south by the road, and on the north by
the Song Tien again, for this river bends sharply to the
west after flowing north for about six kilometres. Between
Chop Vum and these boundaries, just beyond which rose
an encircling range of two- to three-thousand-foot mountains, spread a landscape of tiny forested hills, seldom more
than fifty feet high, standing like chains of islands in a sea
of small terraced rice fields. A few of the knolls and knobs
were smooth-topped and rolling, but most of them were
very steep, and rose abruptly from the rice fields, like
miniature models of the mountains surrounding them.
Most of the houses were not in villages but stood scattered
among the fields. Wherever the land was only gently
inclined, it had been terraced and planted with crops.
Along the sharp ridge of one small hill, a footpath ran to a
small pocket of flat land near the top. In this pocket,
farmers had planted rice and built several houses that
commanded a view of most of the valley and the mountains beyond. Nearly all the houses near Chop Vum had
front yards where chickens and ducks could run about,
vegetable gardens in back, and a ring of hedges and trees
around house, yard, and garden. One species of palm tree,
which had a single crown of leaves and grew to be fifty or
sixty feet high, was particularly common in the gardens.
Small, winding paths ran from house to house on top of
the field divides and up and around the knobby hills, and
every crevice or fold in the skirts of the mountains seemed
to have a house tucked in it. The arrangement of the
houses allowed a dense population to live separate lives
with considerable privacy. In only a few places were as
many as fifty or sixty houses grouped together to form

villages, and even in these places the houses were not lined up side by side on streets but were separated by yards and by groves of bamboos and palms. The layout of the villages conformed to the bumps and hollows of the landscape, instead of dominating it with a symmetrical design. The village houses were linked by paths, and these paths led, ultimately, into an indistinct, curving main path that ran near all the houses. The village of Phai Tay stood at the base of Chop Vum, within the fork of the Song Tram and the Song Tien; the village of Duc Tan stood on the north bank of the Song Tien about two kilometres northeast of Phai Tay; and the village of Thanh Phuoc was sprawled along both sides of the road that formed the southern boundary of the area. In Thanh Phuoc, two stone churches stood within fifty yards of each other on opposite sides of the road. Each of them was about three stories high and seventy feet long, was faced with intricately carved stucco, and had a cross on the roof.

The afternoon I flew over this landscape with Major Ingersol, several herds of water buffalo were wallowing in the clear water of the rivers. There were people bent over at work in the water of the rice fields, and in the yards. The area had been heavily battered at some earlier date, and gray and red squares of what had once been houses dotted the landscape. Roughly one house in twenty had been destroyed. Many fields were totally taken up by craters, and the forest on the hillsides was blackened and pockmarked. On two adjacent knolls, perhaps a hundred feet high and five hundred feet wide at their bases, the woods had been almost entirely destroyed by bombs that had left overlapping craters. Each type of terrain—the mountains, the fields, and the yards of the houses—seemed to have received the same amount of bombing, as though the fighter-bomber pilots' intent had been to cover with equal quantities of explosives the areas marked out by the squares on their maps. Smaller craters, from artillery fire, spotted the fields and yards but were not large enough to show up in the thick forest. Many of the artillery craters were yellow and fresh, but all the bomb craters were partly overgrown with bushes and vines, and so must have been at least several months old.

I asked Major Ingersol when these bombings had occurred, and he answered, "Well, only the Marines were operating around here before Task Force Oregon arrived, but I don't think they got up this far. But it looks like they did. I don't know. It looks like it happened quite a long time ago, anyway."

Having surveyed the future area of operation, Major Ingersol flew south across several ridges of mountains toward the Song Tra Khuc Valley, in northern Quang Ngai Province. On the way, he indulged in his favorite pastime of viewing waterfalls. "You can see that FAC-ing *can* be pretty boring, especially on these strictly V.R. missions," he said. "V.R." stands for "visual reconnaissance." "I'll show you some of the waterfalls up here. They're just beautiful. This is some of the most beautiful mountain countryside I have ever seen." Before we came to a waterfall, he would describe it to me in detail from memory, telling me whether or not it had a pool at the bottom, whether it cascaded over a cliff or flowed down the rocks, and how many tiers it had. One of his favorite waterfalls—a long, cascading one with a large, clear pool in a rock bed at the base—had been bombed since he last saw it; he pointed out a crater on its lip.

By the time we started back to Chu Lai, it was late afternoon, and the sun was large and red beyond the dark mountain ridges. Over the plane's radio, a voice from somewhere said, "Hey, we're having a party over in D 19 tonight, with lots of free booze. Come on over."

Another voice answered, "I'll make it if I can, but I don't know if I'll be able to get over tonight. Thanks a lot."

Early the next morning, Operation Benton was launched in the area I had just flown over with Major Ingersol. The men of the 1st Brigade of the 101st Airborne Division were beginning their fifth consecutive week in the field. On the evening of the twelfth, the FAC pilots for the 1st of the 101st had only one drink each before dinner and did not drink at all after dinner. During a final planning session at quarters that evening, the lower officers called their superiors "sir" regularly, for the first time in the two days I had spent with them. Their mission for the next day was to guide air strikes onto the four initial landing zones, or L.Z.s, for helicopters bearing the troops into the area. These air strikes were a general practice, and were termed "L.Z. preps." Just before the troops were landed, the landing zones were "hosed down" with machine-gun and rocket fire from helicopters.

During the first two days of the operation, the back seat of every FAC plane that went up was occupied by an artillery observer, so I was unable to fly, but in the evenings the FAC pilots told me something of what they had seen. They said that, at the last minute before the L.Z. preps were to start, one flight of planes had been cancelled, owing to mechanical failure, so one landing zone had received only the machine-gun and rocket fire from helicopters. At a second landing zone, the L.Z. prep had been applied to a plot of high fields, according to plan, but the troops had mistakenly landed a kilometre away, on a hilltop that had not been blown up for them in advance. Meanwhile, seven or eight kilometres away, at an artillery battery that was to give support to the L.Z. preps and to the operation itself as it got under way, a helicopter had crashed into an ammunition truck, setting off the ammunition and blowing up the battery and inflicting several casualties, so no further artillery support could be given to any of the landing zones from that position. The installation of the command post for the operation, on top of a small mountain just north of the Song Tien at the point where it starts to bend north, had gone smoothly at first, but then a fire had broken out on the landing zone. (According to the FAC pilots, the air strikes they directed never started fires. It was the helicopters, they maintained, that started the fires, with their machine guns and their rockets.) When more than a hundred men, several artillery pieces, and several crates of ammunition had been landed, the fire had got out of control. Artillery shells had begun to explode in the flames, and the troops had evacuated the spot and set up a camp on a nearby hilltop, temporarily leaving several damaged artillery pieces and mortars behind. The men and equipment of the command post itself had been removed by helicopter to the top of a mountain about five kilometres to the east. Artillery shells had continued to explode sporadically on the flaming hilltop of the old command post for several hours. Over the next two days, seven more landings were completed without serious accident.

The first afternoon, the troops received occasional

sniper fire as they dug their positions into the hills. The ground commander on the hill next to the abandoned command post judged that the snipers were N.V.A. troops firing from the village of Duc Tan, which was about a kilometre west of the hilltop, and he requested that the village be bombed. A grave, wooden-faced young FAC pilot, whom I will call Lieutenant Moore, guided the air strikes, and later reported that twenty or thirty houses had been destroyed. In telling his fellow-pilots about the air strikes, he said, "I flattened the whole place, but I just couldn't get this *one* hootch." "Hootch" is the Army term for a Vietnamese house. "I kept telling them to put it right on this one hootch, and there must be six thousand-pound-bomb craters right around there, but I just couldn't get it," he went on. "Now it's a matter of *principle* with me to get that hootch. You watch—I'm going to get it." That day, several other bombings took place, in scattered parts of the area of operation. When night fell, an enemy force of undetermined size attacked the troops that had moved from the original command post to the adjacent hill. Some of the enemy went up on the evacuated hill and fired the mortar shells that the men of the 1st of the 101st had left there when they moved to their new position, and at the same time enemy soldiers attacked the new position. Ground commanders requested artillery strikes, and they also called in the principal weapon for air support at night—the AC-47 (this was the military version of the DC-3, and was nicknamed Spooky) armed with three 7.62-mm. machine guns, called miniguns, which could fire a hundred rounds per second. The AC-47 dropped flares, which, as they parachuted down, illuminated the ground below them as brightly as daylight, yet not even rough accuracy was possible in these conditions, and the technique was to spray with minigun fire the entire area in which the enemy was presumed to be operating. On the first night of the operation, one Spooky expended all its ammunition, which amounted to 21,300 rounds. It was later reported that four Americans and thirty-five of the enemy had been killed in the fight. During the preceding day, a helicopter had been downed by enemy fire. (Throughout the rest of the operation, which lasted about two weeks, an average of one helicopter a day was downed by enemy fire. Some of the wreckage was airlifted out of the area by large Chinook helicopters, and other wreckage was demolished on the ground by rockets from helicopters still aloft, to prevent the enemy from getting the guns, radios, and other equipment. In at least one case, the enemy entered a downed helicopter and took some of the equipment before the helicopter could be destroyed. The downing of the dozen or so helicopters during the operation was not mentioned in the press releases of the final week, and the Army would not confirm a total figure, but it extended every hospitality to any reporter who wished to see the operation himself, from the air or on the ground, or to talk with the men who had taken part in it. While I was aloft over the area of operation, I often saw Chinook helicopters heading back over the mountains toward the base with the wrecks of the smaller Huey helicopters hanging from their bellies by cables.)

A press release from the Information Office of the 1st Brigade of the 101st Airborne Division, titled "Paratroopers Maul NVA Battalion," described the encounter with the enemy:

> NUI CHUONG, Vietnam (101-IO)—Fires from exploding artillery shells blossomed around the hill. Flames leaped high in the dry elephant grass sending a black plume of smoke into the cloudless sky.

Captain Ronald G. Odom, San Francisco, looked out the helicopter door at the burning hilltop. . . .

After recounting several light contacts with the enemy during the day, the release continued:

Moonlight played across the hilltop casting grotesque shadows that kept the eyes of every paratrooper strained, nerves taut.

The moon disappeared at 11:30 P.M. Minutes later the enemy attacked!

"They opened up with everything they had," Odom recounted. "We were hit with 81- and 60-mm. mortar fire. Off our flank, their heavy machine guns began firing and their infantry moved in."

Odom previously had made a map reconnaissance of likely locations for enemy mortars and Nemetz called in artillery. Despite the artillery support, the enemy continued to rake B Co. with mortars and automatic weapons.

On the northwest flank, a Bostonian, Lt. Robert Berry, and his 4th platoon were taking the brunt of the attack. He radioed: "Some are ten meters away. Good hand grenade range. Out."

Odom recalled how he responded to Berry's report: "He was so damn cool, I couldn't believe it, and he stayed cool and calm all night long."

Lt. Thomas J. Courtney, Knoxville, Tenn., had the 3rd platoon firing into the enemy pushing toward his flank. The tracers from their rifles criss-crossed their perimeter with streaks of red.

The enemy mortar fire continued to blast

away on the hill. Suddenly, a report from
Berry's platoon announced the location of the
Communist mortars—barely 100 meters from
his platoon.

Forward observer Nemetz pinpointed the
location and called in a thundering volume
of fire. . . .

Throughout the night, Col. Puckett encouraged his men. He braved mortar fire to aid the
wounded, walked the perimeter to talk with
the troops.

At 2 A.M., nearly nine hours after the battle
started, it stopped.

Silence surrounded the paratroopers as they
waited for dawn.

When day came, the tired men of B Co. surveyed their perimeter. Thirty-five NVA lay
dead, their weapons scattered over the battlefield.

On the second day, the 1st of the 101st began to spread
out into the countryside in small units; several of them
met heavy resistance from the enemy and suffered casualties. That night, the FAC pilots said that the unit ground
commanders had called for an unusually large number of
air strikes throughout the area of operation. The pilots
described the targets to each other in terms of topographical features, or by coördinates on their maps, because they
did not know the names of any of the towns or rivers in the
area. One FAC pilot remarked that the units involved in
Operation Benton must be "really kill-hungry," for three
of the companies had chosen as code designations for themselves the names Cutthroat, Marauder, and Assassin.

On the morning of the third day of Operation Benton, I

flew over the 1st of the 101st's area of operation with
Major Billings, whom I had flown with during Operation
Hood River. I saw that, except for two or three houses,
the village of Duc Tan, which had stood below the evacuated command post, had been destroyed. Some groups of
houses in Duc Tan had been completely annihilated by
bombs; the only traces of their former existence were
their wells or back gardens. Other houses had been burned
to the ground by napalm. Most of the fields around the
destroyed village had been eliminated by the deep craters
of delayed-fuse bombs or else had been covered with
debris. More craters were scattered across other fields in
the Chop Vum area and across mountainsides, and the gray
squares of freshly burned individual houses dotted most
of the landscape. Major Billings told me that these houses
had been burned by phosphorus rockets fired from helicopter "gunship" patrols. A few minutes later, I watched
a gunship cruise low over the landscape. It wheeled suddenly and fired several phosphorus rockets into a group
of three houses that stood in a clump of palms. White
smoke puffed up, and the houses burst into flames. The
helicopter circled and then charged the houses again,
firing more rockets into the fields and gardens. Several
hilltops and small mountains that had been green and
wooded when I saw them three days earlier were burned
black by napalm. Fresh artillery craters were spattered
over the fields around the landing zones. At that point,
approximately twenty per cent of the houses in the Chop
Vum area had been destroyed.

Major Billings had been assigned to guide a "preplanned
strike," but before he could locate the target on the ground
a ground commander called for an "immediate" strike,
which meant a strike carried out a few hours, at most, after

it was requested, whether by a ground commander or by a FAC pilot. "We picked up some sniper fire earlier this morning from a couple of hootches down below us, at about 384 297, and we'd like you to hit it for us," the ground commander said. Major Billings flew over the hundred-metre square described by the coördinates, and found that it included the two large stone churches along the road, in the village of Thanh Phuoc. The ground commander was in charge of a hilltop landing zone that was a little over half a kilometre from the churches. When he had received the sniper fire, he had apparently scanned the horizon, noticed the two church steeples, which were the only buildings that stuck up above the lines of trees, and decided that the snipers were firing from the churches. In front of one church, a white flag flew from the top of a pole as high as the church itself.

"Let's have a look and see what's down there," said Major Billings. He took our plane on a low pass over the churches. The churches were surrounded by twenty or thirty houses. About half of these had stone walls and red tile roofs. The others had clay-and-bamboo walls and thatched roofs. One thatch-roofed building was perhaps fifty feet long and thirty feet wide, and appeared to be some sort of gathering place. Flower gardens were in bloom in front of both churches. Behind both, plots of vegetables stretched back through glades of palm trees to rice fields. After climbing to fifteen hundred feet again, Major Billings got into contact with the ground commander and said, "Two of those structures seem to be structures of worship. Do you want them taken out?"

"Roger," the ground commander replied.

"There seems to be a white flag out front there," Major Billings said.

"Yeah. Beats me what it means," the ground commander replied.

An hour later, three F-4 fighter-bombers reached the target area, and the flight commander radioed to Major Billings—who had spent the time trying to spot suspicious activities—to say that they were prepared to strike with seven-hundred-and-fifty-pound bombs, rockets, and 20 mm.-cannon strafing fire.

"We can use all that good stuff," said Major Billings.

"What kind of a target is it?" asked the flight commander.

"They're military structures. You can tell by how they look that they're military structures," Major Billings answered. Just then a fleet of ten helicopters moving in tight formation arrived at the hilltop landing zone. Major Billings went on to say that he would have to wait until the helicopters left before he gave clearance to bomb.

I asked him whether he thought it was necessary to bomb the churches.

"Well, if the V.C. don't care and just go in there and use the place to fire on our troops, then we've got to wipe it out," Major Billings said. "And the V.C.—the V.C. are *the first ones to blow up a church*. They go after the churches on purpose, because the churches won't always go along with what the V.C. are doing. *They* don't care at all about blowing up a church and killing innocent civilians."

As the helicopters rose from the hilltop, Major Billings said to the flight commander, "Believe it or not, two of those big buildings down there are churches. I'll check with the ground commander again to see if he wants them taken out."

"No kidding!" said the flight commander.

"Say, do you want those two churches hit down there?" Major Billings asked the ground commander.

"That's affirmative," the ground commander replied.

"O.K., here goes," said the Major. Then, addressing the F-4 pilots, he said, "Make your passes from south to north. I'll circle over here to the west."

The Major brought the O-1 into a dive, aiming its nose at the village, and fired a phosphorus rocket. Its white smoke rose from a patch of trees fifty yards to the south of one church. "Do you see my smoke?" he asked the flight commander.

"Yeah, I got you," the flight commander said. "I'll make a dry run and then come in with the seven-hundred-and-fifty-pounders."

A minute later, an F-4 appeared from the south, diving low over the churches in a practice run. As it pulled out of its dive, it cut eastward and began to circle back for the next pass. A second F-4 made its dive in the same way, and released its bombs. A tall cloud of brown smoke rolled up from the vegetable garden in back of one of the churches.

"That's about a hundred metres off," Major Billings said. "See if you can move it forward."

"O.K. Sorry," the flight commander said.

The third plane also sent its bombs into the vegetable garden. The first plane, on its second pass, sent its bombs into rice fields about sixty yards to one side of the churches. Three pillars of brown smoke now rose several hundred feet in the air, dwarfing the churches and the houses. On the second plane's second pass, a bomb hit the back of one church directly—the church with the white flag on the pole in front.

"Oh, that's nice, baby, real nice," Major Billings said. "You're layin' those goodies right in there!"

When the smoke cleared, the church was gone except for its façade, which stood by itself, with its cross on top. The white flag still flew from its pole. The third plane sent its bombs into the rice fields to the side. The first plane fired rockets on its third pass, and they landed in the vegetable garden behind the destroyed church, leaving it smoking with dozens of small brown puffs. Several of the rockets from the next volley hit the other church, obliterating its back half and leaving two holes the size of doors in the roof of the front half. Four or five of the houses around the church burst into flame.

"That's real fine!" said Major Billings.

"Where do you want the twenty mike-mike?" asked the flight commander. ("Twenty mike-mike" is military slang for 20-mm.-cannon strafing fire, which fires a hundred explosive shells per second.)

"Lay it right down that line you've been hitting," Major Billings said. "Put it right down across those hootches, and we'll see if we can start a few fires." (Strafing rounds often set houses on fire, whereas bombs rarely do.)

As one of the F-4s made the first strafing run, the path of fire cut directly through the group of houses around the churches, sparkling for a fraction of a second with hundreds of brilliant flashes.

"Goody, goody! That's right down the line!" exclaimed Major Billings. "Why don't you just get those hootches by the other church, across the road, now?"

"Roger," answered the flight commander.

On the second strafing pass, the flashing path of shells cut across the group of houses on the other side of the road.

"Real fine!" Major Billings said. "Now how about getting that hootch down the road a bit?" He was referring to a tile-roofed house that stood in a field about a hundred yards to the west of one church. The path of fire from the third strafing pass—the final pass of the strike—cut directly across the house, opening several large holes in its roof.

"Right down the line!" Major Billings said. "Thanks, boys. You did a real fine job. I'm going to give you ninety-per-cent Target Coverage."

"Did I get any K.B.A.s?" the flight commander asked. (The number of killings credited to each pilot is not kept as an official statistic, but most pilots try to keep track of their K.B.A.s informally.)

Major Billings, who told me he had not seen any people in the area, either before or during the strike, answered, "I don't know—you'll have to wait until ground troops go in there sometime. But I'd say there were about four."

As the two men were talking, perhaps a dozen houses in the strafed area began to burn. First, the flames ate holes in the roofs, and then they quickly spread to the walls, turning each house into a ball of flame. Most of the houses burned to the ground within a few minutes, leaving columns of black smoke rising from the ruins.

Major Billings called Chu Lai to give his Bomb Damage Assessment Report. "There were two Permanent Military Structures Destroyed, ten Military Structures Destroyed, and five Damaged," he said.

I asked him whether he considered the houses and the churches military structures.

"Oh, that's just what we call them," he replied.

A few minutes later, the ground commander on the hilltop got in touch with Major Billings to request another immediate strike. "There's a row of bunkers down below our hill here, along a tree line, and we've seen the V.C.s down there," the ground commander said. "We see their heads poppin' in and out. We'd like to get an air strike put in down there."

Major Billings flew over the spot the ground commander had indicated, and found a line of trees about half a kilometre from the hill. The dark openings of several bunkers showed on the near side, and a row of several houses was standing on the far side.

"I've got you," Major Billings said. "Do you want us to put 'em in along that tree line down there? There are a couple of hootches down there, too."

"Affirmative. We've been getting trouble from that whole general area down there."

"O.K.," said Major Billings wearily, pronouncing the first syllable long and high, and the second low. "We'll do that as soon as the fighters come in."

Three F-4s arrived in the area twenty minutes later, and the flight commander announced that they were carrying napalm and thousand-pound bombs, which are the largest normally used in South Vietnam.

The first bombs of the strike landed about a hundred metres off target. One bomb turned an entire rice field into a crater about thirty-five feet across and six feet deep, and splashed mud over the surrounding fields. The next two bombs annihilated two houses with direct hits. Two more bombs landed next to the tree line, breaking most of the trees in half and hurling one palm tree fifty or sixty metres into a field.

"O.K., you got that tree line real good," Major Billings said. "Now let's get some of those hootches to the south of it with the napes." He directed the pilots to a group of a dozen houses that stood about forty yards from the tree line. The first canister landed beside two houses, which were instantly engulfed in napalm. When the smoke cleared, only the broken, blackened frames of the houses remained in the intense blaze, which continued after the houses were burned to the ground, because the napalm itself had not yet finished burning.

"Beautiful!" cried Major Billings. "You guys are right on target today!"

The next canister did not land directly on any of the houses, but it landed close enough to splash napalm over four of them, and these houses immediately burned down.

With the strike completed, Major Billings told the fighter-bomber pilots, "I'm giving you a hundred-per-cent Target Coverage. Thank you very much. It's been a pleasure to work with you. See you another day."

"Thank *you*," the flight commander answered.

Major Billings' three hours of flying time were up, and he turned the plane toward Chu Lai. Fifteen minutes later, we landed.

After we had taxied to a halt at the fuel pump, a young mechanic asked, "How'd it go, Major? Did you get some of 'em today?" He spoke with a nonchalance that failed to disguise his intense interest in getting an answer.

Instead of just replying "I dunno," or "Real fine," as he and the other pilots usually did, Major Billings burst out "We bombed two churches!" and gave a laugh that seemed to register his own surprise and wonderment at the act.

That afternoon, back at the FAC pilots' quarters, Major Billings, scratching his head and staring into the faces of the other pilots, exclaimed, again with a laugh, "I put in a strike on two churches!"

"No kidding," said one.

"They had a white flag in front of them. That damn white flag is still standing," the Major said.

"Yeah, I saw the white flag when I was out today," Lieutenant Moore said. "We'll have to get that white flag. It's a matter of *principle*."

The conversation turned to the subject of accidental bombings, and Major Billings, who had been a bomber pilot in both the Second World War and the Korean War, told of an ill-conceived bombing run he had once made over North Korea. "There was a big building right in the center of a town, and they told me it was a real important military headquarters," he said. "The target was so important that they sent two reconnaissance planes to guide me right to it. I laid my stuff all over it. About three days later, I found out that the place was really a school, and about a hundred children had been killed. They weren't going to tell me about the mistake, but I found out."

A man I have called Major Nugent said, "In early '65, there was a pilot who accidentally bombed an orphanage and killed a lot of kids. When he found out about it, he was so shook up that he voluntarily grounded himself for good. He said that he'd never fly again."

"That's the way you feel when something like that happens," said a man I have called Captain Reese, whom I'd also flown with during Operation Hood River.

"No—I mean, you can't let it get to you, or you couldn't go on," Major Billings objected. "It gets completely impersonal. After you've done it for a while, you forget that there are people down there."

"Yeah, everything looks so calm up where we are," Major Nugent said. "We can't even tell when we're getting shot at. We forget what's going on down on the ground. It's the guys on the ground—the ground troops— that really have it rough. They really know what's happening."

The extreme solemnity that had descended on the group seemed suddenly to generate an opposite impulse of hilarity, and small, irrepressible smiles began to appear on the pilots' faces.

Captain Reese turned to me and asked if I had ever

heard the songs about the war that they occasionally sang.
I said that I had heard one such song.

"Shall we tell him?" he asked the other pilots. They all
looked at each other, and before anyone could answer,
Captain Reese sang rapidly:

> "Strafe the town and kill the people,
> Drop napalm in the square,
> Get out early every Sunday
> And catch them at their morning prayer."

Major Billings then recited the words of another song:

> "Throw candy to the ARVN,
> Gather them all around,
> Take your twenty mike-mike
> And mow the bastards down."

At dinner in the Marine dining hall that evening, after
a few drinks, the pilots began to make jokes in which they
ridiculed the idea that the bombings they guided were
unnecessarily brutal by inventing remarks that might be
made by men so bloodthirsty that they took delight in
intentionally killing innocents. The joke-tellers appeared
to bring out their remarks with considerable uneasiness
and embarrassment, and some of the pilots appeared to
laugh unduly long in response, as though to reassure the
tellers. All the jokes seemed to deal, indirectly, with the
conflicts of conscience that had arisen in the conversation
at the pilots' quarters during the afternoon.

When the main course was nearly finished, Major Nugent asked Captain Reese, "Git any woman and children
today?"

"Yeah, but I let a pregnant woman get away," Captain
Reese answered.

Lieutenant Moore's heavy-browed, serious, wooden face began to reflect a struggle between his usual gravity and a rebellious smile. "When we kill a pregnant woman, we count it as two V.C.—one soldier and one cadet," he said.

Everyone laughed loudly.

"Bruce got a bunch of kids playing marbles," said Major Nugent.

The group laughed again.

"I got an old lady in a wheelchair," Lieutenant Moore said, and there was more laughter.

"You know, when I flew over Japan, *anything* was fair game," Major Billings said. "They really were merciless, and they shot at everything. I remember I once saw an old guy riding a bicycle down the road, and I came up behind him, putting my fire in the road. The guy's feet started going faster and faster on the pedals, and just before my fire caught up with him you would never believe how fast the old bugger's feet were flying!"

The idea that civilians were often killed in the bombings they guided rarely arose in the pilots' conversation, and now that it had come up—if only to be debunked—the pilots made their jokes in the casual, familiar tone that marked most of their conversations. Yet the laugh that followed Major Billings' story erupted with a sudden force that seemed to take the men themselves by surprise. I sensed that their laughter eased a tension that had been building up during the session of jokes—eased it, perhaps, because this usually straightforward, informal group of men had found it a strain to have a largely undiscussed subject standing between them. Lieutenant Moore was so severely racked with laughter that he could not swallow a mouthful of food, and for several seconds he was convulsed silently and had to bend his head low with his hands over his mouth. Tears came to his eyes and to Major Nugent's.

"Oh, my!" Lieutenant Moore sighed, exhausted by all the laughing. Then he said, "I didn't kill that woman in the wheelchair, but she sure bled good!"

Nobody laughed at this joke. A silence ensued. Finally, Captain Reese suggested that they find out what movies were playing on the base that night.

The next afternoon, I flew on a FAC mission with Captain Leroy, a tall young pilot with a cocky, boyish smile, who was almost always relaxed and cheerful but, when the situation called for it, could pull himself together to speak in the responsible, measured tones of a soldier addressing his superior officers. When we arrived over the Chop Vum area, I noticed that the destruction of the houses had increased considerably. Most of the village of Phai Tay, inside the fork of the rivers, was now in ruins, and so were some additional houses to the east of the churches on the road running below Chop Vum. To the west of Chop Vum, a greater number of scattered individual houses had been destroyed than when I was last there, presumably by phosphorus rockets fired from helicopters, or by artillery fire. The high-flying white flag that had stood in front of the remains of one church was gone.

Captain Leroy had been given the coördinates of two pre-planned strikes, and these turned out to be situated on the southern and eastern flanks of the hill that had been evacuated by the command post on the first day of the operation. The southern flank was heavily wooded, and the first air strike, which consisted of both napalm and bombs, blew several gaping holes in the trees, but no further effect was visible. The eastern flank, a broad, gently inclined slope, was terraced at its based and wooded above that, except for the summit, which was blackened and bald, having been bombed and burned during the L.Z. prep. Halfway up the eastern flank, where the terraced fields came to an end, small paths curved up to several groups of three or four houses ranged around courtyards in small clearings in the woods. Starting at the base of the hill, Captain Leroy guided the F-4s up the slope, giving instructions to the pilots to "get those hootches." Napalm splashed on two groups of houses, and they immediately began to burn, but a number of napalm canisters landed far from their mark, and Captain Leroy was displeased with the performance as a whole.

As though to set things right, he announced to me, "O.K., now it's *my* turn to get me a hootch," and brought the plane into a dive and lined up in his front windshield a group of houses that were about three hundred yards from the original target area. He fired a rocket—the only one he had left—and white smoke puffed up about twenty yards from the houses. "Damn! Missed!" he exclaimed. But about thirty seconds later the houses burst into flames. "Hey, I got it!" he said, in a surprised voice. "It must be as dry as hell down there."

Three people ran out of one house and along a narrow path toward a line of trees, where they disappeared from sight. "Look! See those people?" Captain Leroy said. "They're running for their bunkers. See the bunkers where they're running to?"

He reported to Chu Lai that six military structures had been destroyed.

A minute later, I asked him if he judged that the people who had run out of the house were members of the Vietcong.

"All the innocent civilians have had a chance to get out

of here if they wanted to," he answered. "They're always warned. I saw a Psy War plane dropping leaflets."

I asked where all the civilians that had left had gone.

"Oh, they go to friends' houses—places like that," he said.

I remarked that there had been almost no people in sight on the roads since the operation began.

"They got out before the operation began," he said. "Look. Those villages are completely infested with V.C., just like rats' nests, and the only solution is to burn them out completely. That's the only way we can do it."

Captain Leroy continued to circle, watching the countryside below.

A few minutes later, a flight commander called him on the radio. "We've got some twenty mike-mike up here left over from another strike, and we wondered if you could use it anywhere," the pilot said.

"I'll check with the ground commander," Captain Leroy answered, and he did so, whereupon the ground commander said he would check with his unit commanders. Ten minutes later, he called back and said, "They don't have any place you can use it right now, but I wondered if you could put it on top of the old command post to explode any artillery shells that are still up there, so that the V.C. can't get them."

Captain Leroy directed the fighter-bombers to the target. The 20-mm.-cannon shells sparkled briefly on the hilltop as the planes made three passes, but there were no secondary explosions.

As Captain Leroy turned back to Chu Lai, his radio picked up a conversation on the ground.

A voice from a ground unit said, "We killed four V.C. this morning, sir. We turned around and saw that these guys were following us. They saw that we had spotted them, and we fired, and they took evasive action. We got all four of them, though. They didn't have weapons, but they were wearing the short V.C.-type black-pajama uniforms, and they were definitely of military age. No question about that, sir."

On the way back to the base, I asked Captain Leroy how the FAC pilots liked their assignment in Vietnam.

"At the beginning, they'd probably prefer to be zooming around in the F-4s, but after they get the FAC assignment, they like it all right. There's no complaining," he answered.

The next morning—the fifth day of Operation Benton—I flew on a mission with Major Billings. On the third day of the operation, elements of the 196th Light Infantry Brigade had been lifted into a valley east of the 1st of the 101st's area of operation and adjacent to it, in the hope of intercepting enemy units that might attempt to flee in that direction. We flew over this valley, and Major Billings pointed out what appeared to be a wisp of fog hanging over fields and houses. "See that haze down there?" he asked. "That's gas. It's not lethal, though—it just makes them nauseated, so they throw up, and generally puts them out of action. The troops were getting fire out of that area, so they put the gas in to clean the place out. Then the troops went in with gas masks."

When we arrived over the Chop Vum area, I saw that bombing, rocket fire, and artillery fire had destroyed more houses there. On the north side of the mountain, a dozen or more lines of smoke rose from the villages along the Song Tien—the usual sign that troops on the ground were burning houses. Presently, Major Billings flew over these villages, and I could tell from the smoke and ashes that at that point two dozen houses had been burned down.

Major Billings, weaving the plane back and forth to confuse the aim of snipers, brought us to below a hundred feet and made several passes over the burning villages. Families stood in their front yards watching their houses collapse in the flames. Some American troops stood in the yards next to the villagers, and others were pressing ahead through the trees, setting more houses on fire.

I asked Major Billings whether the men on the ground might not be annoyed with him if they knew he had brought a member of the press down low while they were burning a village.

"Oh, no! They *like* it!" he answered.

Major Billings flew out ahead of the troops and over the unburned part of the village and its fields. At one point, he said to me, "Look, here's what I want you to see—spider holes. They'll all be interconnected, and you will have a perfect position for Charlie to fire at our troops from here." He brought the plane down to fifty or sixty feet as we rushed over an embankment that had three or four black holes in it, spaced about ten yards apart. The fields were marked with craters, and several houses had been obliterated or half destroyed by artillery shells. A water buffalo lay dead on its side in the center of a rice field.

Major Billings' assignment for the day was to guide a pre-planned strike whose coördinates turned out to indicate the flat, broad top of a hill in the Chop Vum area. There were houses and crops on the hilltop and part way down the sides—until the slope became too steep for terracing. Ten or fifteen houses had already been destroyed, but on the very top—two rounded peaks, where the land was flat enough for a few rice fields—five or six large houses remained standing. Because the coördinates described the target only as a certain square a hundred metres on a side, the whole top of the hill, including patches of fields and woods, was included in the designation for the strike. Major Billings decided to concentrate the strike on the houses.

I asked him what type of target this was, and he said that he had been given only the coördinates, and no description, but that he guessed the most appropriate one would be "Suspected Enemy Troop Concentration," or else "Enemy Base Area."

A flight of F-4s arrived in the area, and the flight commander announced to Major Billings that they were carrying five-hundred-pound bombs, napalm, and 20-mm. cannon for strafing fire.

Major Billings brought our plane into a dive and fired a phosphorus rocket directly into the rice fields. One F-4 made a practice pass over the target, and the next F-4 began the air strike with two five-hundred-pound bombs. The pair of bombs exploded in the woods a hundred and fifty metres down the hill. The bombs from the second plane landed two hundred metres down the hill.

"They're nowhere *near* the target today," Major Billings said to me. Then, addressing the flight commander, he said, "Try and bring it up the hill some—about a hundred and fifty metres."

"Roger. Sorry," the flight commander answered.

The bombs from the next three passes landed between a hundred and a hundred and fifty metres away from the target area.

"Jesus, they haven't got one bomb anywhere near the target," Major Billings said to me. Then, adopting a patient tone, he told the flight commander, "The area I want you to hit is right up there next to my smoke, up where those hootches are."

"I see it," the flight commander answered. "I'll see if we can put these last loads on it."

Napalm canisters from the next two passes also landed down the hill in the woods. The canisters from a third pass tumbled down onto the hilltop, landing in one of the rice fields.

"Now you're on," said Major Billings. "Now try to lay twenty mike-mike across the same area."

When the heavy black cloud from the third load of napalm cleared above the rice fields, two houses were on fire. Their black frames showed briefly through the brilliant-orange flame and then crumpled. All three strafing passes cut across the fields and the houses, ending the strike. Soon two more houses burst into flame.

"I'm only going to give you twenty-per-cent Bombs on Target and fifty-per-cent Target Coverage," Major Billings told the flight commander. Then he radioed to the control desk at Chu Lai the information that four military structures had been destroyed.

With the strike over, Major Billings made a brief flight to the northern edge of the 1st of the 101st's area of operation, and beyond its borders I noticed the flames of burning houses and several lines of smoke rising from both sides of a small valley. The Major explained that the Marines had launched an operation named Cochise just to the north of Operation Benton and timed to coincide with it. We flew back over the Chop Vum area, and I found that the ground troops I had seen moving about north of the mountain had pressed about half a kilometre eastward, leaving a path of burned houses behind them.

As we were flying over Chop Vum, a unit commander

somewhere on the ground addressed a superior officer on the radio. "I've got an old lady here, sir. What should I do with her?" he asked.

"The important thing is to keep moving ahead here. Don't get bogged down with the refugee thing," the officer answered.

"Should I send her home again, or is there a safe area to send the people we find to?" the unit commander asked.

"No, there isn't, but the important thing is to steer clear of the refugee problem," the officer said. "Otherwise, you'll just get bogged down, like C Company did."

"Yes, sir," the unit commander said.

Major Billings turned back toward Chu Lai, and I asked him what percentage of the houses in the 1st of the 101st's area of operation he judged to have been destroyed during the first five days of Operation Benton.

He looked down at the landscape and answered, "Not half. Maybe forty per cent."

At the central control desk the next day, a captain compiled a report for me on the tonnage of explosives used, the number of air strikes carried out, and the results of the strikes during the first five days of Operation Benton in the area around Chop Vum that I had selected for observation at the beginning of the operation. I described the area to him in terms of its coördinates on the aviation maps, and for much of his information he drew on the Bomb Damage Assessment Reports, or B.D.A.s, turned in by the FAC pilots. The report reads:

> 5 DAYS/NIGHTS OPERATION BENTON
> PARTIAL COVERAGE OF BASE AREA 117
> 43 Strike Missions Actually Flown.
> 20 of these with accountable B.D.A.
> 23 of these with no B.D.A. due to heavy foliage, darkness, smoke

ACCOUNTABLE B.D.A. FOR 20 MISSIONS
139 Military Structures Destroyed
33 Military Structures Damaged
17 Military Bunkers Destroyed
3 Military Bunkers Damaged
4 Secondary explosions
125 metres Trenchwork destroyed
1 Tunnel Complex destroyed
1 Tunnel Destroyed
1 Automatic Weapon Position Silenced
1 Large Rice Field Destroyed

ORDNANCE EXPENDED

Bombs	Napalm Cans	Rockets
251	93	339
20-mm. Cannon		Flares
25,600 Rds.		145

7.62-mm. (miniguns)
21,200 Rds.

I was unable to determine the number of artillery rounds fired into the Chop Vum area, but two thousand and five rounds had been fired into the 1st of the 101st's whole area of operation, which was about ten kilometres on a side, and included the Chop Vum area. There was no damage assessment available for artillery fire, helicopter machine-gun fire, or phosphorus rockets, nor could I learn how many houses had been burned by troops on the ground.

During my stay with the FAC pilots, they and other officers said again and again that we could win the war quickly if only we weren't under so many restraints. They spoke mainly of three kinds of restraints. First, they said that except where troops were engaged in battle, villages could not be bombed until the villagers had been warned by a leaflet drop or a loud-speaker announcement. Second, they said that when we wanted to turn an area into a "free-strike zone"—that is, an area in which we could bomb at will, and without warning —the villagers had to be evacuated. Third, they said that we could not destroy an area until we had cleared the action with the province chief. To find out about the warning system, I spoke with the Psychological Warfare Office for Task Force Oregon; to find out about evacuation I spoke with the Civil Affairs Office for the 101st Airborne Division; and to find out about the clearance system I spoke with the province chief. Having flown over Operation Benton during its first five days, I confined my inquiries to that operation in that period. All in all, my investigation disclosed that the procedures for applying these restraints were modified or twisted or ignored to such an extent that in practice the restraints evaporated entirely, though enough motions were gone through to create the illusion of restraints in the minds of the officers.

At the Task Force Oregon Psychological Warfare Office, the lieutenant colonel in charge told me that his people had dropped 1,515,000 leaflets over the area of operation and had made one announcement, but that all these had been of a very general nature, and none had warned of impending air strikes. He showed me a copy, in the original English, of each of the leaflets that had been dropped, including a group that the men at the Psychological Warfare Office refer to as "the Chieu Hoi mix" ("Chieu Hoi" means "Open Arms"), which consists of various leaflets encouraging members of the Vietcong to defect to the side of the G.V.N.—that is, the South Vietnamese Government. Some are threatening, showing

photographs of the naked corpses of Vietcong soldiers
riddled with bullet holes and heaped in piles, and others
are conciliatory, showing photographs of smiling defectors
along with signed statements saying that life in the government camps is prosperous and happy. The Psychological
Warfare planes also dropped a hundred and eighty thousand copies of Leaflet No. 47-65, which is titled "Vietcong
Mines Cause Senseless Deaths" and shows a cartoon drawing of several farmers reeling from an explosion in a rice
field. The caption reads, "The V.C. mine your rice fields
and cause you to go hungry. You must help the ARVN and
the Marines to stop the Vietcong and deny the Vietcong
any of your own rice." On the back is this text: "Vietcong
mines kill Vietnamese on the roads, in the villages, and in
the rice fields. Help your friends and neighbors by reporting such V.C. activities." Finally, they dropped a hundred thousand copies of Leaflet No. 167-66, which shows a
cartoon drawing of a boorish Communist Chinese official
laughing cruelly and spilling food all over a table as he eats
a lavish meal while at his feet a moronic-looking Vietnamese with a Vietcong star on his tattered conical hat
crouches under the table and picks up scraps of food from
the floor. The text on the back reads:

APPEAL TO THE V.C. TO REJECT THE RED
CHINESE AS THEIR MASTERS
The Red Chinese Communist masters of
the Vietcong have declared that the South
Vietnamese people must pay more and more
to support the unjust war of the Vietcong. Still
the Vietcong soldiers go hungry and they are
not paid. Where does the rice and money go?
Think about it! Refuse to give your rice and
money—don't let the Chinese Communists
make fools of you.

The colonel gave me a short briefing on the activities of his office over the previous three months. "We drop leaflets based on the desire to exploit their vulnerability," he told me. "We drop more than a million a day. We use mostly Cessna O-2s for the drops, but now we are getting in C-47s, and they can drop two million leaflets in one flight." (Later, I looked at the office notebook of leaflets—well over a thousand of them, of different types. The book is divided into "Campaigns," such as "Support G.V.N.," "V.C.," "Instructions to Civilians," "Chieu Hoi," and "Health." The "Health" leaflets give tips on personal and public hygiene. For example, they advise the villagers always to boil water before drinking it, to cover their garbage, and to sleep under mosquito nets. The leaflets usually end with the assurance that the G.V.N. "cares for the people.")

The colonel went on to say, "We also have a new aircraft that carries an eighteen-hundred-watt bank of loudspeakers effective up to five thousand feet. We've got several standard tapes that we can run off here. We played the national-reconciliation tape for a couple of hours over Benton. We make our own tapes here, too, using *hoi chanh*"—returnees, that is—"the way we do with the leaflets. Sometimes we play a tape *and* drop the leaflets. The *hoi chanh* tell how well they've been treated, and that kind of thing."

I asked what the national-reconciliation tape said.

"Well, I don't have a translation of the actual words, but the general idea is to get them to return to the government cause," the colonel said. "We get the targets for the different kinds of leaflets through intelligence and interrogation of *hoi chanh*. We try to cause disaffection between the top V.C. and the V.C. rank-and-file, and we advertise the Chieu Hoi Program. One of our big problems here is lack of support for the government, but this problem exists for the V.C., too. A lot of the people are in the V.C. because of force, and there are a lot in because it is the thing to do—because the neighbors are doing it. Last year, there were a hundred and sixteen defectors in Quang Ngai. I Corps, which includes Quang Ngai and four other northern provinces, has a high rate of defectors."

"Do you estimate the rate of defectors as the number of *hoi chanh* in the population of the province or as the number of *hoi chanh* in the estimated number of enemy troops in the area?" I asked.

"I don't know the precise details of how they measure it, but anyway it's very high here," the colonel answered, and he continued, "We've also got posters that we put up in the area. On the fourth of May, the V.C. blew up some houses at Ly Tra and Li Tinh, a few kilometres southeast of Tam Ky, in Quang Tin. So we made up some atrocity posters." The colonel got up from his desk to show me some large posters on an easel that stood at the back of his office. They featured photographs of the burned or blown-up bodies of women and children, and scenes of destroyed houses followed by scenes of Vietnamese reconstructing a village. The colonel, however, was not sure that the destruction of villages and the killing of villagers was always an unsound tactic on the part of the Vietcong, and after gazing gravely at the poster for a moment he smiled and said, "But the distribution of atrocity posters has to be limited. Sometimes they influence the people the wrong way, and help out the V.C. Sometimes it is just what the V.C. want."

The colonel then said that many ground units were aided by loudspeaker teams who broadcast ahead of the American troops, encouraging the enemy to surrender. In combat, the Psychological Warfare Officers preferred to play tapes rather than use live voices. "That way, the guy is sure to sound confident, and we avoid fluttery, scared-sounding voices," the colonel explained. "Sometimes they use the tapes to broadcast from the perimeter of the U.S. troops. Mostly, we play music and interrupt it with what we call our commercials. We use nostalgic music to make the V.C. feel lonesome and want to go back home. We know from research that flute music is nostalgic to the Vietnamese. We've got three main pieces—one with a man, one with a woman, and one with a flute. The man and the woman sing of their lovely home. The Vietnamese are very closely related to their land. There is an old Vietnamese legend about a commander who was so good on the flute that all the enemy dropped their weapons and went home when he played it. We haven't had that happen yet. But I want to emphasize that in all our leaflets and pamphlets we *tell only the truth.* This is, of course, to establish our credibility, so that the people can depend completely on the truth of what we say."

I pointed out that we had destroyed about forty per cent of the houses in the Benton area of operation during its first five days, and asked him how he viewed this.

"We do destroy villages, and we have to," he answered. "But there are rules of engagement that prevent us from just arbitrarily bombing any friendly village. Whenever there's time, we get a Psy War bird out there to warn them. That way, we keep from hurting as many civilians as we can. Also, when the V.C. set off a mine in the road, and someone innocent gets killed, the V.C. exploit us and say, 'See what the American artillery has done!' So we drop our standard leaflets about V.C. mines."

The colonel also told me about units called audio-visual teams, which showed movies in the camps and villages when they got a chance. "They show American films, usually—mostly Westerns," he said. "Once, they showed 'The Swinger.' That wasn't too good. That was a mistake. They won't show that one again. But we try to show pictures that portray the American way of life. We're careful to show them things they understand. For instance, if you show them a science-fiction movie, they won't know what's going on. Walt Disney pictures are good, because the words aren't too important. In between reels, we show cartoons and shorts that liberally assert our propaganda. A lot of these are made by the South Vietnamese Ministry of Information. One shows a North Vietnamese soldier goofing up—falling into a canal, and that kind of thing. Another shows how a *hoi chanh* decided to defect. Sometimes we get the village chief to address the people between reels. You see, they don't have any TV or movies or record-players, or anything. So when we show them something, they gobble it right up. What we are accomplishing is to leave a good taste in the mouths of the children, so that when they grow up and the V.C. try to persuade them they'll remember the nice things the Allies did for them."

As I passed out of the colonel's private office into a larger room, which was filled with the desks of other Psychological Warfare Officers, a captain was calling out to a lieutenant, "Hey, Ray, what about a nice nostalgic tape by a woman?"

"Fine!" answered the lieutenant. He was peering at the Psychological Warfare Office target map, which was enclosed in a folder decorated on the outside with two *Playboy* Playmates of the Month.

A minute later, the captain handed the lieutenant the English original of a leaflet to read.

The lieutenant objected that a curfew that was announced in the leaflet should read, "From sundown to sunrise," instead of "From 6:00 P.M. to 6:00 A.M." "The

Vietnamese don't know what time it is," the lieutenant said. "They don't have any watches."

"Sure they do," the captain replied. "You look around the bases and you'll see they've all got watches."

"Yeah, on the bases," the lieutenant said. "But you go out on Route 1, where they're carrying wood and rice and stuff, and I'll give you a double mixed drink for every watch you see."

"All I know is we announced the last curfew by the hours," said the captain, and the two men moved on to another question.

A chart on the wall next to the captain's desk showed in one column the number of leaflets dropped each month so far in 1967, in a second column the number of defectors for each month, and in a third column the number of defectors for each month of 1966. The captain told me, "We keep tables on how many defectors we get every month to gauge how effective we've been, and we feel pretty good about the fact that we've had more *hoi chanh* this year than in the same months last year, because this is where we measure the results. This is where we can see we are really doing something." There was, however, no correspondence between the number of leaflets dropped during the months of Task Force Oregon's operations and the number of defectors in those months.

I visited a small tent serving as the Civil Affairs Office of the 1st Brigade of the 101st Division, to ask how many people had been evacuated from the Benton area of operation, and learned that Operation Benton was not supposed to "generate any new refugees." Apparently, word that the camps had been able to provide care—and then only minimal care—for only a fraction of the area's dispossessed people had reached Saigon, and Task Force Oregon had been requested to conduct operations in a way that would not result in a great increase in the number of people arriving at the camps. During the first week of Operation Benton, Task Force Oregon's solution to the problem was to conduct the operation as usual but omit the step of evacuating the villagers, either before or after their villages were destroyed. I learned this when, on the sixth day of the operation, I asked the major in charge of the Civil Affairs Office how many of the seventeen thousand people who lived in the area of operation had been evacuated, and he told me that fifteen people had been lifted out by helicopter and that a hundred more were waiting for transportation. I pointed out that about forty per cent of the houses in the area had already been destroyed without any warning to the villagers, and the major told me that, with the help of the Psychological Warfare Office, the Civil Affairs Office had devised a more flexible plan, which would be put into action during the second week of the operation; this was intended to offer the inhabitants of the area what the major described as a "free choice" between going to the government camps and remaining on the sites of their homes. Each American soldier would be given a handful of leaflets designed expressly for Operation Benton, and would himself pass them out to the people of the area when his commanding officer instructed him to do so. The leaflet to be employed—No. 244-133-68—was titled "Move to Ly Tra Refugee Camp," and read:

> The American soldier who handed you this is here to help you free yourself from the Vietcong and the North Vietnamese invaders who bring upon you the ravages of war. He will take you and your family to Ly Tra, where the G.V.N. will protect you. There you can live a

peaceful, prosperous life without fear for the lives of your beloved ones. You will go to Ly Tra by helicopter and will be able to take only the personal possessions you carry. The G.V.N. has a refugee center at Ly Tra that will give you aid until you can reëstablish yourself.

If you desire to go to Ly Tra, touch the American soldier on his shoulder. He will understand. Get your belongings together and follow the American's instructions. If you do not wish to go to Ly Tra, tear this leaflet in half. He will understand that you do not wish to go.

I asked the major in charge of the Civil Affairs Office what he thought the purpose of Operation Benton was.

"The province chief has told us this is pretty much a hundred-per-cent V.C. area," he answered. "We consider just about everything here to be a hard-core V.C., or at least some kind of supporter. Before they bomb an area, a Psy War bird always goes in ahead. This is an operation to catch the V.C., not to clear the area. You can't just go around moving everybody out all the time."

I asked if the Civil Affairs Office had any further plans for the people in the region.

"Now you're getting out of our area," he answered. "*We* don't have any plans for the immediate future. It's the responsibility of the G.V.N. and the ARVN to carry out Pacification and Revolutionary Development."

While we stood talking, a captain at a desk nearby received a phone call, and after he hung up he said to the major, "That was the colonel, and he wants those two villages burned. He said the province chief requested it."

A tall young lieutenant in fatigues and an undershirt,

on the other side of the tent, interrupted the conversation to ask, "What about the people?"

"The colonel said we're not supposed to bring out any refugees," the captain replied.

"What do you mean? How can we burn a village if we're not going to bring out the people?"

"Well, those are the colonel's orders."

"Look," the lieutenant said, standing up. "We have our rules of engagement, and we can't just go around burning villages without taking care of the people. That's just ridiculous! Can you have any respect for a colonel who gives an order like that? I mean, no kidding—can you?"

"The province chief ordered us to do it," the captain said.

The lieutenant sat down again.

A sergeant from the Operations Office spoke up to say, "The Vietnamese can relocate themselves. That's the way they are. Every two years or so, they'll just pick up their sticks and move on to somewhere else on their own. That's the way it was in Korea, too. The villages got wiped out there, too, and everybody just picked up their stuff and went somewhere else. Those aren't houses. They're just huts. Take, for instance, all those people who came down from North Vietnam for religious reasons. The North is Catholic and the South is Buddhist. That's one reason why they don't like each other." Actually, of course, both North Vietnam and South Vietnam are predominantly Buddhist, with a Catholic minority.

The next day, I drove to Tam Ky, the capital of Quang Tin Province, to see Lieutenant Colonel Hoang Dinh Tho, who is the Province Chief, and ask him about his role in providing clearance for Task Force Oregon's activities for the first five days of Operation Benton and in his province generally. His office was in a large two-story building in the ornate, pastel-colored colonial French style, which stood in a large courtyard at the end of a long driveway lined with trees, on the outskirts of Tam Ky. At the entrance to the driveway, two three-story modern-style stucco towers stood like giant bookends on a plain that had had its trees bulldozed away for security. There was a guardhouse beside one of the towers, and beyond them coils of barbed wire stretched out into brown fields. A Vietnamese officer there explained to me that an arch was to have stretched between the towers but that materials had run out. He said that the trees had been planted as a special project in an effort that President Diem had made to beautify the country. Flanking the office of the Province Chief were two long, low buildings occupied by officers of the ARVN and their American advisers. Just as I arrived—it was shortly after noon—a pickup truck pulled up to one of these buildings. In the back of the truck, an American soldier holding a shotgun guarded about twenty Vietnamese, whose heads were covered with muddy sandbags. In their blindness, some had clasped hands and others had their arms around each other. A Vietnamese officer shouted something to them, and they removed the bags and looked about them, blinking in the whitish noon sun. Five of them were young women, eight or nine were young or middle-aged men, three were old men, and two were young girls with still boyish figures. When they had helped each other climb shakily off the truck, they were delivered into the hands of a tall, young, collegiate-looking American soldier with a shock of straight dark hair, who appeared to be intensely irritated by something. "Get over there!" he shouted to the people, pointing with a sheaf of papers he was holding toward one end of the building. The people looked in the direction he indicated but did not move. "I said *get moving!*" the young soldier shouted, and struck an old man—who happened to be standing near him—in the face with his sheaf of papers. The old man fell back, his gaze riveted on the young American, who then turned away and stalked ahead of the group, his face red and furious. Four American officers who had been standing on a porch talking and watching the prisoners get off the truck went inside the building. The people filed around a corner of the building and were led toward a small, white-washed, windowless structure that stood alone in a withered field. Several ARVN officers who had been loung-ing outside it began to pick themselves up sluggishly as the people came in sight.

I asked an American officer passing through the square who the Vietnamese prisoners were.

"Detainees," he answered. "They picked them up back in the mountains somewhere, and now they're taking them out back for interrogation." (Several times during my stay in Quang Ngai and Quang Tin, I saw groups of detainees, always with sandbags over their heads, being herded into airplanes or trucks under the guard of Americans carrying shotguns. I learned at the Task Force Oregon Information Office that ninety-three per cent of them were eventually cleared as innocent and released.)

In due course, I was received by Colonel Tho, who is about forty and is shorter than most of his countrymen. He has strikingly clear and handsome features, he was im-maculately groomed, and he displayed a solid, if inelegant, command of English, which he had acquired during two years of military training in the United States. It had recently been reported in the Vietnamese military press that Colonel Tho had insisted that several air-conditioners intended for his own spacious offices be installed in an ARVN hospital instead. I mentioned this to him when I met him. and he laughed in delight and embarrassment, brushing the matter away with a sweep of his hand. Colonel Tho then motioned to an American officer standing behind him, who stepped forward for a few seconds to introduce himself, in a hushed voice, as Lieutenant Colonel Robert O. Lynch, Senior Adviser for Quang Tin Province, and then stepped back, solemn-faced, like a well-trained butler. Throughout the interview, Colonel Tho laughed often and gesticulated expansively, and Colonel Lynch sat silent, apparently to avoid cramping the Province Chief's style with an overbearing American presence.

We sat down around a small coffee table, and I asked Colonel Tho what his role had been in the planning of Operation Benton, and whether he had restrained Task Force Oregon from any bombings or shellings during the first five days of the operation. I learned that his method of giving clearance in an American military operation was not to review the targets of individual air strikes or shellings but to give the American ground commander a blanket clearance before the operation was launched. The Chop Vum area had been covered by such a clearance, and Colonel Tho had received no information on the results of any American air strikes, except in terms of enemy casualties, since the beginning of Operation Benton.

"The American Army comes to me to ask my permission for running the operation, and I tell them the areas they can't bomb," Colonel Tho told me. Later, I learned that he had been called to a meeting two days before the operation and had been asked to specify the no-strike zones. It had then been agreed not to operate within several kilometres of the town of Phuoc Tien. "Outside of Phuoc Tien, the ground commander decides where to bomb," he went on. "Sometimes I give permission to burn a fortified village on the ground, but not so many in this operation. Just one or two. Sometimes the villages support the V.C., and they are *too strong,* so they must be destroyed."

I asked him about his plans for the civilians in the area.

"No refugees this time, unless they *ask* to come," Colonel Tho said. "We take out only villagers who are friendly to protect in the government area. For relatives of the V.C., maybe they have to suffer some."

At this point, Colonel Lynch looked up, and, after asking and receiving the Province Chief's permission to speak, he said, "Of course, when we *do* have to destroy a village, in almost every case we warn the people in advance with announcements or leaflets. We're very careful about that."

I asked Colonel Tho if there were any plans for securing the area after Operation Benton was over.

"Well, maybe, sometime, but now we don't have enough troops," Colonel Tho said. "This operation is just to get the main-force V.C. units. This war has many faces. Sometimes we find V.C., and move some people for economic war. Sometimes economic war is most important. Population control. Change the population patterns."

I observed to the Province Chief that the two churches in Thanh Phuoc had been bombed, and asked if he had heard about that.

"Oh, yes," he said. "I got the report this morning that V.C.s blow up two churches."

I said that I had seen American planes bomb the churches.

The Province Chief laughed for several seconds, and said, "Well, in the fighting you cannot always tell what is happening, and you cannot always tell the difference between just regular houses and church."

Later, I spoke with a captain in the ARVN who had been in and out of the northern provinces since the end of the Second World War, and he expressed alarm at the policies that our military had developed in I Corps over the past year or so. "The Americans are destroying everything," he said. "If they get just one shot from a village, they destroy it. We have an expression: The American S-5 builds a village and the American S-3 destroys it." S-5 is the Civil Affairs Office, and S-3 is the Operations Office. "I helped give out rice and building materials in one village, and three days later it was completely bombed. They bomb villages with the families of our troops living in them. A soldier comes back from Saigon and finds that his family has been killed. They bomb the rich and the poor. The rich man is the V.C.'s enemy. We should protect him. But now he has two enemies: the V.C., and the Americans who bomb all the houses. They even bomb the houses of the local militia. Who has made this new policy? The Americans never try to protect a village. Just one V.C.—*just one* —can enter any village with a machine gun and the people are helpless against him. What can they do? Nothing. He shoots, and then their village is bombed."

On my way back to Chu Lai from Tam Ky, I had an opportunity to talk for fifteen minutes or so with several members of a group of about a hundred civilians who had been brought to a staging area from the Benton area of operation the day before. According to plans worked out by the office of the Province Chief, villagers who might be brought out of the area would enter the government camp at Ly Tra, but when the officials at Ly Tra heard about this they refused to accept any new arrivals, declaring that they already had far more people than they could supply with food and shelter. The evacuated villagers were split up and shunted off to a number of smaller camps. The jeep I was riding in happened to stop at the staging area. The hundred-odd villagers, who were from several different parts of the Benton area, were grouped on a concrete platform the size of half a basketball court, which was covered by a tin roof mounted on metal stilts. The platform stood in the center of a vast, treeless, sandy, scrubby expanse. There was a good deal of this type of terrain on the shore side of Route 1 in Quang Tin and Quang Ngai, but it had not traditionally been a living place for the Vietnamese; they had always built their houses near trees and water, and had reserved the arid fields of white sand and coarse grasses as sites for tombs. Next to the platform stood several rows of huts with roofs of tin or thatch and walls of straw or cardboard. These housed people who had left their homes earlier in the year.

There were no Americans at the site, but, with the aid of an interpreter, I discovered that a group of people who had lived around the two bombed churches in Thanh Phuoc were present. I approached this group, and attempted to address myself to a young woman who was crouching on the concrete with three children holding on to her, but this proved impossible, for ten or twelve other people immediately crowded around me and all answered my questions at once. The interpreter was overwhelmed by the hail of answers, and succeeded in interpreting no more than a fraction of them. There were only two or three young men in the entire assemblage of civilians, but there were quite a lot of old women, and they were by far the boldest in speaking out. I asked the group around me where they had gone when the bombing began, and I received a hail of answers.

"We went in our caves."

"We didn't come out for three days. We ran out of food."

"I want to go back to find my sister."

"My house was bombed."

"We don't have anything to eat here."

"Three people were killed."

"Can I have some rice?"

"We don't have any blankets here."

"All the houses were bombed."

"We hid in the caves and brought the children."

"We couldn't bring any possessions."

I asked whether they had been able to reach the camp with their families intact.

"I am thankful to say that all my children are here."

"I don't know where my daughter is."

"My daughters are here, but my son is gone."

"My husband isn't here."

"We couldn't bring anything."

"I want to go back to find my father."

I was apparently the first American who had spoken to them, and they naturally mistook me for someone in charge, who could help them. When one woman said she wanted to go back to find other members of her family, there was an immediate outburst of enthusiasm from the group.

"Will you send the helicopters back to bring more people?"

"Can I go back?"

"I don't have any food."

"Will you bring out more people?"

When they asked me to send helicopters back for their

relatives, some of the villagers pointed to the blue mountains on the edge of the hot plain.

The men present did not answer unless they were addressed specifically. Upon being asked about his family, one old man, who was wearing a pith helmet and the black pajamalike garment that most Vietnamese farmers wear, told me with exaggerated politeness that his son was an ARVN soldier, and immediately several women chorused that they, too, had sons in the ARVN.

"My son went into the ARVN four years ago and I haven't heard anything from him since," another woman added.

"My son went with the Vietcong," said still another.

Some of the women, apparently not putting much trust in my interpreter, resorted to gestures and pantomime to gain my attention. They stretched out empty palms to show that they had nothing, pointed to dirty children or pointed to their stomachs, and made theatrically exaggerated piteous faces, mimicking their own suffering. One woman grabbed me by the sleeve and tugged me a few yards to a tiny pile of clothes and blackened pots, and told me, "This is all I could bring."

Among the people assembled on the platform were some who stood with glazed eyes and parted lips. I asked a woman about one of these, and she answered, "He has a fever. Many of the other people have fevers." She shook her head and said, "It is not good to have a fever."

Several other people took no interest in my presence, and one young mother, who was squatting barefoot among her children, turned her back with a sorrowful, angry look when I addressed her through my interpreter.

Children from the nearby huts had mingled with the newly arrived people, and these children were extremely bold. In the manner of most Vietnamese children who have lived anywhere near Americans for very long, they thrust their hands in my pockets and shouted "Chop-chop souvenir!" (which means, in effect, "Give me something to eat!"), or "Chewing gum! Chewing gum!," or simply "O.K.! O.K.! O.K.!" But four children from the Chop Vum area whom I attempted to talk to ran away and, when I followed them, would not meet my gaze.

After I had spoken with the people from Thanh Phuoc, I was approached by a thin middle-aged man in clean black clothes, who introduced himself as a former pastor of one of the two bombed churches. He said that he himself had left Thanh Phuoc a year and a half before, and had now come to the staging area to help settle the new arrivals. One of the churches had been Catholic and the other Protestant, he explained, and the people of Thanh Phuoc had built both churches themselves, about a decade earlier, under the guidance of missionary groups from Saigon, which had made the materials available.

As we drove away, a helicopter landed and a fatherless family climbed out onto the bare field, each person carrying a small bundle.

O̲n August 27th, the day before Operation Benton was brought to a close, I flew on one more FAC mission over the Chop Vum area to see what had happened to it during the remainder of the operation. I flew with Captain Reese. As we crossed the 196th Light Brigade's area of operation, Captain Reese pointed out an avenue of brown trees and fields that was about two hundred yards wide and ran for three kilometres down the center of a cultivated valley. He explained that Operation Ranch Hand had sprayed the valley with defoliants three days earlier. As we approached the Chop Vum area, I found that during the nine days since I had last flown over the region about fifty per cent of the houses in the villages just north of the Song Tien had been destroyed. To judge by the appearance of the ruins and the density of the craters, the houses had been destroyed by bombing and artillery. In some places, a single house stood untouched in the center of a scene of devastation; in other places the ruins of a destroyed house lay in the center of an untouched group of houses. On the south side of the Song Tien, where ground troops had been burning houses when I last flew over the area, the houses had been systematically burned in a path that curved around to the eastern side of Chop Vum. Approximately sixty-five per cent of the houses in the Chop Vum area as a whole had been destroyed.

Captain Reese had been assigned to guide two pre-planned strikes during his three-hour mission that day. On our way to the first target, I noticed five or six people on the roads and in the fields. When Captain Reese spotted three people in a rice field, he said to me, "They're down there around their houses, harvesting the rice. They oughta know better'n that. They're liable to get hurt." A minute later, having spotted a lone figure walking along a road, he said, "There's some guy. He probably lives here."

Over our radio, someone on the ground said, addressing someone else on the ground, "I went over, found a couple of people in the open, and took a couple of shots at them. They went away."

Another voice said, "We've got some suspects here. A couple of them look a little *old,* but the others look real good."

"Keep them for us," said an answering voice, with a heavy French accent. Captain Reese explained that the Intelligence Officer of one company was a former Frenchman who had fought with his countrymen in Vietnam before their defeat in 1954.

The first target turned out to be a patch of forest that was bordered on two sides by fields and houses. Someone walked quickly from a yard into a house as our plane approached.

Captain Reese asked a ground commander who was two or three kilometres away which part of the woods to bomb.

"Why don't you pick the best area for exfiltration?" the ground commander suggested.

"I really like that little knoll over to the west where you can see the exfiltration trails in the woods there," Captain Reese said. "I think we can expose it for you."

Just then, another ground commander interrupted to request an immediate strike. That afternoon, he explained, C Company was going to be landed by helicopter on a bare hill that stood among wooded hills and vegetable fields in the Chop Vum area. He gave Captain Reese the coördinates, and we flew to the designated place. Then Captain Reese asked the second ground commander if he wanted to have any particular spot hit.

"Well, C Company is going in there, and we want to give them preparation in any likely areas of enemy troop concentration," the ground commander answered.

"Well, I can see a valley that might be good, and another hill with some trails running up into the woods. Which place do you want?"

"Both of those places sound good to me. Pick the one *you* want."

"O.K. I think I'll put it in on the little hill. There's some trails going up there, and there might be something up there," Captain Reese said. He was looking down at a small, steep hill that was already marked with five or six large bomb craters. After checking for clearance, he waited for the fighter-bombers, and when they arrived he brought our plane into a dive and fired a phosphorus rocket. The puff of white smoke appeared about thirty yards from the summit of the hill.

The target was small, but in the ensuing air strike the fighter-bombers succeeded in sending three loads of bombs and one of napalm almost directly on the phosphorus smoke. Two final loads of napalm landed within fifty yards of the smoke.

When the strike was finished, Captain Reese congratulated the pilots on their unusually excellent aim. Then he made several low passes over the smoking hill, and remarked to me, "There ain't nothin' there."

Captain Reese turned back toward the first of his preplanned targets but was once again interrupted by a ground commander who wished to request an immediate strike. His company was operating about three kilometres north of the Song Tien and one kilometre north of a small road that ran east and west, parallel to the river. Instead of giving coördinates, the ground commander guided Captain Reese to the target by describing it in relation to landmarks on the ground.

"It's five hundred metres east of that pagoda on the road there. Have you got the pagoda?" the ground commander asked.

Captain Reese flew over the road from west to east for a minute, and answered, "I see a church but no pagoda."

"It's right under you now," the ground commander said.

"I don't see it," Captain Reese said.

"O.K., well, there's one hootch down there about a klik south of us that we want you to get," the ground commander said. "Klik" is military slang for a kilometre. "We've got sniper fire out of that tree line."

Captain Reese flew over the area indicated, and found

that it was occupied by a village of sixty or seventy houses. Many of the houses that remained standing here and elsewhere along the road now had white flags flying on poles in their front yards. "I see a village down there," he said.

"No, this is just one hootch," said the ground commander, who was apparently unable to see the village from his spot on the ground because of a thick cover of trees.

"Well, I'll put in a marker round," Captain Reese said, and he sent the plane into a dive. He bore down on the village and fired a phosphorus rocket into its center. "How's that?" he asked the ground commander as he brought the plane out of the dive.

"No, that's not it," the ground commander said. "I'm talking about that *one* hootch in the tree line over to the east a couple of hundred metres."

"I'll put in another rocket," Captain Reese said.

The second rocket exploded to the east of the first rocket but—from the point of view of the ground unit—several hundred yards behind it.

"That's the general area," said the ground commander, apparently tired of trying to pinpoint the one house.

"Do you want us to pretty well cover this general area?" Captain Reese asked.

"Affirmative. Hit the whole area. We've seen activity all through this area."

"The activity I see down there is all Charlie—is that right?"

"Roger. We're the only friendlies around."

"O.K., I'll put in a can of napalm and see what it looks like," Captain Reese said. Addressing the flight commander of three F-4s that had arrived overhead during the conversation with the ground commander, he said,

"Would you put your napes on those hootches down there, about a hundred yards from my smoke at ten o'clock."

"Roger," the flight commander answered. "I'll make my dry run now."

Shortly afterward, an F-4 cut through an opening in some large, puffy white clouds that were floating in a clear blue sky, and made a pass over the village.

"O.K., I've found a hole I can come down through onto the target," the pilot said.

On his next pass, the pilot sent two canisters of napalm down onto the western edge of the village. Two houses were immediately incinerated.

"Real fine. A real good hit," said Captain Reese.

The second plane sent its napalm into some vegetable fields next to the village. The napalm burned furiously in the brown earth and belched black smoke for about a half a minute. The napalm from the next pass again landed on the edge of the village, setting another house on fire.

"Yeah, yeah, yeah!" exclaimed Captain Reese.

"We've got two seven-hundred-fifty-pound bombs for this next run," the flight commander announced.

On the next pass, the two bombs landed in the vegetable fields, with the result that two small fields were eliminated by deep craters, and dirt was sprayed over the adjacent fields.

"We sure put some holes in their rice paddies there, didn't we?" Captain Reese remarked to me.

"Where do you want the strafe?" the flight commander asked.

Captain Reese referred the question to the ground commander.

"Try to get that one hootch," said the ground commander, who had not seen the results of the strike so far, because of the trees blocking his view.

"We'll try to get that hootch for you," Captain Reese said. "Shall we pretty much cover the area?"

"That's a roger," the ground commander said. "Any civilians in this area are Charlies, or Charlie sympathizers, so there's no sweat there."

"We'll work around through there with the twenty mike-mike," said Captain Reese. Addressing the flight commander, he said, "We'd like you to work around through this whole area." Then, apparently bringing his attention back to the problem of hitting the specific house that the ground commander was interested in but that the Captain himself had never identified, he seemed to decide, upon seeing a house with an especially large roof, that that was it. He said to the flight commander, "I'd like you to get that one big hootch north of where that first nape went in."

"The one with the big roof?" asked the flight commander.

"That's it," Captain Reese answered, not bothering to specify which of several big-roofed houses he had in mind—perhaps because any of them might have been the one the ground commander wanted destroyed.

The first strafing pass cut a sparkling path across the entire village. Three fairly big holes appeared in the red tile roof of a large stone house on its western edge. In back of this house, a tall palm tree was cut cleanly in half by one of the explosive shells, and its leafy top half slammed violently into a nearby yard.

"That's not the hootch I was thinking of," Captain Reese said. "Try to get the big one with a brown grass roof in the tree line to the right of it."

"Roger," answered the flight commander.

"Did you see that palm tree go down?" Captain Reese asked me. "That's how powerful those shells are."

On the next pass, the strafing fire cut across the entire village once again, this time drawing a flashing line through the large thatch-roofed house that Captain Reese had described to the flight commander. The house burst into flames, and a person ran out. Then two more people ran out, and then they all ran in again, to emerge once more, still at a run, with bundles in their arms. For about a minute, three or four people ran in and out of the house, bringing out bundles. Then the entire house was aflame and the roof fell in. As Captain Reese circled over the house, he watched the running people and remarked, "They're really gettin' it outta there. I don't blame them." Then, as though addressing the people carrying their belongings out of the house, he added, "Git it outta there! Git it outta there!"

When the house had collapsed entirely in the flames, Captain Reese headed away from the village and called the central control desk at Chu Lai. "We destroyed an Enemy Sniper Position. Seven structures were destroyed," he said in his Bomb Damage Assessment Report. After that, he asked the ground commander, "Did we get that hootch you wanted?"

"Well, you pretty much covered that whole area," the ground commander said.

The flight commander radioed to ask, "Did we get any K.B.A.s?"

"There's probably some K.B.A.s there," Captain Reese said. "We hit a hootch that they saw some snipers running into, but the ground unit probably won't go in there to look for bodies. That was real good work. I appreciate it."

"Well, thank you," the flight commander replied. "I enjoyed it."

Before returning to Chu Lai, Captain Reese had to

perform a final task—that of observing a "Will Adjust" artillery mission. The target was a patch of forest next to a rice field in which thirty or forty water buffalo stood grazing. A fence near one edge of the field had been intended to restrict the water buffalo to a narrow strip of it, but the buffalo had made a breach in the fence and were feeding on the rows of rice shoots.

"We're gonna scatter some cattle down there," said Captain Reese.

The first round of artillery was a smoke shell, and it landed in a field some three hundred yards short of the target. Captain Reese advised the battery, which was about ten kilometres away, of the degree of its error, and the next round, which was an explosive shell, landed some fifty yards from the target. The next salvo, which consisted of several explosive shells, landed in the target area. The water buffalo lifted their heads together to look at the smoke from the explosion, and then moved to the opposite edge of the field. At that point, another FAC plane arrived to guide the rest of the artillery mission, and Captain Reese headed our plane back to Chu Lai.

O<small>n</small> one wall of their quarters, the FAC pilots had pinned a chart listing the K.B.A.s that were credited to missions guided by the various pilots in the past week. Major Billings was credited with four "points," Major Nugent with three, Captain Reese with four, Captain Leroy with two, and Lieutenant Moore with eleven. "Moore's got all the K.B.A.s," Major Billings remarked that evening. At the bottom of the chart, a carefully hand-lettered explanation of the point system read:

POINTS AS FOLLOWS:

MEN	WOMEN
old 3	old 3
crippled 3	crippled 3
children 3	children 3
military age 1	military age 1
	pregnant 5

Special this month: combination of two or more may also be counted.

In actuality, of course, the pilots rarely knew the age or sex of the people killed in air strikes, and this chart, like their joking at dinner the week before, seemed intended to ridicule the idea that innocent people were often killed by the bombings.

While I was looking at the chart, Major Nugent approached me with a troubled look and, shaking his head in disgust, said in a low voice, "Yeah, well, you know a couple of days ago a unit on the ground got some sniper fire from a hootch, so they called some phosphorus rockets on it. Then the guys on the ground rushed the place, and when they got there, there was nothing but two women and four kids in the hootch, all messed up real bad with shrapnel and phosphorus, and the V.C. had just plain disappeared. They couldn't find them anywhere, or find out where they went. That's the kind of war it is. That's what we're up against. Maybe those women were shooting. I don't know. It's the civilians who always get it. They get it in every war."

On August 28th, when Operation Benton came to a close, Task Force Oregon announced that the troops taking part in it had killed, and counted the bodies of, three hundred and ninety-seven of the enemy, and that forty-seven American soldiers had been killed. Into an area of ten by twenty kilometres they had dropped 282 tons of "general-purpose" bombs and 116 tons of napalm; fired 1,005 rockets (not counting rockets fired from helicopters), 132,820 rounds of 20-mm. explosive strafing shells, and 119,350 7.62-mm. rounds of machine-gun fire from Spooky flights; and fired 8,488 artillery rounds. By the end of the operation, the Civil Affairs Office had supervised the evacuation of six hundred and forty of the area's seventeen thousand people, to the vicinity of government camps.

The reports that were sent back to Saigon to form the over-all statistical picture of the war could be divided into two kinds. One kind measured the achievements of the American efforts in Vietnam in terms of materials expended—whether these were bombs dropped, artillery shells fired, Psychological Warfare leaflets dropped, pounds of rice distributed, or gallons of defoliants sprayed. Like the Psychological Warfare Officer for Task Force Oregon at Chu Lai who was encouraged by the fact that his people had stepped up the rate of leaflets dropped over Quang Ngai Province to a million a day, and like the artillery officer in Duc Pho who took pride in the fact that his men had fired sixty-four thousand and forty-four shells into two districts in three and a half months, most American officers and officials found cause for optimism in the sheer scale of the outputs of our efforts. The other kind of statistical report measured American achievements in Vietnam in terms of some of the effects of all this activity. The Bomb Damage Assessment Reports filled out by the FAC pilots were a good example. The terms "Military Structure," "Suspected Enemy Troop Concentration," "Percentage of Target Destroyed," and "Percentage of Bombs on Target," which described the bombing targets and the bomb damage, were devised by higher-ups, and the FAC pilots' only track-keeping duty was to write figures into the blanks. With this system, only results of the kind we intended to bring about were reported to Saigon, and the vast "side effects," such as the destruction of villages in large areas, went unmentioned. It is perhaps not very surprising that the Bomb Damage Assessment Reports supplied no blanks for "Homes Destroyed" or "Civilians Killed."

A further problem was that the terms employed in the Bomb Damage Assessment Reports often did not correspond to what the FAC pilots saw on the ground. When a FAC pilot guided an air strike onto a target that was defined by his coördinates only as a patch of jungle a hundred metres square, and was termed a "Suspected Enemy Troop Concentration," or guided an air strike onto a village that was described as an "Enemy Sniper Position," there was no meaning in a figure for the "Percentage of Target Destroyed," and little meaning in a figure for the "Percentage of Bombs on Target." Since the pilots could never know how much of the real target—the enemy troops—had been destroyed, they fell back on simply reporting how many houses had been destroyed, or how much of the hundred-metre-square patch of jungle had been torn up, as though this had been the objective of the bombing. Also, since the enemy was fighting primarily a guerrilla war, and built virtually no "military structures," the FAC pilots came to apply this term to any building that the planes happened to bomb. (Some of the bunkers and caves used by both the N.L.F. and the civilians might accurately have been called "military structures," but the Bomb Damage Assessment Reports listed these in a separate category.) Most of the terms used in the Bomb Damage Assessment Reports seemed to have been devised for something like a bombing raid on a large, clearly visible, stationary military base, and not for the bombing of guerrilla forces in the setting of fields, villages, and jungle which the FAC pilots actually guided. Finding himself having to guide air strikes with the aid of a set of instructions that had little relevance to his actual task, each FAC pilot had to improvise his own ways of trying to tell where the enemy was operating. This was how Captain Reese came to think that he could spot, on the trails, grass that had been freshly bent by the passage of enemy troops, and that he could distinguish enemy houses from civilian houses by whether they were in the tree lines or not; how Lieutenant Moore came to think that he could tell a farmer from a soldier by the way he walked; and how Major Billings came to believe that he could tell enemy soldiers from civilians by making a low pass over the fields and seeing who ran for cover, and that he could judge whether a wisp of smoke hanging over the woods was rising from the fire of a Montagnard or from the fire of a Vietcong soldier.

While some units of the 196th Light Infantry Brigade were helping the 101st Airborne in Operation Benton, other units of the 196th launched a separate, nameless operation along the northernmost five kilometres of coastline in Quang Ngai Province. Because American troops had been fired on almost every time they entered this coastal area, the 196th Light Brigade had decided that the best course of action would be to evacuate its inhabitants, who were thought to number five thousand; to destroy their villages; and to convert the area into a free-strike zone. The first stage of the operation was planned for the morning of August 21st, when elements of the 196th would make a surprise landing in amphibious tractors (usually called Amtracs) at Tuyet

Diem, a fishing village on a small peninsula. During the next three hours, the population of the village, estimated at six hundred, would dismantle their houses and take the beams and roof thatching, and also all their possessions and animals, down to the beach and aboard two landing craft that were to be brought near the shore in front of the village. Then, according to the plan, the landing craft—making as many trips as necessary—would sail down the coast to a lot that had been cleared in preparation for the operation, and the villagers would set up their village in the new spot. The newly cleared lot had formerly been the site of a large village called Son Tra, which had been shelled by the Marines about two years before. At that time, its people had been evacuated to a roadside a few kilometres away, where they erected huts to live in. A week before the operation that was to destroy Tuyet Diem was launched, the Army arranged to employ the villagers of Son Tra to level the ruins of their old village in preparation for the arrival of the villagers of Tuyet Diem. The villagers of Son Tra were given hints that they were clearing their old village in preparation for their own return. By conveying these hints, the Army hoped to prevent the National Liberation Front from guessing that the site was being cleared in preparation for a new military operation. The Americans who planned the evacuation of Tuyet Diem and the other coastal villages were much gratified by the neatness and simplicity of their plan, especially when they compared it with other evacuation projects that had been carried out in the province. As they saw it, the evacuation would not create "refugees" of the kind that had proved such a burden in the government camps. One colonel said of it, "We're just going to interrupt the villagers' work for six hours. They're not going to lose their chance to work, like the other refugees we've got. They can just bring their boats down the coast and start right up again with the new village. The real beauty of this is that all we have to supply is one day's food. They're going to bring their houses right along with them, so we won't need to bring any extra supplies for houses. This isn't going to be like those operations where five thousand people come into a camp with nothing to eat and nowhere to stay. This is going to be the best Civil Affairs operation we've run yet. The refugee people have been preparing for it for a full week." Mr. Ernest Hobson was far from happy about any operation that would increase the number of displaced people in the province, but, he, too, said that the evacuation of Tuyet Diem was much the most carefully planned operation of the sort so far.

The American planners were particularly pleased with the arrival of a three-man Vietnamese Cultural Drama Team—a troupe of actors organized by the South Vietnamese government and sent on tour throughout the country—which would perform for the villagers during their first evening at the new site. The evening before the evacuation, the Cultural Drama Team performed for an audience of about a hundred G.I.s in an open movie theatre at one of the base camps of the 196th Light Brigade. Standing under floodlights on a low stage, two youths dressed in the black garments of farmers sang several rock-and-roll songs in Vietnamese, accompanying themselves on electric guitars. They then switched to Vietnamese songs for a time, and wound up with "When the Saints Go Marching In," which they sang in English, in high, reedy voices. The second half of the performance was a magic show. Whereas the singers had remained perfectly deadpan throughout their concert, the magician, who

couldn't have been more than eighteen, never once relaxed a wide, tense smile as he moved through his routine,
and he moved through it as though every step and every
flourish of his hands had been mapped out in advance.
Among other tricks, he made a glass of water disappear;
folded up a dollar bill in a piece of paper, burned the
paper, and pulled the bill, intact, from the ashes; made
three scarves tie themselves together in midair; and produced a bouquet of paper flowers from his assistant's ear.
At the beginning of the magic show, the G.I.s clapped
politely, but their interest soon waned, and then, the
audience having suddenly been attacked by a swarm of
large, bumbling insects that resembled fat dragonflies, the
magician lost its attention completely. After the show, a
colonel who was involved in the planning of the evacuation made a sour face and said to a fellow-officer, "Are *they*
going to play tomorrow night? I don't think *I'd* want to
watch them if *I'd* just been moved out of *my* village."

The next morning, I accompanied the soldiers of the
196th Light Brigade that landed in Tuyet Diem. The
troops assembled at four-thirty at the top of a gently rising
field in front of the base camp, and at five o'clock the men
started walking down a dirt road to the beach in two single
lines, each man keeping ten yards between himself and the
man in front of him. A three-quarter moon faintly illu-
mined the road from behind a high cover of thin, milky
clouds. A deep thumping of artillery shells landing in
rapid series, which had begun at about one o'clock, continued well into the morning at a stepped-up pace, and to
the east, over the peninsula where the troops were to land,
the sky periodically flashed a dull yellow. The morning
was warm and muggy, and the troops, in their battle gear,
began to sweat freely. The double column descended from
the high ground in front of the camp and approached the

horizon. (These fishing boats drew only two feet of water, were about six feet wide and thirty feet long, had long, heavy bowsprits, and sailed under a gaff rig.) Facing the water were half a dozen stone houses of two or three rooms. Some had porches whose roofs were supported by gaily painted stone pillars. The walls of these houses were decorated with molding, and the cornices, windowsills, and door frames were painted with patterns in bright blues, reds, oranges, and greens. Palm trees and bamboos arched above the houses, casting a mottled shade.

Several families stood watching silently as the troops filed into the village. The soldiers, too, were silent. Each of the Vietnamese, male or female, wore a simple black collarless garment with three-quarter-length trousers. Each of the women and the little girls wore her hair long down her back, held in place with a silver oval clasp. Most of the villagers had bare feet, and children under three wore no pants. A few soldiers poked their heads briefly in at doorways, but most of them simply walked along the pathways between the houses, intently scanning the scene around them as they proceeded; they were on the lookout for signs of the enemy. Only the sergeant who had been complaining about Yankees on the Amtrac was more aggressive in his search. He walked directly up to a neatly-groomed, wiry middle-aged man who, with his wife and son, was standing in front of one of the most prosperous-looking houses, and, pointing inside, demanded, "What's in here?" Getting no answer, he went inside, pointed to a large ornate chest, and said, "Open this."

The Vietnamese man looked at him questioningly.

"Dammit, Ah said open this!" the sergeant shouted, striking the chest with his gun butt.

The man opened it, revealing a pile of folded clothes.

The sergeant poked inside with the barrel of his gun and then left.

Outside again, the sergeant demanded, "Where V.C.? *Beaucoup* V.C., hunh?" ("*Beaucoup*" is a standard word in G.I. pidgin Vietnamese.) No one replied. As he passed another house, he noticed that the shutters on a side window were wired closed, and he bashed at them with his gun butt, but they did not break open, and he continued on his way without bothering to enter the house, whose front door stood ajar.

A few moments later, the sergeant pushed aside a curtain over the front entrance to a third house, and found himself facing an old man who was sitting on the floor just inside, bobbing his head and saying something that sounded like "Ow-ow-ow-ow-ow."

"Ow-ow-ow-ow-ow," mimicked the sergeant. "You're fuckin' crazy, that's what. Ow-ow-ow-ow-ow."

A central path wound back through the village, which was spread out on a hill. Directly behind one of the shore-front houses, a pile of rubble lay on a house foundation, and a palm tree about ten inches thick had been snapped in two halfway up, so that its leafy head—still green—was bowed into a neighbor's yard. "Artillery," a soldier remarked when he came upon the scene. Farther up the hill, the houses were poorer and were crowded closer together. Most had one or two rooms, were built of clay packed into woven bamboo frames, and were roofed with thatch. At the crest of the hill, the landscape opened out onto about two acres of flat rice fields. The troops who had headed up through the pasture when they debarked from the Amtracs were sitting on a steep, sandy hill that rose immediately behind the rice fields and gave them a view of the entire village. A dozen houses that were as large and well made as those on the shore surrounded the fields. Two other houses bordering the fields were in ruins. Recent artillery fire had made several big craters in a young crop of rice, and had sprayed mud over what remained of the rice shoots and onto the grassy embankments dividing the fields. The central path that led up the hill from the sea ran along its crest, parallel to the shore, for a few hundred yards, and then descended the hill to the shore farther north, at a place where treeless dunes covered with beach grass swept back from a long white beach.

Half an hour after the troops arrived, a Psychological Warfare Team consisting of an American and a Vietnamese began making announcements with a tape recorder and a loudspeaker. They announced that American troops had arrived to free the villagers from Vietcong domination, and ordered them to dismantle their houses and load the building materials, their possessions, and their animals on the landing craft (which had not yet arrived) within the next three hours. They also announced that the soldiers would help the people carry their possessions down to the boats. The commanding officer did not issue an order to this effect to his soldiers but allowed each man to decide for himself whether he would carry anything. The two landing craft arrived shortly after the announcements, one pulling up in the cove in front of the center of the village and the other at the long stretch of sand to the north. The villagers began to work as soon as they understood the nature of the situation. American troops that had entered other villages in Quang Ngai had usually found few able men, but at Tuyet Diem they found that a third of the families had men at home. Everyone, from the very old down to children of five or six, began carrying bundles to the beach. The villagers kept their stores of rice in waist-high pottery jars, and these were the most difficult objects to carry. Little

girls and old women who were not accompanied by men
importuned the American soldiers for help by tugging at
their sleeves and attempting to pull them along to their
houses. Four or five soldiers consented to help, and at once
three or four little girls and a few old women gathered
around them and tugged at their sleeves, trying to pull
them in different directions, and smiling coaxingly or
making sad faces. Neither the young men nor the young
women ever smiled or asked for help. Most of the villagers
set about carrying their belongings down the hill with a
cold, fierce determination. Working against the three-hour
deadline, they balanced huge loads at the ends of bamboo
poles and made for the beach at a rapid, smooth, dancing
jog. One old woman wept freely and loudly as she walked
down the hill with a load. Other women wept soundlessly.
One young woman's eyes streamed, even though her features were tightly composed, as she bent her energies to
the work. All the children over five or six worked silently
and hard, without any urging from their parents. Children
of nine or ten carried two- and three-year-old brothers and
sisters to the beach, leaving the heavier burdens of food,
cooking utensils, and furniture to their parents. On the
long open beach, the smallest children stood crying in
groups of two and three next to their families' furniture
and bundles of belongings. The four or five Americans
who had taken up shoulder poles smiled and winked at one
another with embarrassment as they passed on the path, in
the manner of adults who have good-naturedly consented
to take part in a children's game. To most of the soldiers,
the villagers' possessions looked hardly worth carrying anywhere. Besides their jars of rice, the villagers wished to
bring down large jars of *nuoc mam*—a major food staple for
them, made of fermented fish, which gives off an odor that
is usually disagreeable to Americans smelling it for the first

time. They also carried bundles of twigs and reeds for firewood. When one American soldier was asked whether he intended to carry any of the villagers' belongings to the boats, he looked around him at the bundles on the beach and said, "What? *Me* carry *this shit?*" The villagers were wiry and strong, and even the women carried loads sufficient to tax a young G.I. (When a G.I. relieved one old woman of two bundles of firewood, he lifted them to his shoulder, and then set them down again and handed one to another soldier to carry and, looking at the frail old woman, put on an expression of amazement for the benefit of the other soldiers.) The combat soldiers in Vietnam are unusually big men, even by American standards, and at Tuyet Diem they loomed over most of the village men by more than a head. Some of the village women, apparently equating size with strength, led American soldiers to absurdly heavy loads and motioned to them to carry these to the beach. One old woman led an American at a half run to her hut, where she began desperately digging with her hands into the packed sandy earth of its floor. At length, she uncovered two huge jars of rice, each weighing about a hundred and fifty pounds. She secured one jar to each end of a shoulder pole with a wire hook and motioned impatiently to the American to take them away. Later, he and a man from the village together carried a jar at a time, with difficulty, down the path, one of them at each end of a shoulder pole.

Around eleven o'clock, the sun began to burn through the clouds, and the Americans who had been carrying belongings sat down and stopped work for the day, almost overcome by the heat. At eleven-fifteen, a sudden burst of machine-gun fire sent up a line of small geysers in the cove, about fifty feet from the shore. The commanding officer sent a patrol out along the beach, but the source of the fire was never ascertained. These were the only shots fired that day. (The Tuyet Diem operation was unusual in its lack of contact with the enemy. The military can almost never predict when the enemy will choose to resist in force, but most operations encounter sniper fire, at least, or small-unit fighting that results in both American and enemy casualties.)

The landing craft had been able to pull up to within ten yards of the shore, where the water was waist-deep. Each time a landing craft departed, many of the villagers, believing that the last boatload of belongings was leaving, waded deep into the water with bundles in their arms, and the soldiers on board shouted at them, "No more! That's all!," and attempted to prevent them from pushing their bundles onto the lip of the craft. Once, as a landing craft pulled away from the shore, a man ignored the protests of a soldier who stood at the rear of the craft, and, wading out up to his shoulders, tried repeatedly to shove a bundle of cooking utensils aboard. The soldier, becoming angry, pushed the man's bundle into the water. Some two dozen ARVN troops arrived late in the morning on one of the landing craft. They did not carry anything to the beach. One of them had brought a transistor radio, and a group of Americans persuaded him to tune it to the American armed-forces radio network. Light music, of the kind usually heard in restaurants or elevators in the United States, issued across the crowded beach. Another group of American soldiers sat on a poncho eating combat rations and drinking the milk of coconuts they had taken from nearby trees. Several soldiers had brought cameras, and they took pictures of the villagers carrying loads to the beach, and also of the landing craft jammed with firewood, furniture, bundles, jars of food, hobbled animals, and villagers. (The military in Vietnam apparently encourage the men to take snapshots of the war to send home. In the photographic department of the Danang PX, there hung a poster showing a picture of houses and palm trees silhouetted against a conflagration that filled most of the poster with red-and-orange flame and black smoke. In the foreground was a larger-than-life-size profile, in black silhouette, of the helmeted head of a G.I.; he was holding a camera to his eye and pressing the shutter. A caption at the bottom read, "SEND HOME A PHOTOGRAPHIC HISTORY OF THE WAR IN VIETNAM.")

To get their belongings from the beach to the landing craft, some villagers made use of large, shallow baskets woven of reeds and waterproofed with a coating of tar or resin. (The fishing villages along the coast in Quang Ngai use baskets of this type as small boats. It was in these simple craft that the villagers had first launched out on the water as children; in front of other coastal villages I often saw the water dotted with children in baskets, who propelled themselves about at a surprising speed with a sculling stroke of a single paddle.) During the morning, men who had been out in their fishing boats returned to Tuyet Diem, and helped carry belongings to the landing craft. By noon, it was apparent that the population of the village was not six hundred, as had been thought, but about fifteen hundred, so the deadline for the dismantling of the village was extended until late afternoon.

At Son Tra, where the villagers were being landed after their journey down the coast, a team of American soldiers had been detailed to help them carry their possessions ashore. Around the newly cleared lot that was to be the villagers' new home, a barbed-wire fence had been erected to insure that everyone checked in through a registration tent, for fingerprinting and questioning, and through a Red Cross tent, for a brief medical checkup.

Perhaps because the number of people so far exceeded expectations, rendering the medical and security facilities inadequate for even the most cursory checking, someone had cut a large breach in the fence, and several hundred villagers had poured through to claim spots on the lot. On the lot, three stone buildings, including a roofless church, remained standing. Children's line drawings of helicopters, cattle, pigs, and gunboats had been scratched into the paint on the inside walls of one building. At one end of the lot was a little rocky hill that had been reduced to a blackened knob dotted with shattered stumps of trees during the Marines' bombing and shelling about two years before. Because of the delay in the schedule, American officers at Son Tra decided to postpone the destruction of the village of Tuyet Diem until the next day, and to blow up only the wells that night, to keep the Vietcong from getting water there. The officer detailed to the task said that because they were good, deep wells, with stone shafts part way down, he would need several hundred pounds of explosives to destroy them all.

An ARVN sergeant had been appointed "village chief," to control and organize the Tuyet Diem villagers at their new site. The Americans present always referred to him by his new title and spoke to him with the same humble deference that I had seen accorded to Lieutenant Colonel Tho in Quang Tin. The village chief was a tall, thin young man with a tight-lipped, impatient air, who wore a freshly pressed khaki uniform, stiff and glistening with starch, and French-style glasses with rims of clear plastic that extended only across the top of the lenses. At about two o'clock, when I arrived at the beach in front of the lot, he was in a state of fury because the gap in the barbed-wire fence had rendered the registration procedure meaningless. He paced up and down just inside the barbed-wire fence shouting through an electric bullhorn, telling the villagers they should remain on the beach, but his order came much too late; about half the new arrivals had already entered the empty lot. At one point, nine middle-aged and elderly men approached him, with their conical straw hats in their hands, and a spokesman for the group told him that the villagers were afraid the Vietcong would come to Son Tra to kill them in the night, because they had not resisted evacuation from their homes in Tuyet Diem. The newly appointed village chief interrupted the spokesman in mid-sentence and, shaking with anger, shouted that he would listen to no demands of any kind at that moment, because no one was supposed to have even come through to his side of the fence yet. The spokesman started to say something more, and the village chief rushed at him and, in swift succession, struck him on the face with the front and then the back of his hand and kicked him on the hip. The spokesman fell back as he was beaten, and said nothing more. Several American officers were sitting nearby in a jeep talking, and one of them—an adviser to the new village chief—remarked to me, "Looks like they're having a little row." At my request, he went over to the chief with his interpreter to ask what had happened, and after returning and explaining the situation to me he observed, "The village chief believes that you have to be tough at first to gain their respect in order to control them."

Because the villagers had had neither the time nor the manpower to dismantle their houses and load the materials on the landing craft, as the Army had originally planned, and no building supplies had been made available, the villagers slept for the next few weeks under pieces of cloth propped up on sticks, or under their tarred basket boats. During that time, they began constructing makeshift dwellings of poles that they cut for themselves in a patch of woods nearby. The first night, they camped here and there all over the lot, but the next day they learned that theirs was only the first of a number of villages to be moved into the enclosure, and they were made to squeeze into one corner at the back. That day, the village chief performed his first administrative act, which was to take everyone's identification card away, so that no one could leave the enclosure. The same day, the Army decided to evacuate another village right away, and consequently a thousand more people arrived on the lot, bringing the official estimate of its population up to twenty-five hundred. Even then, only half the lot could be used, for more villages were scheduled for evacuation in the near future. Later that week, troops of the 196th Light Brigade blew up and then burned the empty village of Tuyet Diem. The Army put off the evacuation and destruction of the other villages until after the Presidential election, on September 3rd, because the troops of the 196th were needed to provide security around the polls.

Like most of the American military in Vietnam, the Army men who evacuated the villagers from Tuyet Diem and then destroyed the village saw what they were doing as only the first stage of a long-range benevolent plan for all of South Vietnam, in which the country would be rebuilt and then would develop a free and democratic government. This first stage of the plan—the destruction of the villages—usually went very smoothly, and gave rise to considerable optimism among the Americans who carried it out, but the second stage—the stage in which the Vietnamese and their American civil-affairs advisers were to rebuild and reorganize villages like Tuyet Diem, and were to stitch the whole society back together again—turned out to be infinitely more difficult than anyone had expected, and the people who were to carry it out could not even begin to match the scale of destruction with their construction. More often than not, the reality of the villagers' new life under the South Vietnamese government turned out to be a crowded tent in a government camp or a bare lot like the one in Son Tra. Many optimistic Americans, including reporters as well as military men and civilian officials, tended to set off the destruction caused by the military effort against the construction resulting from the civil-affairs effort, seeing the two results as separate but balanced "sides" of the war; and, looking at our commitment of men and materials, they were often favorably impressed with the size of the constructive effort, almost as though it were being carried out in one country while the military effort was being carried out in another. But, of course, the two programs were being carried out in the same provinces and the same villages, and the people who received the allotments of rice were the same people whose villages had been destroyed by bombs. The Vietnamese civilians felt the effects of the two programs not as two abstract "sides" of the war but as a continuing experience in the single reality of their daily lives, and, from their point of view, the aid given them by the Americans and the South Vietnamese government amounted to only a tiny measure of compensation (although extravagant promises were made in the leaflets and in other propaganda) for enormous losses and suffering. Many Americans, both civilian and military, tended not to see beyond the particular program they were involved in. Civil-affairs officials, forgetting that it was American firepower that had been the original direct cause of the destitution of the vast majority of the people in the camps, were puzzled when these hungry, tired people showed little gratitude for the help that the Americans and the G.V.N. were giving them. Many of the civil-affairs officials were working exhaustingly long hours and doing the best job they could with their limited time and resources, and they could not see why the people should complain and expect more than they were getting. Many military men, for their part, were loyal only to *their* duty—that of conducting military operations. Having efficiently carried out the "military half," they saw it as the responsibility of the Vietnamese government and of the American civil-affairs advisers to carry out the "civilian half" by taking care of the people who had been hurt or dispossessed in the "military half." (Thus, although, in the two weeks of Operation Benton, Task Force Oregon destroyed about sixty-five per cent of the houses of an estimated seventeen thousand people, the officer in charge of the 101st's Civil Affairs Office had been able to answer my question about the future of the area's population by saying, "*We* don't have any plans for the immediate future. It's the responsibility of the G.V.N. and the ARVN to carry out Pacification and Revolutionary Development." He did not know that the G.V.N. had no plan for these people.) But because, along with the destruction of villages, American military operations brought death to many civilians, American civil-affairs workers, no matter how well intentioned they might be, and no matter how well supplied they might someday become, could never, from the point of view of the villagers, "balance" the sufferings caused by the military, or undo what they had done, which was often absolute and irreversible.

On August 30th, in a wing of the province chief's office in Quang Ngai City, I was granted an interview with Mr. James A. May, a civilian, who was the Senior Adviser for Quang Ngai Province. Mr.

May, who is from California, is forty-seven years old, stands several inches over six feet, and has a long, bushy mustache. On the job in Quang Ngai, he often wore a Mexican sombrero and Western-style leather boots. Mr. May is a voluble talker, and when I asked for his view of the condition of the Pacification Program in Quang Ngai, on which he is the chief adviser, he warmed to the subject quickly, and delivered an impromptu talk that began with a description of the activities of the Marines. "The Marines came in May of 1965," he said. "Task Force Oregon came into a situation where, although the friendlies had made progress for two years, it was only moderate progress. There was quite a bit of forward and back, but, on balance, we nibbled ahead. The problem was that Charlie had occupied large portions of the province since the Japs. As far as Charlie was concerned, until the Marines arrived he had hardly been touched by the war. In many areas, it was easy for him to believe he was winning, and the people were illiterate, so they didn't know what was happening. When the Marines came, the friendly operations could go into an area, but they'd retreat soon, so it was easy for Charlie to say, 'We ran them out.' But since Task Force Oregon arrived, there have been a number of changes that have been very visible to Charlie. Task Force Oregon has had three big advantages over the Marines. First, they have had the manpower to do the job. Second, they have had the firepower, which is also very important, for shock effect. Third, they have had more mobility, with their helicopters. The main thing they've been able to do is to drive Charlie out of his strongholds, keeping a kill ratio of ten to one. They have kept Charlie on the run. Their reaction speed and firepower were unbelievable. Charlie started out by following his usual pattern of shooting down choppers, but this time five more

would come along and go after him. And the artillery was
always there, and we could throw in an armored unit with
tremendous speed. Charlie got everything *and* the kitchen
sink thrown at him so hard that he didn't know what hit
him. Before Task Force Oregon came, Mo Duc and Duc
Pho"—two districts in the south of Quang Ngai Province—
"were Charlie's. But now he's had so many casualties that
he's had to revise all his plans. One big thing we've done is
to repair Route 1 for transportation. Now Charlie can still
snipe and harass, but he cannot effectively overrun a large
village or overrun an outpost. Now he's all off balance.
He's got communication problems, and his food supply
and labor force are drying up. Aside from what he brings
in on infiltration routes, he's had a tough time."

I asked Mr. May if he meant that by destroying the
villages the Army had deprived the Vietcong of their
use.

"In a few areas, the villages have been destroyed," Mr.
May said, "This is a necessary side effect if you're going to
fight hard. We've invited the people to come on out of the
V.C. villages to secure areas where it's safe. The V.C. use
villages as protection, the way a gangster uses a hostage. So
in the process of getting at Charlie it's inevitable that the
village gets it. You'll notice that the undestroyed areas are
the ones that have not seen a G.V.N.-and-Allied Forces-
versus-V.C. confrontation. That's the way war is. To me,
it's just like the Second World War in places in France and
Italy, where the villages were wiped out as far as you could
see. You just can't get at the enemy unless you get at them
where they're at. There isn't any way to get them but level
the villages they are located in. You know, some of these
villages have never known any kind of government other
than the V.C. But we give them an opportunity to get out
and go. Also, these mud houses with thatched roofs can be
built up overnight. You send some people back into an

area, and in a week the place is all built up again. So I expect to see a lot more destruction. But the destruction works both ways. Just two weeks ago, the V.C. attacked a village on Route 1 in Son Tinh District that was protected by the Popular Forces, and blew up about twenty houses, with a lot of civilian casualties. Gradually, we're depriving the V.C. of his labor force and food. Now we've got about fifty thousand people in camps and about seventy-five thousand people who have built their own houses or are living with friends. Little by little, the people are realizing that security lies in the secure zones. They're beginning to see that the business opportunities are here in the cities, and they're coming in by the thousand now."

I asked about the operation I had just seen carried out in the village of Tuyet Diem.

"Well, technically they are not counted as refugees, because they were resettled right there," Mr. May said. "They brought the parts of their houses down and can set them up again. It's amazing with these Vietnamese houses. They can take them down and then put them right back up again, like an Erector set."

I asked him how the Pacification of villages was proceeding.

To answer this, Mr. May pulled out of his desk a map of the province as big as an unfolded newspaper. Along Route 1 and around the town of Duc Pho, the map was washed over in light blue. In the northern part of the province, the blue area along Route 1 was from one to five kilometres wide. "This shows the pacified areas when the Marines got here in 1965," he said. "We could hardly go outside Quang Ngai City. Now the area is much bigger." With one finger he delineated a blue area that bulged out about ten kilometres from the road in Son Tinh District and around Quang Ngai City.

Then Mr. May took me into a conference room down a

hall, where a much larger map hung on the wall. It was dotted with black-headed pins, which indicated the presence of Revolutionary Development Teams—groups of young Vietnamese men sent out to win rural people over to the Saigon government's side. "We've got forty-seven Revolutionary Development Teams," he told me.

Looking at the map, I saw that all but three or four of them were stationed along Route 1 or in the undestroyed region around Quang Ngai City.

"The R.D. Program has proved itself many times over by now," he said. "We have plans to expand Pacification considerably. Even in the worst days, it has been successful. The program has grown steadily."

I asked him what, in his view, it meant to say that a village was "pacified" or had been made "secure."

"Well, it means that it's highly improbable that the V.C. would dare infiltrate into it in the daytime," Mr. May said. "Of course, this is hard to determine, because sometimes the V.C. run out of no place, like Indians attacking a fort on the frontier at night."

I mentioned that in Son Tinh District, where a large number of Revolutionary Development Teams were working along Route 1, an American lieutenant colonel had advised an observer from Saigon against sleeping in any village in the province.

"I heard about that, and I jumped the colonel on that," Mr. May said. "I mean, for an American to be able to sleep in a village would be a very special situation, quite different from a regular Vietnamese sleeping there. It would be more like a village chief trying to sleep in the village. The village is secure for most Vietnamese, but the village chief can't sleep there, because the V.C. have got it in for him in particular. So I'd say that's not a very good measurement. You might say that a pacified area is an area that is more secure than before but not yet completely secure. The villages are not perfect everywhere. What the V.C. have to face is: How much will they pay for a victory? Will they lose more than they gain if they take a city? For instance, the V.C. might be able to come right into the province capital—I'm not saying they couldn't—but it's a question of how much it would cost them."

I asked Mr. May whether he considered the physical destruction of villages in wide areas of the province an impediment to the Pacification Program.

"I don't think it makes a tremendous amount of difference," he replied. "Once we provide security for an area, the people flock right back out and build the place up themselves again in no time. For instance, Charlie took over one village in '64, and we ran him out in '65, and the village got pretty damaged, but when we designated the place a secure area, the people came flocking back by the thousand. Then Charlie overran it again and the people left again. Then, when we took it again, the people came right back again. Then Charlie took the place again, and this time some of the people stayed there, but the point is that if we secure an area the people will come right back in again and build the place right up again in no time. Soon we plan to provide real and lasting security for that village. We keep a record of how the Pacification of each village is going. It's a document with a lot of questions on it, and we feed all the questions into a computer."

Later, I saw a Pacification "point sheet" that had been used by the Marines. It, too, was of a standardized type. The record for one village was as shown on the following facing pages.

High officials who received standardized reports like this one talked of the G.V.N.'s Pacification Program only in terms of progress, trying to judge whether the progress was slow or fast, and when one program (such as the G.V.N.'s Strategic Hamlet Program) failed, and a new, improved

OBJECTIVE	MAX POINTS	POINTS
I. *Destruction of Organized V.C. Military Forces*		
A. V.C. local/main force units destroyed or driven out	15	6
B. G.V.N. forces capable of defending area	5	2
Total	20	8
II. *Destruction of V.C. Infrastructure*		
A. Census completed	2	1
B. V.C. infrastructure discovered, destroyed, or neutralized	8	2
C. G.V.N. intelligence network established	5	1
D. Census Grievance Teams completed interviewing each family	2	1
E. Principal grievance completely processed	3	1
Total	20	6
III. *Establishment of Local Security*		
A. Defense plans completed	2	1
B. Defense construction completed	3	2
C. Permanent local defense forces trained and in place	12	5
D. Communications established with military supporting unit	3	3
Total	20	11
IV. *Establishment of Local Government*		
A. Village chief and council appointed and functioning	2	2
B. Village chief and council elected	2	0
C. Village chief lives in village and is able to sleep there	3	3
D. Hamlet chief's appointed councils functioning	2	0

OBJECTIVE	MAX POINTS	POINTS
E. Hamlet chiefs, councils elected	4	0
F. Hamlet chiefs live in hamlets and are able to sleep there	4	1
G. Permanent Psy Ops and Public Information services established	1	1
H. Village statutes enacted	1	0
I. Social and administrative organization of villages completed to meet immediate needs of villagers	1	0
Total	20	7
V. *Completion of Initial New Life Programs*		
A. Public health	4	2
B. Education	4	3
C. Agricultural	4	3
D. Markets	4	3
E. Transportation	4	2
Total	20	13
Final Total	100	45

program (such as the G.V.N.'s New Life Hamlet Program) was instituted in its place, they always spoke in terms of the G.V.N.'s having a chance to make a fresh start at "winning the hearts and minds of the people," as though the earlier failures had had no effect on the countryside and the situation in 1967 were the same as the situation in 1964 or 1965. But at the lower level, in provinces like Quang Ngai, American civil-affairs officials and workers faced a situation in which the cumulative effect of the many abortive programs—all of them accompanied, from 1965 on, by the full force of the Americans' overwhelming firepower—had been to bring disruption, destruction, and death to the countryside on an immense scale, and to leave among the people an indelible bitterness that no new program—unless it were a program to raise the dead—could hope to overcome. Before American civil-affairs workers in Quang Ngai became optimistic about any new programs for the G.V.N., they had to ask themselves whether the G.V.N. had any presence whatever in most of the villages, and, what was more to the point, whether there were many villages left in Quang Ngai in which anyone could have a presence.

I asked Mr. May about the official policy toward the people who continued to live in the zones of harassment-and-interdiction artillery fire.

"These people have had a choice," Mr. May said. "They still think Charlie's going to win. We've plastered the place with Chieu Hoi leaflets. And when we bring them into secured areas we try to get them to stay, but the pull of the land is very strong. But all the people have to do to keep their village from being destroyed is make sure that their hamlet isn't a fort for Charlie. But, for instance, down in Duc Pho they're not even trying, because Charlie *is* their government right now. Still, we've been encouraged by the number of people who have come to live along the highway, and also by the number who have started living on the beaches. We know they're not dangerous out there, because they haven't got any cover, and they can't dig underground so well there."

I asked if he thought it was a good idea to hold all the villagers responsible when the Vietcong chose to fire at our troops from their village.

"If you let him in your village, you're an accomplice, aren't you?" Mr. May said. "If you're feeding him and working for him, aren't you an accomplice?"

I asked about conditions in the camps.

"There's always plenty to eat, and a roof over their head," Mr. May said. "It does get a little overcrowded. It's not like a first-class hotel, with someone giving you a big welcome. I don't maintain that the refugee performance is like that. But we give them a free choice about whether to come or not. Usually, some want to come and some don't. Some people look and see that everyone else is getting aboard a chopper, so they get aboard, too. And when they go back, sometimes someone just says, 'There's been no fightin' in the village, so let's go back.' But we don't encourage them to go back until their native area is completely liberated. Some people want to know, 'Aren't we going to create a nation of refugees living on the dole?' This has been proved totally without foundation. The refugees have a better standard of living than they did in their villages. Look at the tin on their roofs. It's better than the old thatched roofs—it doesn't leak. And the refugee camps bring the people in closer to the urban centers, where they can have modern experiences and learn modern practices. It's a modernizing experience. The peasant is ignorant, but he isn't stupid. He knows business opportunities when he sees them. But I'll say one thing: You never have any trouble getting them to go back to their villages!" He laughed. Summing matters up, he added, "This is a tough, new kind of war. It's kind of like the Indian wars. There's no fast and easy way to finish it. There are so many places for the V.C. to hide—just like the Indians did. But I'd expect this province to be pacified in three or four years. And if we can pacify Quang Ngai, we can pacify any province. In three or four years, we may not have wiped out all the Charlies, but we will have cut him off from the people and restricted him to the mountains, where he'll be nothing more than a nuisance, like tigers—not a serious threat. Already, Quang Ngai is a bustling beehive of activity. Things are going well. I decided two years ago that I didn't come out here to lose. But if I thought our practice or theory was wrong, I'd get out."

In October, I received a report on the subject of civilian war casualties from a British civilian physician who had been working in Quang Ngai for over three years. In the report, he said that as of October, 1967, the number of patients in the province's only civilian hospital was between five hundred and fifty and six hundred and fifty a day. Of these, about fifty per cent were surgical cases. For example, on October 6th, three hundred and five of five hundred and sixty patients were in the surgical wards. Since the arrival of Task Force Oregon, the average number of war casualties admitted to the hospital each day had been thirty, although there were sometimes only ten admissions and sometimes forty.

> They come by Lambretta, hammock, motorcycle, bicycle, and about twenty per cent by helicopter [the doctor wrote]. The latter [helicopter] presents a great problem, as they bring patients from far away to us that should be going to a hospital closer by—for example, we have patients from Quang Tin Province. To get them back home is nearly impossible. Of our surgical patients, ninety-five per cent are war casualties. War casualties break down:
> 1. Cannon—fifty-five per cent (and higher).
> 2. Bullet—fifteen per cent. 3. Bomb—fifteen per cent. 4. Grenade—three per cent. 5. Mine —two per cent. 6. War burns—eight to ten per cent.

The report explained that war burns were caused by napalm, phosphorus, flamethrowers, and jettisoned gasoline tanks, and continued:

We frequently have patients admitted with blast syndrome from bombing (air displacement) or gas poisoning from tunnels. Ten per cent of the latter usually die in hospital. There are very few home burns—less than one in twenty. We also get cases that have been tortured by ARVN or security police. The following illustrates how many casualties arrive at the province hospital. When shelling occurs, there are those slightly wounded. They stay home, probably five in ten. Of the remaining five, two die at home or on the way to the hamlet aid station or village dispensary. The latter is staffed by a technician, midwife, etc. One is treated at the dispensary and kept till he is well. The other two are taken to the province hospital by the relatives. When the relatives acknowledge the seriousness of the situation, they may take him at once instead of going to the dispensary. This is true for coastal areas. From the other areas very few reach the hospital. Situations in which injury occurs: 1. Innocently at home, working, eating, or sleeping—being shelled or bombed not aware of impending danger. 2. Bunkers, infrequently. 3. Bullet wounds from ground troops caught in the crossfire, or deliberately inflicted by the military.

If the doctor's estimate of the ratio of the number of civilian casualties who reached the hospital to the number who did not was correct, this would mean that there had been about fifty thousand civilian war casualties a year in Quang Ngai since American troops first arrived.

On the night of my interview with Mr. May, the Vietcong overran Quang Ngai City. They freed twelve hundred prisoners from the province jail, blew up two gas stations that served American vehicles, and fired mortar shells into the American military advisory compound, causing thirteen casualties. I spent that night in one of several American compounds in the city, and in the evening, before the attack, I sat talking with Mr. Hobson, the American provincial adviser for refugees, and several doctors and nurses who worked at the province hospital and lived in the compound. Americans all over the city had been informed that there was a strong probability that the Vietcong would attack the city that night. Mr. Hobson, who had spent several years as a parole officer in the United States, passed out guns and taught the doctors how to use them, but he had little confidence that an effective resistance could be put up if the Vietcong chose to attack their compound. "I don't think they're going to attack here, but they can go anywhere they want," he said. "And if they want you, they can get you." The compound was always guarded by four or five ARVN soldiers. At night, these guards had been falling asleep on the job more often than not, and the Americans in the compound had devised a system whereby each American stayed awake for three hours a night, in rotating shifts, in order to keep the ARVN guards awake.

At about nine o'clock, an elderly Red Cross nurse with white hair and a prim, kindly face came into Mr. Hobson's part of the compound to ask his advice about what to do in the event of an attack.

Mr. Hobson advised her to lock herself and the nurses she shared quarters with in their room. Then he asked, "Do you want a gun?"

"Oh, my, no! I wouldn't know how to use a gun!" the elderly nurse replied, in a tone of mixed shock and amusement and delight.

"Well, then, shall I get you my knife?" Mr. Hobson asked, and his joke seemed to catch the mood of this group of reluctant soldiers, for everyone, including the nurse, burst out laughing.

At two o'clock, after most of the group had gone to bed in their rooms in the compound, heavy machine-gun fire sounded from the direction of the prison, which was perhaps two hundred yards down the road, and then came the thumping of incoming mortar shells. Everyone got out of bed and looked out into the darkness. Soon there was the sharp crack of artillery, followed by the faint whistle of the shells going overhead. Mr. Hobson explained that whenever the Vietcong attacked, artillery began to fire all over the countryside at "suspected enemy troop concentrations." The firing down the road continued for an hour and then subsided, and the people in the compound returned to bed.

In the morning, large crowds of the townspeople appeared on the streets and stood around in groups, talking. The city authorities had let the body of one youthful Vietcong, dressed only in a loincloth and sandals, lie in his blood on the street outside the liberated prison, as though to prove an ARVN and American victory. A Vietcong flag remained flying in a schoolyard until ten o'clock, however. When the schoolmaster was questioned by the authorities, he explained that he had been afraid to take the flag down by himself.

In the military advisory compound, several barracks had been damaged, and six jeeps in the central yard were immobilized, their tires punctured with mortar shrapnel. I found two officers surveying the scene.

"Do you think the girls'll come?" one officer asked the other.

"What girls?" the second officer asked.

"The *girls,*" the first officer said. "The whores. On the picnic."

"Oh. I don't know. A lot of our Vietnamese workers in the offices don't show up after these attacks."

"Maybe some of the girls will show. Maybe I'll have to settle for No. 5 instead of the one I like—you know, No. 2."

I learned that one young American soldier had been killed as he ran in his pajamas from his barracks in the compound toward a bunker, and that twelve others had been wounded on their way to bunkers, or in their beds. No helicopters had been able to take off to suppress the enemy fire, because the mortar shells had landed right next to the helicopter pad from the first minute of the attack.

Later that day, I left for Saigon, and, by chance, I arrived there just in time to catch the last few minutes of a press conference that was being held by a high American official in the Pacification Program. He was speaking to an audience of over a hundred correspondents in an air-conditioned auditorium. Toward the end of the conference, a Japanese newsman asked him if there were any provinces that could be held up as models of progress in the Pacification Program. The official mentioned Binh Dinh Province, and added, "Another place where clear-and-hold has been proceeding remarkably well is in Quang Ngai. I think that Quang Ngai is going to turn out to be one of the success stories of 1967."

ABOUT THE AUTHOR

Jonathan Schell was born in 1943 in New York City, where he still lives. His previous books are *History in Sherman Park*, an account of two voters in the 1984 presidential election; *The Abolition*; *The Fate of the Earth*; and *The Time of Illusion*.